BLOWBACK

After spending seven years in prison, Michael Forwell now lives in London with his family. These days Lee Bullman prefers to write about crime rather than commit it. This is his first book.

BLOWBACK

MICHAEL FORWELL

With Lee Bullman

PAN BOOKS

First published 2009 by Sidgwick & Jackson

First published in paperback 2010 by Pan Books

This edition first published 2018 by Pan Books
an imprint of Pan Macmillan
20 New Wharf Road, London N1 9RR
Associated companies throughout the world
www.panmacmillan.com

ISBN 978-1-5098-9201-3

A CIP catalogue record for this book is available from the British Library.

To my family

For May, Nicole, Nicholas, Nigel and Tonia
"Thanks for a second chance"

To my colleagues

This adventure could not have happened without
the quiet genius of Robert Leitzman. R.I.P.

M.G.F

For Janine, and MWC

L.B.

CONTENTS

PROLOGUE

'MICHAEL . . . THEY'RE SHOOTING AT US . . .'

End of the road. Singapore 1988.

After all the years of dope deals, all the boats loaded up on deserted tropical beaches, after all the nightclubs and the hotel suites, after all the helicopters, the first-class plane tickets and the cash and the cars. After all of that, sleep had only just come.

It had finally ridden into town on the back of the last couple of nightcaps, those last two cut-glass tumblers filled with three-finger shots of whisky, the expensive stuff with the smooth bite that was all I seemed to drink these days. Not that I was boozing to pass-out point, but I was definitely drinking more lately, it was going down easy and somewhere over the years my tolerance had shot way up.

The local humidity didn't help, that fierce, unrelenting Asian heat clung to the Equator and radiated out from there in waves that just kept coming, long after the sun had set. For a man born in southern England and educated on the north coast of Scotland, it still took some getting used to no matter how much I travelled, and I'd travelled a lot.

Despite the open window in the darkened bedroom the curtains weren't twitching, the night was far too still for that. The air-conditioning was always on but never seemed to work, the climate beat it hands down. Its soft buzz mixed with traffic noise punctuated by the odd raised voice drifting lazily up from somewhere out there in a subdued monotone hum, providing a blacktop back-drop to whatever it was that I dreamed about. That was another thing with the booze, you could never remember your dreams.

On the bedside table next to me, seconds floated silently by on the yellow-gold Rolex GMT Master, my favourite watch, its perpetual motion and floating hands issuing this unheeded, elegant warning that time was running out. Then my phone kicked in. Its shrill, insistent ring roused me in a single rude jolt, smashing through the sleep and the booze and the dreams and changing everything. Changing it all for ever.

There was a moment of light confusion then as the fog lifted and the head cleared and I padded over thick cream carpet to the new telephone. State of the art, top of the range, best you can get, just like everything else, like the speedboat, the nightclub, the Rolex, the private island and the one-call mobile phone, another expensive toy to keep me one step ahead in the cat and mouse game that was covering continents. The call could only be from one person, and it could only mean one thing. This was bad news, the worst.

'An urgent message has come through for you, Mr

Forwell,' a soft female voice said. 'From the boat . . . There is some trouble, I think.'

I'm Michael Forwell, aka Rodney Wayne Boggs, aka Michael Charles Young, aka Michael Leslie Stocks, aka Michael Escreet, aka The Fox. I'm a successful bar-owner, I'm a millionaire dope smuggler, a dedicated adventurer, and I'm listening to the voice at the other end of the line tell me that a fax marked urgent has just arrived at the office I kept over at the Marina. I took a grateful moment then to register that the call hadn't woken my wife May. I have always been careful to shield her from my business dealings and now May sleeps soundly on in the bed I had just left, blissfully unaware of what was about to befall us as I tried to focus on the message read out to me, even though somewhere deep down, where the fear lives, I already knew what it said: Sammy needs to speak to me. Sammy needs to speak to me right now.

Samuel Colflesh was the gang's logistics man, a tactician par excellence. He'd had the current operation running parade-ground smooth up to that point. Now he was calling from a different time-zone, 600 miles from the edge of America and closing in on the Washington coast manning the bridge of my converted oil-supply ship *Encounter Bay,* the ship that was currently in the process of smuggling over seventy tonnes of vacuum-packed, quality-assured high-grade marijuana into the United States of America.

That was enough dope to keep California high for a month. Every third person in America could have rolled a joint and the whole country could have got high.

If I'd had the time I might have allowed myself the luxury of reflecting on the irony of the situation. I might have taken a moment to consider that of all the operations to go wrong it almost had to be this one, this one last haul, this shipment so big that when the money came rolling in neither I nor my partners in crime would ever have had to work again. And the irony didn't end there. It wasn't even our dope we were moving this time; we were working as hired hands to carry someone else's product, a multi-million-dollar international delivery service, coast to coast. When pay-day came on this final smuggling run we'd have been *weighing* that money rather than counting it.

But those synapses weren't snapping, not yet. This was no time to reflect on what happens when you break my old friend Lietzman's number one rule (Rule 1 - No Outsiders. Rule 2 – No Outsiders). It was too late in the day and too early in the morning for that.

I needed to speak to Sammy on board *Encounter Bay*, to touch base and get to the whys and wherefores, and to see if there was anything left. And it wouldn't be easy.

Communication between members of the gang, especially when we were, as now, in the middle of an operation, was never simple. There were codes, rules and procedures; there was even an operations manual for God's sake, running to fifteen pages, courtesy of Sammy. Mobile phones, still a relatively new and expensive technology in the late 1980s, were often bought by the gang in order to make a single call before being discarded lest the relevant authorities should begin to take an interest in whatever it is that international drug smugglers talk to one another about. The phone in the apartment was unusable for the same reason.

The obsession with security was by now so ingrained within the gang that I knew I could only make the shore-to-ship call from a public call box, but my problems didn't end there. It was 3 a.m. and I was in Singapore. I needed a call box and phone cards. I needed an aspirin, breakfast and a shave, but they could all wait. Calling the satellite phone on the bridge of *Encounter Bay* would be expensive although it is all relative, I suppose – there was, after all, close to three hundred million dollars' worth of dope on the boat.

I dressed in a hurry and left the apartment. My white Jaguar was parked at the kerbside and I gunned it, the stereo and engine springing to life as one, Salt 'n' Pepa's 'Push It' filling the car and throwing me, all Blaupunkt bass and synsonic drum pattern. *Get up on this.* Then it was stereo off and foot down hard as I swerved fast and loose, carving up empty streets, running red lights. I hit town, parked the Sovereign haphazardly and started running, running through Singapore's hot streets still busy with the business of night, ignoring the stares from the few around at that hour as the blood started pumping and the sweat to pour, blind to everything but getting in touch. Focused only on finding out.

I soon found myself three miles from home, in the city's majestic main Post Office, a century old and surrounded on three sides by the Singapore river, still open for business despite the hour. I bought the phone cards I needed, peeling off cash from a healthy roll in my loose-cut Brioni chino pocket, regulation wear for the prosperous local ex-pat, and headed across the marble floor to the neat row of phone booths. My heartbeat was louder by now than the footfalls of my soft leather slip-ons, filling the cavernous space around me with the slow white noise of panic. The jade and gold oval ring I wore, a trademark of sorts, blurred in green and gold as I punched digits, then hung in mid-air for a moment as I took in my surroundings and caught my breath, waiting for the call to connect and Sammy to pick up.

The Post Office was built on a grand scale, shades of European classicism slap-bang in the heart of downtown South East Asia, a mahogany and marble reminder of the city's own profitable excursions into the drug business, paid for by the opium trade back in the colonial days. Yet more irony.

Ring ring click. 'Fox?' When Sammy called me by my nickname – we all used nicknames, part of the fun, part of the secret-keeping, part of the life – the panic that I had been fighting to stave off receded a little. The American at the other end of the line sounded remarkably cool for a man in so much trouble. But that was no more than you'd expect. After all, we'd nicknamed Sammy 'Haig' to reference the general who'd kicked ass all over India.

Samuel Colflesh had sent his message to me as soon as he'd heard the unmistakable whirr of an aeroplane engine overhead, just before he'd changed course and tried in vain to lose the tail. Moments later the distinctive paint-job of the Coast Guard C-130, the white body with the blue and orange stripe, had emerged seemingly straight from the heart of the sun and buzzed *Encounter Bay* from the west, getting a lock on its position and radioing in that the target was in sight. But even then, even with the Coast Guard plane doubling back and swooping overhead, Sammy had kept it together. There was always plan B: they'd change course again, they'd keep going, reverse and run, just like the manual said they should.

As far as Sammy was concerned, although the arrival of the Coast Guard wasn't great news, it wasn't a cause for too much concern. He was still safely navigating the no man's land of international waters while flying the red, white and blue of the Panamanian flag and still operating outside of any single nation's jurisdiction. But lines had been redrawn for this one; neither the Drug Enforcement Agency nor the Coast Guard was about to let my ship full of dope slip through their fingers. They'd worked too hard and too long for that.

In meeting after meeting they'd rehearsed the smuggler's possible evasive actions and how they would counter them. As well as the 148-strong crew aboard the Coast Guard cutter, they'd taken twenty armed DEA officers along for the ride. The ship they'd selected for the job, the *Boutwell,* was appropriately equipped for the task in hand, fitted with two 25mm machine guns with laser sights, a 76mm anti-aircraft gun and a state-of-the-art weapons system for firing tracers and shells. If the smugglers tried to run, they could catch them, if they panicked and decided to ram then the cutter's reinforced hull would stay solid.

By the time my call connected, the *Boutwell* had Sammy in range and had begun to tell him via the ship's radio to prepare to be boarded. Sammy's faith in the safety of international waters was shattered; the flag he was currently flying was Panamanian, and the exiled government of that country had acceded to the Coast Guard's request to use the stretch of ocean to ambush the smugglers and use whatever force it took to bring them down.

Sammy's message bounced off satellites, his voice echoing through the thousands of miles of empty air between us. 'Michael, Michael, they're shooting at us.'

And sure enough, as Sammy held the satellite receiver at arm's length I heard the huge explosive splashes of 50-calibre anti-aircraft shells fired as warning shots just off the hull of *Encounter Bay*. The Coast Guard voice booming out over the radio was losing patience and began threatening to turn their sights on *Encounter Bay*'s engine room. I heard Sammy's defiant announcement to the Coast Guard, heard him yell into the radio, military to the end, 'The flag still flies and the city has not fallen.'

But the cause was lost and it would take far more than bravado to get out of this one. When Sammy asked what he should do next, I gave the only advice I could.

'Just . . . Just come back, Sam.'

CHAPTER ONE

BECOMING THE FOX

Itchy feet and a genetically inherited taste for adventure.

With hindsight, the fact that I ended up heading a smuggling operation that made millions of dollars moving tons of weed around the world isn't so strange. In the years leading up to my first forays into the dope trade a number of disparate elements combined to make me ideally suited to the calling. I inherited a love of danger from my father, I developed a healthy disregard for authority at school, which never left me, and I always loved to travel. On top of this I found myself unimpressed by the options open to me in the straight world, quickly tiring of the crappy jobs on offer and constantly searching for something, even if I wasn't sure at first what that something was.

I entered the world against the backdrop of a Europe at war. In March 1944 the skies over Britain, France and Germany raged, cities burned and fell as the bombs dropped and the bullets flew. The US alone dropped 30,176 tonnes of bombs on Germany and occupied

Europe during over 20,000 missions in the month I was born. Hitler's bunker suicide and an Allied victory were still a year off, and Britain's young men were still giving their all for King and Country. One such man was my father, Squadron Leader Ernest Forwell, an experienced RAF fighter pilot, missing in action at the time of the birth of his only child having been shot down during a night-time Spitfire raid over enemy-occupied France. The Spitfire he was flying spun out of control, my father turned through hellish three sixties as night sky and dark earth blurred into a whole mess of danger. With seconds to spare he ejected and deployed his parachute, floating serenely back to solid ground as he watched the plane explode into a ball of flame, lighting up the night sky for miles around. Somehow he managed to evade capture, despite looking and sounding every inch the typical RAF flyboy sporting full uniform, flying jacket, clipped accent and handlebar moustache. He moved through France across country, stealing chickens and sleeping in hedges, avoiding the Nazis by travelling only at night. He was taken in and hidden by a French family who provided him with the forged papers he needed as a cover and clothes that wouldn't attract quite as much enemy attention as his RAF uniform. While there he met and befriended a New Zealand pilot who had also been shot down and both men stayed to fight with the resistance, my father not returning to Britain until the war ended in 1945.

As my father was surviving in occupied France, earning his Distinguished Flying Cross and his mention in dispatches, I screamed my first scream and settled into a life of what would soon become postwar privilege as the son of a hero. But that adventurous spirit inherent in the Forwell gene had not begun with my father. Way back when, at the turn of the twentieth century, my ancestor William. L. Forwell had written his 215-page opus, *A Thousand Mile Cruise In The 'Silver Clouds'*. The book provides an account of his journey from Dundee to France and back again in a small boat (the *Silver Clouds* of the title) and features evocative chapter headings such as 'The French Ladies – Paris Drink' and 'Our Ship Sunk – Drowned in the Cabin'. I never met William Forwell, but I think I would have liked him.

My background was resolutely upper-middle class. My paternal grandparents owned rubber plantations in Malaysia and Singapore and growing up I'd often travel to visit them during school holidays. It was on these trips that I developed an enduring affection for South East Asia and was as happy there as I ever was in England, which always seemed somewhat grey and tired on my return after a summer spent among the world's most laid-back people and – increasingly important to a restless teenage boy – its most beautiful women.

My father had stayed on in the RAF after the Allied victory. Once reunited on his return he and my mother, Jacqueline, moved to wherever he was stationed as he performed a number of tours of duty in far-flung corners of the Far East and Asia. As well as spending holidays with my grandparents, I thought nothing of jumping on a plane to catch up with my parents and spending the weeks between term time being indulged by my father and his comrades in arms, even being allowed to drive in their armoured vehicles and fire off their automatic machine guns.

With no brothers and sisters and having what was, compared to other children my age, an itinerant lifestyle, I turned into a self-sufficient young man, with little need for companionship and a growing awareness that, despite what others at home in England would have me believe, the world was a very small place, shrinking by the year.

When I was thirteen years old my parents moved me out of the school I was boarding at, Knossington Grange in Rutland, and sent me to complete my education at Gordonstoun, an imposing seventeenth-century mansion set into 150 wild acres in Moray in the north of Scotland. My parents had saved hard to enable me to go to Gordonstoun and I was excited at first by the prospect of starting at this prestigious school. Famous as the institution responsible for educating future kings and princes, Gordonstoun's reputation is world-class. Prince Philip so enjoyed his own time at the school that he would later send his sons and partners in the family business, Charles, Edward and Andrew, to board there.

An odd crowd mix at Gordonstoun, the place acting as a catch-all for new and old money alike. As well as the British royal connection the school was chosen by David Bowie to educate his son Zowie; Sean Connery, one of Scotland's most famous exports, sent his son Jason there; and Balthazar Getty, great-grandson of the world's richest man, also passed through its hallowed halls as did countless of the handmade Savile Row suits and stuffed shirts who ended up running this and many other countries. Fittingly enough, bearing in mind the Connery connection and the life of adventure I would soon embark upon, the school filled out the fictional back-story of another great British ducker and diver with a taste for the high life and a love of toys, one James Bond.

The regime at Gordonstoun soon highlighted my problem with authority. In those days, the school was strict; it had a set of punishments in place for infractions of their many rules and, me being me, I soon fell foul of the system. Breaking the rules earned the miscreant what was called 'penalty drill'. Lasting for anything up to two hours, penalty drill took place at five o'clock on Saturday mornings while the rest of the school slept soundly and involved laps around a triangular patch of grass surrounded by a track on the school grounds, followed by a cold shower and a Dickensian breakfast of bread and dripping and a cup of tea. Pupils called for penalty drill were required to complete laps of the triangle, running around once and then walking them twice. The amount of time you were required to take part in this pointless pursuit depended on the crime committed. Towards the end of my time at Gordonstoun I could be found walking and running the triangle for the full two hours pretty much every Saturday morning.

Another punishment doled out by the school was the silent walk to the nearby town, the hike to be completed alone and in silence; the time spent walking supposedly offering a chance for us to reflect on what we had done wrong. Again, I soon became very familiar with every bump in the road between the school and the town, using the time to dream of escape and adventure.

Corporal punishment was seldom administered at

Gordonstoun, the cane being saved for those pupils who most exasperated the teaching staff and on whom the other punishments seemed to have little or no effect. I was picked out as one who might benefit from the administration of the cane after being accused of one infringement of school rules too many.

Despite its reputation as the school of the rich, Gordonstoun was far from ostentatious. The big stone buildings always seemed cold, even in the summer, but a hardy ruddy-cheeked demeanour and resistance to the elements was built up in the pupils by the weekday morning routine of a cross-country run through the grounds. Although academically the school was second to none, I never really excelled in the classroom. The education on offer was in the classical tradition, learning Latin by rote, studying ancient history and theology, subjects which seemed chosen to highlight my short attention span.

My time at Gordonstoun wasn't all doom and gloom though. I enjoyed sport, playing in the school rugby team and becoming school javelin champion. And there were other extracurricular activities that captured my imagination. The school actually ran its own corps of Sea Cadets and housed a fire engine that it was the pupils' duty to maintain and man, should fire break out in the vicinity.

The Gordonstoun school motto, written within a golden scroll beneath a rendering of a Viking ship in full sail, is *Plus est en vous,* which translates as 'there is more in you than you think', and I set out to prove it.

*

By the time the sixties rolled around, my father had left the RAF and my parents were ready to escape the black and white kitchen sink austerity of postwar Britain and become 'ten pound poms', taking up the Australian government's offer of a £10 fare to emigrate to that brave new sunny world. Australia needed an influx to help the country reach its fast-growing economic potential, part of the 'populate or perish' policy. I happily finished my last term at Gordonstoun, packed up my school trunk and followed my mother and father to the new world.

On arriving in Australia I completed my education in Queensland on the north-eastern corner of the mainland, eventually managing to leave school with a respectable batch of eight O levels and a vague but insistent desire for travel and adventure. I had forged a few friendships at my new school, in particular embarking on a teenage love affair with a girl called Cheryl.

Despite hailing from a background cushioned by the dual safety nets of money and privilege, I was determined to find my own place in the world, and to do so without relying on my family to finance my entrance into adulthood. As soon as I left school my working life began in earnest following a skip across the Coral Sea to Papua New Guinea, where I began training as an electrical technician on the island's Lae Airfield, itself the scene of much wartime action. I learned quickly at my new post, fitting aerials atop DC3s while roasting in the unforgiving sun, or sheltering from the ferocious monsoons that could blow up from nowhere.

Island life managed to capture my imagination for

only a year, though, for by 1963 I was feeling the pull of the metropolis.

Winding up next in Sydney, I spent the following two years furthering my involvement in all things electrical (and indulging a growing fondness for *kit,* big boy's toys), working as a sound recordist and technician at local radio stations and film studios. I also enjoyed a brief tenure at the Post Office, which, if nothing else, taught me how to type.

On a visit to my parents in 1965, I took a job on board the prawn boats, dodging crocodiles in the sweeping Gulf of Carpentaria off Australia's northern coast, and began a lifelong love of all things nautical. I did so well I was offered an apprenticeship by the South Australian Fishing Cooperative, who had boats in the area, gaining nautical experience aboard their fleet of boats based in Port Arthur in Adelaide.

But a pattern was emerging. Soon I was beginning to feel the familiar itchy feet and headed back to Papua New Guinea, ostensibly to earn the money that would finance my travels on a wider scale. I had an idea that I wanted to see more of the world, and a well-paid job with few distractions would allow me to save the money I'd need for my dream trip.

My new employer was Kennecot Exploration who took me on as a surveyor's assistant and charged me with helping the conglomerate map the huge swathes of uncharted jungle that would soon play host to the Ok Tedi copper mine. I was twenty-three years old. The environment I found myself working in for the next year was home to tribes only recently catalogued and filed by the prying anthropological eyes of the West. I witnessed first hand the several indigenous tribes, counting among their number the Head-Hunters, Mud-Men and the Cargo Cult. It was dangerous work; the Head-Hunters were believed to have once possessed cannibal tendencies, and the Cargo Cult had amassed a collection of weaponry scavenged from Second World War air-drops to the island. Neither group was particularly enamoured of its new visitors.

In 1967 I headed back to Queensland and for the first, but not final, time in my life went underground, working as a driller deep below the scorched earth in the copper mines of Mount Isa.

It was there that I met an American by the name of Cliff Ball. We became firm friends and began to make vague plans for a trip throughout South East Asia, an area still ravaged by the conflict of the Vietnam War.

My parents meanwhile had settled into their life in the new country. My mother was living up to her nickname of 'The Duchess', throwing and attending parties and generally indulging her taste for fun and sociable frivolity. Dad had simpler tastes and was much happier with informal nights out in the local pub than at the dressy affairs Mum so enjoyed. Since I'd left home and started my wanderings, my father had taken up work as a bush pilot, finding the job the ideal opportunity to indulge his passion for aircraft. The work was often dangerous, the low-flying over inhospitable outback terrain calling for him to bring into play all the skills he had learned while flying fighter missions in the war. The distances involved for the pilots were immense as they carried farm labourers and supplies over thousands of miles of desolate bush land and dense rainforest. Often the ground was flooded and the pilots would find themselves navigating across newly formed lakes not charted on any map.

Sadly, my father's dangerous choice of occupation was to have tragic results. On 18 July 1967 he set off to take two stockmen back to the farm they worked in the Cape York Peninsula, making the trip in a small Cessna 172, a journey of over a thousand miles. Despite the fact that the weather was beginning to act up my father decided to go ahead with the journey anyway, fulfilling the bush pilot's job description as a kind of outback taxi service. Somewhere deep within the Forwell gene there is perhaps a predisposition to take risks regardless of the possible outcome of the venture. In this case the risk-taking was fatal. During the flight Dad found himself having to take off and gain altitude in the middle of what was by now an almighty thunderstorm in order to negotiate a mountain range. The plane couldn't climb fast enough to clear the terrain and he and his passengers crashed into the side of a mountain in the middle of a tropical forest.

The news that the father I idolized so much had died in an air crash came as an awful blow, which shocked and saddened me to my very core. To my eyes, Dad had always seemed larger than life, a heroic figure whose bravery, humour and compassion marked him out from every other man I had ever met. I just couldn't believe he was dead. What made the event harder to take was the fact that because of the inhospitable nature of the terrain he worked and the sheer scale of the distances involved, it took almost a full year to locate the crash site, which was by then a half-overgrown selection of barely recognizable plane parts. The pin my father wore on his uniform, a pair of metal wings sprouting from the side of a crest, showed the horror of the crash in miniature; it had been bent almost into a circle while he was still wearing it by the force of the crash. The only saving grace was the news from the investigators at the crash site that the accident would have happened so quickly and been so ferocious that the men aboard the plane would have known little or nothing about it.

My father's fatal accident temporarily quenched my desire for the dangerous work that was becoming my stock in trade. As a result I slipped down a gear and rather than return to the work at the mine I stayed at home, near to the mother with whom I shared the awful burden of grief. But my thrill-seeking drive hadn't gone for ever: I still used some of the cash I had saved to buy myself the two-seater sports car that became the first in a long line of fast white motors.

After a few months I was ready to hit the road again with little more than my cocked thumb and a stubborn resolve to find adventure and, perhaps in the process, myself. I spent the next three years hitchhiking around South East Asia, wandering through a war zone and picking up cash wherever the opportunity to do so presented itself. I managed to make my meagre travel budget of $250 stretch for eighteen months. During the course of the road trip to nowhere I felt the streets of Saigon rumble beneath the tracks of American tanks and suffered fuck-you-for-not-fighting abuse from the

American soldiers who mistook me for a hippie trail peacenik. But the GIs had me all wrong, marking me as protesting against a war I knew very little about.

Arriving in the Maldive Islands I collected live seashells for a marine biologist and elsewhere found casual work as a barman and waiter wherever and whenever I found it in order to eke out my existence as the solitary traveller. In Singapore I put on a wetsuit and worked as a salvage diver, after which I returned to Sydney.

This was the sixties, the decade we hear so much about – Vietnam, Hendrix, Woodstock and free love, man – a decade that apparently touched and changed anyone lucky enough to have lived through it. In cities all around the world freethinking radicals were turning on, tuning in and dropping out with the help of the illegal substances that I would eventually move around the globe. But my experience of the time was markedly at odds with those of others who were there. I didn't even know what a hippie was, and certainly wouldn't have numbered myself among them. The counter-cultural revolution passed me by and probably wouldn't have excited much interest in me even if I had been aware of it.

My sixties were spent building up a dissolute CV of jobs taken wherever I happened to end up on my open-ended wanderings. Not that I was always alone. My journey through the dust and heat of South East Asia often meant sharing parts of my trek with similar adventure seekers. I embarked on the trip I'd planned with Cliff Ball. At one point during our wanderings through Vietnam and Cambodia we were lost in the middle of nowhere without food or water and suffering on that seemingly never-ending Cambodian sand-track from the crippling effects of the heat, which refused to let up even at night. At the side of one of the unmarked roads criss-crossing that part of the world, we came across a peasant shack built on stilts, a type of dwelling typical of that area.

The sun had long dropped though the fierce heat remained and by now we were hungry, hot and desperate, ready to try anything as we approached the humble shack. Cliff rapped on the door while I began babbling in loud English about our dire needs and peaceful intentions. After a few minutes of this desperate pantomime the makeshift wooden door swung inward to reveal a beautiful young Cambodian female amid the bare-bones minimalism of the peasant home. We accepted the girl's invitation to enter and not until the door had closed shut behind us did we notice her fiery-eyed father hiding behind it, armed and ready to swing at these strange nocturnal visitors, a hatchet raised high in his right hand. Quick thinking and a further babble of panicked pleas across the language barrier illustrated with manic hand gestures and pleading eyes calmed our suspicious host to the extent that that he soon relented and began to share with us his meagre resources, even offering us his daughter as a parting gift.

We refused of course, and left the old man a transistor radio as a thank you token, a simple act of gratitude that bought tears to his eyes. But the incident had cemented in my mind the divisions in culture you can't show on a map, differences that run deeper and further than mere geographical distance.

Back in Australia, I did what was expected of me and

decided to settle down. I swapped the shorts and backpack of the free spirit for the businessman's collar and tie in order to become head commercial salesman for B&D Roll-A-Door, Australia's largest producer of modular garage units. I dealt with the firm's larger corporate clients, mainly builders and property developers, living the nine-to-five life of a working stiff. I even took the plunge and got married to my high-school sweetheart Cheryl.

I was actually good at my job, but after four years of suburban life, four years of sales conferences and team targets and a future stretching predictably in front of me, I couldn't fake it any longer. Then fate stepped in and I was offered a new job in Western Australia. I took the job and my itchy feet hit the road once again, this time leaving Cheryl and the last four years behind. The marriage ended as amicably and uneventfully as it had progressed. Four years with me, particularly in view of my recent history, would have armed my wife with the expectation that one day I would move on.

For a while I threw myself into my new post, although the job held little real interest for me. My duties revolved mainly around helping to import radios and cigarette lighters from China, learning in the process the ins and outs of the paperwork and arrangements required to ship goods overseas, knowledge that would later prove invaluable. The two million lighters my new employer imported turned out to be so cheaply made and unstable that they could only safely be half filled with fuel, lest the pressure of air travel release their explosive potential. In order to shift the imported lighters my boss and I took offices on a weekend let and began wholesaling the goods. Unfortunately the lighters were so dangerous that as soon as they hit the Australian market, they were banned.

Of course the job didn't last. One year and a few hundred thousand lighters later I began to feel it again, that pull, that nagging desire for the next horizon, for something, *anything* else. I was thirty-two years old and I'd tried the world of legitimate business and found it severely wanting. Now I gave in once more to the thirst for adventure that was as natural and vital to me as breathing.

I cashed in my savings, left the job in Perth and set off again with a job lot of Chinese transistor radios bought from my now ex-boss to sell along the way in search of my future, a future which soon turned up in the unlikely shape of a mysterious American called Robert Lietzman.

CHAPTER TWO

1976. ROBERT LIETZMAN

A moonlight flit and an introduction to the dope trade.

I'd used a portion of my savings to invest in a caravan, a rugged V8 utility vehicle, plus some fishing rods, a Pink Floyd tape and a collection of the outdoorsman paraphernalia I thought I may just find use for on my newest venture. The plan was to indulge the taste for the road I'd developed hitchhiking through South East Asia with an extended solo trip around Australia's 2,941,299 square miles - just me and my batch of radios for company, points of interest and planned stops t.b.c.

Leaving Perth, I headed north along the coast road keeping the sun to my left and the windows fully rolled down and my shirt sleeves rolled up to compensate for the lack of air-con in the vehicle.

By now the 1970s were in full swing and King Disco's crown was slipping. On the other side of the world, in the New York and London demi-monde, punk rock had begun its snarling assault on popular culture. The Sex Pistols, The Clash and a host of others were spearheading the movement, looking the established social order dead in the eye and daring, in the face of economic depression and social hypocrisy, to ask *why*. The social phenomenon beginning in the cities and spreading quickly through the dry tinderstick suburbs encouraged anyone who would listen that self-expression and a maverick spirit were more valid and vital than blind allegiance to a failing, unfair system, and that in order to move forward as a whole, we first had to take on the challenge as individuals. Robert Lietzman didn't know it, and he sure as hell didn't look it, but he was punk rock through and through.

I first met Lietzman in the summer of 1976 in the quiet Australian port of Geraldton, the latest stop on my V8-powered walkabout, 420 kilometres from my start point. Geraldton was beautiful; it had begun life as a small mining and farming town and served briefly as a convict settlement, but its idyllic Indian Ocean beaches and temperate climate soon ensured its standing as a popular tourist stop. Beneath the picture-perfect waters off its coast lay clues to the town's nautical history in the decaying old wrecks of Dutch merchant ships run aground centuries previously on the shore's protective reef. The nearby Abrolhos Islands, 60 kilometres to the west, were the site of the area's most infamous historical event, the famed attempted hijack and mutiny aboard the *Batavia* in 1629, which had ended when the ship struck the reef and forty people fell beneath the surf and drowned.

By 1976 Geraldton had become a popular spot for surfers working their way around the circuit and bringing with them their own brand of sun-bleached bohemia in the never-ending search for the perfect wave. The laid-back feel of the small town made it the ideal spot for me to park up my caravan and unwind after my recent adventures in the real world of the working week, and I was soon so taken with the place that I decided to stay awhile.

After asking around I found part-time work and pocket money serving behind the bar of the local pub and set about serving and meeting locals and tourists alike. In Australia at the time my story was not unusual, men like me were drifting through towns like Geraldton every day, hitching rides on boats and in cars to and from the small port and picking up whatever work they could find before heading off again on their merry way. Some travelled in groups of three or four in the favoured VW Kombi vans, usually complete with a roof rack full of psychedelically decorated surfboards, then the de rigueur accessory on young Australia's rites of passage tour.

The pub where I found work happened to be the very one in which the unknowing spirit of punk rock, Robert Lietzman, liked to pass the time while land-locked. As I began my first shift, emptying ashtrays and cleaning glasses, a man entered the pub and took a stool at the bar. So far he was my first, and only, customer,

'Bourbon,' he ordered in an American accent. 'With Coke.'

'Coming right up,' I said with a friendly smile.

He looked coolly back. 'You new here?'

'Yeah, just arrived. My name's Mike.'

'Uh huh. You English?'

'Yeah.'

'So what's an Englishman doing in Geraldton?' He shook a Marlboro from his pack and stuck it between his lips.

'Oh just – shit!' I yelled, stumbling back as he pulled out a familiar-looking lighter and thumbed it, expecting an explosion, flaming paraffin, third-degree burns.

'What the fuck!' He was gaping at me over the innocent blue flame.

So I told him about the Chinese lighters, not a career highlight, and my decision to pack it all in and go travelling. And he told me about his beloved boat, the *Diana*, a fifty-foot trimaran that he was single-handedly navigating around the world. Trimarans, he told me in a doting tone of voice, are fast, strong and reliable. The lightweight boat consisted of two smaller outlying hulls connected to the central main hull via lateral struts.

'I'm Lietzman,' he said, reaching over to shake hands. I'd obviously passed some kind of test.

I soon noticed that unlike most of the regulars who congregated at the pub, Lietzman always drank alone. He was a big tipper; keeping his drink topped up and being ready to listen while he worked his way through his never-ending list of gripes could double my evening's pay. This rangy, sparely built American had a way of talking that seemed to just drag you in to the easy, half-whispered narrative. The two of us would quietly set the world to rights from our respective positions behind and in front of the pub's makeshift wooden bar.

About ten years my senior, Lietzman was tall and lean, with short brown hair he'd push back from his tanned face while talking or listening or just watching.

Sartorially he went for an eccentric mix and match approach, favouring belted drip-dry polyester slacks in grey or brown, often slightly too short for him but with an immaculate stitched-in crease, which he would team with faded blue slip-on moccasins, odd socks and whichever clean polo shirt he'd found that morning. He looked like a country and western singer on a golfing holiday. Everything about the man seemed to scream outsider, albeit very quietly.

I saw the mysterious loner I met in that bar as something of a kindred spirit, and although – perhaps because – Lietzman didn't say much, the pair of us clicked immediately. I liked his stories of the sea and the way he told them. One of the first admirable characteristics I noted in him was his immense capacity for his beloved bourbon. The man could drink the stuff all day long and yet never seemed to suffer any ill effects. Indeed, it was his fondness for sipping whisky, in particular that lovingly produced at the Jack Daniel's distillery in Lynchburg, Tennessee, that earned Lietzman his nickname among those few who knew him well. Whether downing his first shot or emptying his second bottle, 'Bourbon' always seemed somehow in control, always aware of his surroundings yet never fully part of them, a rock-steady study in seen-it-all-before detachment.

You knew just by looking in his eyes that Lietzman had a razor-sharp intelligence, and the balls to back his hunches. But, clever or not, he would not suffer fools gladly, was stubbornly difficult to get along with – playfulness and joviality formed no part of his character repertoire whatsoever. Drunk or sober, he was a serious dude.

Throughout the opening act of our blossoming friendship I found myself chipping away at the face of his personality every bit as hard as I had in the mines way below Mount Isa. Even at the parties we went to in Geraldton peopled by locals, tourists and surf bums, soundtracked by the new Rolling Stones album *Black and Blue* or Queen's drawn-out 'Bohemian Rhapsody', which seemed to be playing everywhere that summer, Lietzman would sit apart from the throng, happily ensconced on the edge of the action nursing his bourbon and eyeing the scene before him with a noncommittal, aloof air. Often, I got the feeling that it was what Lietzman wasn't saying that held the key to unlock his inscrutable character.

'You see, Michael, once you've been to sea nothing's ever the same again,' he said, swirling the ice cubes in his drink and taking a long pull on his Marlboro. 'Out on a boat you keep your country with you, you make your own laws and keep your own counsel. It's one of the only places left in the world where you can call yourself a free man and mean it. Seems to me you're the kind of guy who'd appreciate that.'

My ears immediately pricked up as Lietzman leaned across the bar, always seemingly on guard against being overheard even if we were the only two people in the room. His journey had hit a temporary snag he told me, while the *Diana*, currently in a sad state of repair in dry dock, underwent necessary maintenance. Unforeseen circumstances had conspired to put a halt to his travels, hence his short-lived stay in Geraldton.

There was obviously more to the story – there always

was with Lietzman – but for the moment at least he wasn't prepared to divulge his secrets, and I was happy to ignore them. He asked me if I'd care to help get the boat in order, perhaps park my caravan up at the boatyard and lend a hand in her renovation when I wasn't working at the bar. I agreed, and set about learning the workings of the boat close-up, helping out as much as my limited experience would allow and generally enjoying the weather and the company.

Lietzman then added to his air of mystery by suddenly disappearing. Somewhat bemused, I decided to hang around Geraldton anyway, and Lietzman was gone just long enough for his absence to feel less like an impromptu holiday, and more like what it was. My suspicions were confirmed when I was taken to one side by the boatyard owner.

'Hey, Michael, how long were you intending to stay here in Geraldton?'

'I hadn't given it too much thought. Why do you ask?'

He passed me a cold beer from the cooler, took one for himself and we both popped them as we watched a group of surfers stroll by, headed for the beach.

'Well, it's not me that's asking. Bourbon's in a little trouble, he's being held for questioning in Melbourne.'

I thought it wiser not to ask why, and listened as his proposition was relayed to me via this intermediary.

'They'll almost definitely grant him bail, though, so he should be back here in around a couple of weeks. The boat should be ready to go by then and he'll be taking off pretty much straight away. He's gonna need someone to crew for him. You interested?'

Yep, I was interested.

On his return to Geraldton, Lietzman was tight-lipped about his absence, and if he didn't care to divulge the reasons behind his temporary incarceration, then I wasn't going to press him on the subject. While he was away I had managed to offload the last of my Chinese radios and was beginning to tire of life in the caravan. Australia had started to feel small to me by now, the lure of the outback waning. The prospect of joining Lietzman and hitching a ride to anywhere on his boat was becoming more attractive with each bourbon I poured. Maybe it was his tales of the sea, or perhaps it was the way he told them, or maybe it was just that I didn't want the conversation to end, but all Robert Lietzman had to do was say the word.

Lietzman was eager to move on. His bail would not last for ever and his scheduled court appearance would certainly have resulted in a prison term. I knew he needed to get away, but although we spent our spare hours working side by side to make the *Diana* seaworthy, and most evenings in the bar listening to tinny FM rock on the last Chinese radio, there was still one little talk we had not yet had. What he neglected to tell me in those early conversations was that he smuggled marijuana for a living.

Lietzman's involvement in the Australian dope trade went way back. Specifically, he had been running loads of weed from Thailand into Australia aboard the *Diana* and despite starting out strictly as an amateur had, until pretty recently, been doing it successfully. His run of good luck had bottomed out though, in the midst of a sting operation set up by the Australian authorities. He'd spent a couple of months in the holding cells, dodging the drug squad's questions for as long as he could until through some nifty legal manoeuvring he finally secured a release on bail, a circumstance he fully intended to capitalize on.

Lietzman had originally wanted a crew of two to accompany him on the next leg of his voyage and asked me if I could possibly recruit the second crew member. I duly asked around the few contacts I had made in town but had no luck in finding an extra pair of hands for our planned voyage. It was, it seemed, destined to be just the two of us.

The date we were to leave Australia was set. I began cutting the few cords that bound me to my life on the open road in outback Australia, phoned my mother and said I may be away for a while, and threw myself wholeheartedly into this new caper, wherever it was to take me.

I had sold my car, my caravan and my fishing equipment and the few possessions I had been travelling with and embarked on a new adventure with the proceeds safely stashed in my travelling bag, an envelope of cash containing just over three thousand Australian dollars. I was instructed to meet my new captain for a midnight rendezvous at a nearby secluded beach that Lietzman had selected as our departure point. The owner of the boatyard had come through with the food and basic provisions that we would need on our journey and soon, beneath a full moon on calm seas, the *Diana* was ready to sail.

'Welcome aboard, Mike. I hope you've said your last

goodbyes to Australia; you may not see the place again for a while.'

I knew, but didn't care, that we would be bypassing official immigration and customs on the trip and apart from neglecting to load in the new battery that Lietzman had asked for, I did precisely what was asked of me. The battery problem came to light once he had made his final checks aboard the boat and attempted to start her engine.

'There's no power, Mike. You installed the new battery, right?'

I hadn't. Rather than lose his temper though, Lietzman merely phoned the boatyard owner and had him locate a working battery for us that we then duly fitted.

'Okay, Mike, take two.'

The battery problem had put the scheduled midnight launch back until dawn and there was enough light for me to see the coastline shrink in the distance as we headed out to sea. It would be many years before I would again travel to Australia under my own name. As far as Australian passport control knew, Michael Forwell, a British citizen whose parents had emigrated to the country in the late fifties, had entered but never left. As far as they're concerned, I might still be there.

It didn't even occur to me that by embarking on a journey with a man who was wanted and on the run, I had stepped up to the line that separated me from illegality. Soon, I would take a decent run up and leap right over it. Years later I read that my hooking up with Lietzman was one of the defining moments in the Thai dope trade. At the time, it felt like anything but.

*

A good way to get to know someone very well very fast is to sail with them. The *Diana* was a comfortable boat but she wasn't huge, and the close proximity Lietzman and I shared on that short journey served to cement our unlikely friendship and foreshadowed many of the high jinks we would take part in for the next decade. The journey was quiet, we bonded in mutual silence, happy to live an almost monk-like existence in our cramped environment.

By the time we had sailed past Christmas Island we were working smoothly together. I had proved myself a fast learner and an able seaman, and Lietzman was obviously pleased with me as his choice of crew. It was while sailing the Indian Ocean en route to Singapore that we felt the dynamic between the two of us shift slightly but crucially, and soon, rather than working *for* the American (despite the lack of anything like wages) I began to feel I was working *with* him as an equal. It was in this spirit that Lietzman finally confided in me.

Now I learned the reason for his arrest. I can't say I felt too surprised, although I genuinely hadn't thought too much about it. But a man who owns a boat, has recently spent time as a guest of the Melbourne constabulary and just absconded while on bail is likely to be smuggling something. Lietzman also told me that thanks to his arrest he was financially somewhat embarrassed; that is to say, he was totally flat broke, unable even to pay the money he still owed on his chandlery bills back in Geraldton.

But Robert Lietzman was used to being backed into a corner and all was not lost. He had a plan, he said, a foolproof method of turning the last of my ready cash, the three thousand Australian dollars that I was carrying, into a healthy return, doubling my money with sugar on top. I was no gambler, but a return like that had at least to be worth a look. Lietzman needed money to get back in the dope game, to get started up again, and I had it. In that simple equation lay the seeds of a partnership that would last for just under ten years and result in us earning millions of dollars moving boatloads of dope to an enthusiastic Stateside market.

Even with my limited exposure to the world of the weed, I knew that trafficking in the stuff held the distinct possibility of real and specific dangers. But Leitzman was very persuasive. The plan he suggested to me had worked for him before, and it would work again.

The advantages of smuggling Thai dope were sold to me as far outweighing the dangers. The market we were tapping into was huge; there were estimated to be almost twenty million regular pot smokers in America by the mid seventies, but the trade supplying many of them had yet to attract the undivided attention of an experienced official body dedicated to stopping it. The American Central Tactical Units (CENTAC) set up by the DEA to specifically target high-level narcotics smuggling were barely a year old and still concentrating mainly on the trade in the Class A drugs heroin and cocaine. The DEA itself had only been in operation for three years since President Nixon oversaw its formation in 1973 when it took over the duties of the Bureau of Narcotics and Dangerous Drugs, and its 1,470 officers had their hands full attempting to stop the tidal wave of violence that accompanied the burgeoning South American cocaine trade.

At the same time as Lietzman and I were sailing the *Diana* to Singapore, over in Colombia Pablo Escobar and his contemporaries, the Ochoa brothers, Carlos Lehder and Jose Rodriguez Gacha, were beginning to build empires on the profits they were amassing by smuggling first marijuana and then cocaine over the borders. By comparison to what the Colombians had planned for the decade ahead, the dope that Lietzman and I were about to start moving was a drop in the ocean.

Cocaine was becoming big news in America and for a while it seemed that everybody was doing it. There were no reliable figures charting how much white powder was being smuggled into America at the time, but demand was growing at a staggering rate within the generation that followed the burnout of the summers of love. In 1975, the year before Lietzman and I met, American authorities had estimated that five to six hundred kilos of coke per year were being snorted up American noses, a figure that underwent a radical rethink when Cali police stumbled across a single shipment of some 600 kilos aboard a plane headed for Miami.

In the same year, President Ford's Domestic Council Drug Abuse Task Force, chaired by Vice President Rockefeller, claimed that 'all drugs are not equally dangerous. Enforcement efforts should therefore concentrate on drugs which have a high addiction potential. . .'.[1] Their report went on to claim that the use of marijuana was not a major domestic problem and that resources were better employed in attempting to crack the trade in hard drugs.

1 http://www.deamuseum.org/dea_history_book/1975_1980.htm

The trade in cocaine pulled in far more cash than moving dope, a single kilo of coke in America selling for up to forty thousand dollars while weed went for between one and two thousand dollars per pound. The huge profits on offer proved irresistible to men such as Escobar and his contemporaries, men who preferred money to adventure and established early on a rule of unmitigated sensational violence in order to safeguard their share of the burgeoning new market. So the authorities were looking the other way, focusing the bulk of their efforts southwards and giving Lietzman and me the room we needed to manoeuvre. If we were sensible and careful, Lietzman's reasoning went, if we kept a cool head and our mouths shut, then all would be well. And who knows, we may even enjoy it.

It was still no duck walk. The coast was far from clear for potential smugglers intending on getting their product into the US from South East Asia, but customs and DEA attention was far more likely to be concentrated on the so-called Golden Triangle, the point where Laos, Thailand, Burma and Vietnam overlap and where a huge percentage of the world's heroin was cultivated and grown in the form of opium poppies. Steering clear of the area as much as possible was a must.

Frank Lucas, the superfly so-called 'Haint of Harlem', had revolutionized the heroin trade in New York in the late sixties and early seventies by visiting the source of the heroin and negotiating to buy his product direct from the producers in the Golden Triangle. In the process he cut out rogue elements in the Mob who had controlled much of the trade up to that point. Once his deal was done in Asia, Lucas got his trademark 'Blue Magic' smack into America hidden in the GI coffins flown into Fort Bragg. Designated to bring home the remains of the unfortunates killed in action in Vietnam via United States Air Force landing strips, the fix was in with enough members of the military at all levels to make sure the coffins containing the heroin were waved through with no questions asked. When Frank was finally taken down, he made a deal for a reduction in his sentence. Frank Lucas's testimony was directly responsible for the indictment and conviction of almost three-quarters of the New York law enforcement officers who were charged with corruption and drugs charges. There is very little black and white in the world of drug smuggling, and an awful lot of grey.

By the time we hit Singapore me and my three grand were in, though there had been no conscious decision on my part to join the ranks of the criminal class, no initiation ceremony, no more drama than a toast and a handshake. My decision to go along with Lietzman's plan was driven far more by a desire to keep the adventure going and see where it led.

My own personal experience of cannabis was minimal. I'd smoked it once on my travels while travelling economy class as deck cargo, also, ironically, en route to Singapore, when I had fallen in for the duration of the journey with a group of bong-toting hippies. I thought it looked like fun and was tempted by the merits of an expanded consciousness as outlined by our new and very stoned hippie friends, but was still less than sure. In the end I decided to have a go, but a couple of hits and a mild case of the dizzy giggles were enough to convince me that smoking pot wasn't for me, and despite going on to make millions of dollars moving the stuff around the world, I would stick with the booze and the nicotine and never smoke weed again.

Back on board the *Diana* and invigorated now by a fresh sense of purpose, Lietzman and I sailed from Singapore to Phuket, where we moored the boat. Then we flew to Bangkok and Lietzman hit the phone, showing for the first time his feel for the deal, his quick and ready skills in the quiet art of dope negotiation.

'Okay, Michael, lesson one. This is important so never forget it. When you're doing business over the phone always call from a number that can't be traced back to you. Public call boxes are best, phones in bars and hotels are okay too, so long as it's in the lobby, not in your room.'

'Call boxes. Right. Got it.' I nodded.

'Always carry a pocketful of phone change and wherever and whenever possible, always use code. Assume from this point on that every call you make is being monitored, whether it's about dope or not.'

'Right. Call-change, code, and permanent phone paranoia. Got it.'

Standing back and watching my friend pull the thing together only deepened the respect I felt for Lietzman, and further convinced me of his expertise and experience as a smuggler.

Once Lietzman had made the call we returned to our hotel room and waited for our supplier to visit. Leitzman's wholesale connection was named Kamol, a local Thai would-be gangster currently supplementing his income by working as a tour guide. Kamol arrived ten minutes later and was not what I expected at all. The man standing in our hotel room in sandals, bright-red Adidas shorts and multicoloured Hawaiian shirt and accepting a glass of Johnny Walker had one of the broadest, most infectious smiles I had ever seen, and it seemed he was in a position to help us.

'I can happily provide what you are searching. You come to right guy. Many falangs go to wrong man and lose out big-time. You pay money and I find sticks for you, best in Thailand, as many sticks as you have dollars. We drink to business now, yes?'

Cheers.

In those early days, the dope we ran came in the now outmoded shape of Buddha sticks. Buddha sticks are hardly ever seen now; in the dope game as in any other, fashions come and go, and Buddha sticks have long since gone the way of flared trousers and kaftans. In America the customers liked the sticks; it was what set Thai dope apart from that which was being smuggled into America from Mexico and South America. Thai sticks cost more on the street but for good reason – the quality was better, they provided a smoother, longer-lasting high, and weed wrapped around bamboo was a sure sign that anything sold as Thai weed was the real thing. A public warning had been issued regarding Thai sticks when the DEA was just a year old following a Hawaiian bust in 1974, but their cautionary tale didn't have quite the effect they were hoping for. When a DEA spokesman claimed that Thai sticks were three times stronger than domestic or South

American weed, stoners' ears all over America pricked up and the demand for genuine Thai was assured for years to come.

The sticks took the form of leaves of marijuana wrapped around a four-inch length of bamboo, wholesaling from the source at ten sticks to a brick. The new form of a very old drug had made its first appearance in America with the arrival home of soldiers from the Vietnam War, soldiers who had acquired a taste for the potent strain of weed on tours of duty in South East Asia.

Kamol would deliver the pot at a price of fifty dollars a pound. We were paying over the odds and Lietzman knew it. If we were less picky about our source and less worried about our liberty and security then we could have paid as little as fifteen dollars a pound. But at that price we wouldn't have had the peace of mind that working with the ever vigilant Kamol brought us, and we would have been taking far more of a risk.

It is not unheard of when buying dope in bulk to have the shipment laid on, for the supplier to hand over the dope knowing they won't receive the money for the shipment until it has been landed and sold. Weed is more likely to be supplied in this fashion if it is being smuggled by air; flying is far quicker than sailing so the turnaround and payment to the supplier will take a matter of weeks as opposed to the months it can take to load and sell the dope when smuggling it by sea. If at any point the shipment is busted the supplier will almost always expect to see proof of the seizure such as newspaper headlines or arrest sheets. Once satisfied that the loss is legitimate the supplier will often write off the loss and look for new partners with more chance of getting their product through. Some of the heavier guys though would want payment in full no matter what the excuse. We had paid for our first shipment together ourselves; we weren't splitting the risk with anyone, but we weren't splitting the profit either.

Two nights after Lietzman had put in his order for the weed, we got another knock at our hotel room door.

'I am Fah. You will come with me, please.'

Fah was Kamol's brother and business partner. He smiled less than Kamol and those two introductory statements pretty much exhausted his supply of English phrases, so for the rest of the night we communicated with our nocturnal visitor through a series of nods, grunts and hand gestures. Fah was a nervous, shifty man who seemed to avoid eye contact, his gaze flitting around the room from windows to door, taking in our few clothes and possessions until it finally came to rest on the bottle of Johnny Walker and two half-filled glasses on the bedside table. I had never met anyone quite like him and wasn't sure at first if I wholly trusted him.

'Where are we going?' I demanded. 'Where are you taking us?'

'You will come with me, please. You will come with me.'

I looked over at Lietzman, who was busily tying the laces on his deck shoes and preparing to go. It seemed we would be leaving with our odd visitor.

'You come with me, please, you come with me.'

In the dead of night Fah led us down to his clapped-out old car and drove through the Bangkok city limits and out into the country. Lietzman and I sat in the back.

'You sure this is okay, Bourbon? You comfortable with this?' I asked in a low voice.

'You can't just walk into a store and buy what we're buying, Michael. As dope buys go, I've seen weirder. Welcome to Thailand, buddy.'

After a journey that was as much off-road as on, Fah eventually parked up at the edge of what looked, by the light of the moon shining through the canopy of trees overhead, to be a small village. We were led to a hut at the edge of the village and once inside, motioned to sit. Besides Fah, Lietzman and myself, three Thai women sat cross-legged on the floor of the small hut around a black plastic bin bag exuding a sweet smell that filled the small dwelling and would soon become very familiar. The women looked up we entered and smiled broadly in welcome, before returning to their task.

The bag in front of them was filled with weed, and it was all ours. The women were busy, working to the soundtrack of the surrounding jungle, noisy even at night. They were reaching into the sack and pulling out handfuls of the green plant, painstakingly wrapping the dope around short lengths of bamboo, making sticks and bundling the sticks together into bricks of ten.

As the bricks were prepared and piled in the corner of the hut they occasionally handed one over to Lietzman and me for inspection. Lietzman held the bricks to his nose and inhaled, pulled off small pieces of the buds and rolled them between his fingers until they broke up and smelled them again, encouraging me to do the same. For all I knew about dope at the time he may as well have been handing me privet cuttings, but I followed his lead and tried to look as though I knew what I was doing, pulling what I thought were connoisseur faces as I broke up the weed in my hand and noticed its occasional tinges of orange and what looked like crystal. Each time after completing his quality-control ritual Lietzman looked over at the women, nodded enthusiastically and, unusually for him, even smiled.

'This ain't the best Thai stick in the world, Michael,' he said breezily, 'but it's a long ways from being the worst.'

Though dope in stick form was popular with stoners at the time, smuggling it was wasteful. First there was the time and expense involved in having these local Thai women painstakingly wrap the leaves around the bamboo. The second factor, and far more important to the would-be smuggler, was that much of the weight and space of the freight was taken up with sticks of bamboo that would eventually be discarded rather than the pot itself, which would eventually be smoked. The sticks cut an unnecessary swathe into potential profit. As always though, the forces of supply and demand won out. You demand and as sure as night follows day, someone, somewhere, will supply.

Cannabis's star was in the ascendant, and was fast becoming a mainstay of American social and cultural life. Dope was no longer the well-kept secret it had once been on the streets of San Francisco and New York, it was no longer the dividing line between hip and square society. Weed had infiltrated every echelon of American culture, and its growing fan base was not yet fully hip to the myriad forms dope could take. There was a whole new audience out there and they wanted sticks, so in a spirit of profitable largesse, we gave them sticks. Having said that, of course, smoking dope was nothing new; people have been using the drug for medical, spiritual and religious reasons for thousands of years, not to mention those who just want to sit back, relax and get high. For my part, not belonging to any of those groups I was initially nonplussed upon seeing my first load of dope close up, amazed that there was an audience out there who were ready to part with their hard-earned money for what I saw as nothing more than slightly tired-looking weed. I was staggered that the scruffy contents of the bin bag that Lietzman had procured would be of interest to anyone, let alone at the prices he was quoting. At first, not being a pot smoker myself, I just didn't get it.

We sat for hours in the small hut watching as our first shipment of dope was lovingly prepared. At one point the women took a break from their work and bowls of rice and fish were handed out to everyone there. Gradually, sunlight began to seep into the hut as night turned into day and the last of our bricks was prepared and added to the pile. By now Fah had curled up and fallen asleep on a mat on the floor. Lietzman poked him awake and we thanked the women as well as our limited vocabulary would allow and with our weed safely hidden in the boot of Fah's car, headed back into Bangkok.

'Now comes the fun part,' Lietzman told me, as the pair of us sat in our hotel room, staring at twenty pounds of Thai stick, 'disguising the stuff and getting it into America.'

We set about trying to figure ways to smuggle the dope, swapping ideas but coming up with nothing workable. Looking around the room my gaze alighted on the framed print hanging on the wall depicting a beach by night, lit by a full bright moon, not unlike the one we had so recently left behind in Geraldton.

'I know how we'll do it,' I told Lietzman. 'Come with me.'

After a visit to a few local Bangkok hardware stores and a liquor store for a fresh bottle of bourbon and a carton of cigarettes, we wandered the streets looking for the last item we'd need to realize my idea. We stopped at a tourist stall stocked with packed shelves full of local souvenirs, dolls in traditional Eastern dress for the kids back home, flashy trashy costume jewellery with a hint of the exotic for the wife and a thousand other brightly coloured knick-knacks that no one could ever need. Gathering dust beneath the glittering array of curios I spotted a pair of pseudo-ceremonial carved wooden temple masks in vivid greens, reds and golds featuring wild devil-made-me-do-it staring eyes and gratuitous extended tongues that completed their look of mischief, a look that seemed somehow to sum up the enterprise they were about to become embroiled in.

Clutching the masks we returned to the hotel and got to work destroying the wardrobe in the corner of our room with a selction of newly acquired saws and hammers. Working diligently we set about deconstructing the frustratingly sturdy wardrobe in order to create two large and elaborate hollow picture frames. These surrounded a pair of ceremonial masks mounted on squares of deep black velvet, hasty works of local art of dubious merit that we hoped would fox customs at the American end and conceal our first joint shipment of Thai marijuana.

God only knows what our hotel neighbours made of the racket created by the handymen in the next room, or the maid, sent in to clean following our swift departure. There are touring hardcore rock bands who cause less damage.

The hollow frames were filled with Thai stick, the masks set in place and first-class Stateside flights were booked. Two days later I was carrying the fully laden fruits of our labours as hand luggage onto the flight into America.

The walk through customs at San Francisco airport was probably one of the dumbest moves I made in my entire smuggling career. Travelling under my own name, heading towards the grim-faced official waiting to question me, I was wired on a heady cocktail of fear and adrenalin. Time seemed to slow almost to a halt, my throat dried, my pulse quickened and my palms began to sweat. It felt great.

'Purpose of visit?' he barked. During the few brief seconds when our eyes met I was convinced he knew precisely what I was up to.

'Holiday,' I said, surprised my voice was so calm.

Luckily for me, the customs official on duty that day made a split-second decision about the six-foot-plus sandy-haired Englishman with the decidedly odd-looking picture frames and decided not to pull me into the small side room encased in frosted glass for a few more questions. If I had been detained, my life would have panned out very differently indeed.

CHAPTER THREE

MARK, GEORGE, DIANA AND CHARLIE SUPERSTAR

Leitzman's contacts came through on both ends of the deal. Kamol's weed was good quality and the hippie guys he knew in California were as good as their word and paid cash on the nail for the dope.

Lietzman knew the Californian connection from his adventures in the dope trade prior to our meeting. They were a mellow bunch whose relaxed half-asleep approach belied the determination with which they avoided the straight world. They dealt the dope we brought them in order to finance a life on the fringes of normality. They were both trustworthy and trusting in their bellbottoms and sandals, but they were no woolly stoners. They dealt regularly with cash in amounts that many legitimate businesses could only dream of making, and were typical of many hippie businessmen still managing to operate before the guns moved in. I liked them.

The buyers, Rod and Alfie, headed a loose community based in San Francisco that offered spiritual enlightenment and a steady supply of good strong weed to their retinue of followers. They styled themselves after the Sadhus, the Indian holy men they had encountered on trips to the Ganges who devote their lives to the pursuit of cosmic liberation through meditation and worship and in the process eschew all and any trappings of materialism. The Californian chapter of the cult was not so into living without worldly goods and, despite their occasional taste in lavender turbans and long flowing robes, always kept an eye on the bottom line. The amount of dope we'd smuggled into California was small by their standards.

Once I had cleared the load through customs Lietzman and I emptied out the picture frames and headed to a hotel car park where we had arranged to meet Rod and make the handover. We lurked behind a pillar until Rod's car appeared. From what Lietzman had told me about him I expected a cross between a Hare Krishna devotee and a member of the Grateful Dead. I got neither. The only thing that slightly gave Rod away as being anything other than a regular businessman on our first meeting was the long hair he tied back in a ponytail and the sandals he wore with his three-piece suit and striped tie.

The handover went without a hitch. Our cash came in crisp notes and Rod, the would-be guru and dispenser of the vibe of inner peace, didn't so much as look at the product we had delivered to check on its quality. Trust, man. Before driving off to divide up his haul and sell it on, Rod assured us that our dealings didn't have to end there.

'We can take as much weed as you can supply. Business between us will be good. Go in God's light and return with more of this righteous crop. The more the better.'

We had earned over forty thousand dollars for a week's work, a healthy amount of working capital in 1976 and I was duly impressed. A business was born, and from day one, business was booming.

Once I'd walked the gauntlet of that first customs check there was no turning back. The feeling was too good to give up, the rush that crashed over me like a wave as I realized I'd got away with it was too euphoric. I was hooked. I felt like my search was over and I had finally found what I had spent all those years looking for. And I soon discovered I had a natural talent for inventing ingenious ways of disguising the dope that Lietzman procured in order to land it safely in America.

Returning to Asia once again and basing ourselves in Singapore hotels with the profits from the first job as cash collateral, we set about planning another job. By taking care who we worked with and who we talked to, we were planning to build the chain we'd hang a future from. The plans we were formulating would have proved a lot for two people to carry out unaided, but fortune smiled down on us and we had the good luck to hook up for a while with Mark and George.

In Thailand at the time there were many others just like Lietzman and me, good-humoured chancers and perennial outsiders who found the local temperature agreeable and enjoyed the Wild West feel of South East Asian streets where anything could happen and, if you stuck around long enough, usually did. Us and those like us. We responded well to the Asian culture, we were warmed by the sun and the smiles and the easygoing atmosphere, charmed by the fact that here, with just a little luck, a good idea and a modicum of hard work we could become whoever we wanted to be.

Mark and George were footloose and fancy free, passing the time at Changi yacht club when Lietzman and I met them. Like many of the boat people who hung around the yacht club and the harbour in Singapore, they divulged few details of their past. Lietzman and I were the same, itinerant nomads with an eye for the main score who knew that the less you told someone about yourself, the less they could then tell about you.

Mark and George had just purchased a fishing boat, which they were currently living on, and which, as luck would have it, proved to be just the kind of vessel that Lietzman and I needed in order to make our own operation run a little smoother. We began to bump into Mark and George socially, drinking with them in the bars around Changi yacht club frequented by the workers from the local oil fields. One night, all of us a little the worse for wear, the conversation turned to smuggling.

'So, this boat we've bought,' Mark said, watching our reaction, 'it needs to start paying its way soon. We need to start moving a load or two and earn a little money.'

Lietzman's eyes and mine met. As usual in the early days, he took the lead. 'We might be able to help you guys out there. How would you feel about moving something for us? Just from Thailand to Singapore?'

It seemed this was the response they had been hoping for. A smile passed between them as Mark questioned Lietzman as to the nature of the work we had in mind.

'We could do it, be glad to, depending on what it is of course, and what the money's like. We don't want to get into anything too heavy.'

'It's marijuana,' Lietzman said bluntly. 'We'll pay you fifty thousand dollars in cash for every shipment. You pick up our product in Thailand and sail it over to the *Diana* in Singapore. We take it to America and sell it and pay you when we get paid at that end. You'll be waiting two weeks for your money, tops.'

As our four glasses raised in a toast to future success the deal was done. Lietzman and I now had a transportation network in place in South East Asia.

As our dope business began to expand, Mark and George proved reliable couriers, picking up our weed in Thailand and sailing it to Singapore where we would ready it for its journey to California. We were never a gang of four, more two gangs of two who worked together for our mutual benefit, but Mark and George were, as far as Lietzman and I were concerned, the right guys in the right place at the right time. But although we liked them, we always maintained a little distance from them, and vice versa. Aside from their enthusiastic consumption of Thai weed, they had one or two other habits that didn't fit in with our lifestyle. Mark and George liked cocaine. What they did in their own time was their own affair but we worried that their propensity to party could one day jeopardize all that we were setting into motion and so with this in mind we never considered bringing the pair onboard as full partners.

As time went on Robert Lietzman, by nature a secretive and guarded soul, began to trust me more and more. The nature of the work we were doing tied our lives together for the foreseeable future. We liked each other, sure, but we quickly realized that for our business to succeed we needed one another too. With this trust in me growing, the American began to reveal secrets from his past, much of which had been spent in the business of smuggling dope. During his career in the weed game Lietzman had made some enemies. As happens with depressing regularity in the dope trade, deals had gone wrong, people had been pissed off and passed over, causing grudges and resentments to simmer and boil. He was owed money all over town from smuggling operations that had gone sour and went out at one point on a mission to collect, with me in tow.

'See, Michael, in the dope game, it isn't really the weed you have to worry about, it's the money. Smuggling dope is pretty easy, you buy it, you hide it, you ship it and you sell it. Do all that carefully with a little common sense and you're home and dry. But when the money starts to roll in, that's when you've really got to start watching your back. The guy you thought was your partner, soon as he's got paid for the shipment you've helped him move then suddenly he's not so eager to come across with your cut. Always work with friends, Michael, people you know. Rule number one: no outsiders.'

Lietzman never caught up with his debtors on that long night trawl that took us from busy bars to deserted beaches, but the message in his catalogue of cautionary tales was clear: be careful, always be extra, super careful, of who you work with. Even if we had caught up with Lietzman's debtors that night it is questionable as to what would have happened. I took pride in the fact that throughout my career I never carried a gun, I never had need to use violence or even to threaten it. It was a point of pride for both of us.

At the time, most smugglers operating out of Thailand worked in syndicates, carving up any given deal within a loose affiliation of partners, the cash return dependent on the amount of money invested in the operation. Most of the smugglers who worked in this way were strictly hands-off, little more than venture capitalists whose field happened to be the black market. The lion's share of the deal's profits would be earned by the men who had put the deal together and taken the most risks. Because of this method of working it was theoretically possible for someone with the right contacts but no money or resources to turn a profit on a deal simply as acting as the middleman between X and Y, but the downside of the syndicate system meant there were a lot of faces around, a lot of deals being done by people with no history together, deals motivated often by greed or status within the smuggling world rather than a desire for the thrill of the stunt. Lietzman and I vowed early on not to work in this way and instead always keep a tight rein and a cool eye on every aspect of the operations we initiated. Control was the key.

The picture-frame scam had gone without a hitch but attempting anything that brazen again would have been stupid, and we would have deserved to have been caught. We were forty thousand dollars in the black, but we knew that if we were to turn the cash into a long-term proposition we needed a new plan, a method by which we could send our dope as normal freight, throw it in with the tonnes of legal cargo shipped in and out of ports around the globe every day.

In order to get our next shipment into the United States I hit upon the idea of packing the Thai stick stealthily in a series of false-bottomed crates of swimming tropical fish. Once Mark and George had picked up fifty pounds of weed from our supplier and delivered it to Lietzman and me in Singapore, the idea was to create a shipment that would have looked to be more trouble than it was worth opening for any over-zealous customs official at the other end. The devil is in the detail, and I soon became an expert on the habits and species of live exotic fish I was sourcing in Sri Lanka and exporting to America. We had the crates constructed, the weed loaded and the shipments sent as normal air freight.

In order to pack the weed into the crates we squashed the sticks into five-pound slabs and secreted anywhere from twenty to thirty slabs into the crates per shipment. It was then merely a case of booking a flight to America under one of the assumed names we were beginning to collect and signing for our package once it had been cleared through customs at the American end. Our buyers were in place and still more than happy to purchase as much weed as we could provide, and always paying cash. The method was far from foolproof and there were still risks, but they were far outweighed by the addictive thrill of success.

The fish-tank scam revealed one logistical problem that would need solving if we were to sustain it for any length of time. Mark and George had sailed all the dope down in one hit, a substantial amount, and we were now in the not ideal position of being in Singapore with a huge amount of weed that we intended to fly to America piece by piece hidden in the crates over the coming months. Storing the consignment of weed became a problem and when the solution presented itself, it was a killer.

We set about breaking the dope down into twelve separate, manageable loads. We then went and bought ourselves twelve lengths of thick plastic industrial piping, with two end caps per length that ensured anything stored inside the pipes would be completely water- and airtight. The pipes were filled with weed and the caps put into place at either end. We tied lead weights around the lengths of pipe to ensure that they would sink. The pipes were then loaded onboard *Diana,* sailed out to a carefully chosen location and dropped straight down to the bottom of the ocean. To retrieve the dope we simply had to return to the spot, dive overboard with a sharp knife and cut loose the weights. Once the pipes were no longer weighed down by the lead it became a case of raising the pipe full of weed to the surface, dragging it aboard the *Diana* and taking it to the workshop we had hired where we built and loaded the crates. The plan worked beautifully and we never lost a single load.

We worked conscientiously, Mark and George helping out at the Singapore end. The crates carrying the fish and concealing the dope were well made, having been designed specifically for the job, and the longer the scam ran the more efficient it became. We did have one close shave though. On one shipment suspicious customs officials decided to examine further the construction of one of the crates. They sawed off a corner to ensure nothing was secreted inside, missing the hidden compartment hiding slabs of weed by mere centimetres. As Lietzman and I waited to sign for the crate at the bonded customs warehouse, adrenalin kicking in at the unexpected delay, we were approached by an officer.

'Sorry for keeping you waiting, gentlemen,' he said. 'We've been taking a closer look at your delivery today. Never can be too careful with stuff sent over from Asia—' He paused, hard eyes staring at us. I forced myself not to react. 'It's all in order though, sorry for your wait, and have a nice day.'

We waited until we were well out of the officer's ear-shot before bursting out laughing.

The fish scam lasted for a full, happy year, with crates being sent to America weekly and constantly getting through. It went so well that our buyers on the West Coast set up their own infrastructure to receive and unpack the crates at their end, hitting upon the idea of opening their own pet shop. This was ideal because it meant that any documentation relating to the transport of the fish would appear all the more kosher. It also meant that as well as making money from selling the dope we were sending them they could earn a little extra on the side by selling the fish.

So all we had to do now was dive for the weed, pack it and send it, and then travel on a plane to collect our cash. We took the money back as hand luggage. After extensive market research, we picked large chrome Halliburton briefcases to carry our loot. They were sturdy and roomy, favoured by businessmen abroad, and they looked great. Business was so brisk that year that we soon lost count of how many trips we made to California and the number of suitcases we bought.

But variety is the spice of life, and we were always on the lookout for new ways to get the dope in and the money out. Another idea that worked well for us as a one-off was the Four X smuggle. The Four X was a mini speedboat, a zippy black-and-red job that would fit easily into most living rooms. It was powered by an outboard motor that, despite its diminutive size, made the boat capable of great speeds. The Four X was resolutely unstable, wholly unsuitable for racing, but it was a fun toy, and with its painted numbers and flashy decals it looked good, which counted for a lot.

Both Lietzman and I loved speed, the faster the better, and we were hooked the minute we opened up the Four X and experienced first hand just how plucky the little craft was as we put it through its paces in the waters around Singapore harbour. Our fun over, we loaded it on to a trailer and moved it to a rented warehouse where we packed every available inch of the boat full of weed, then crated it up for shipment to America as normal freight. Once it left for California we flew first class to San Francisco.

We spent the night drinking aboard the houseboat Lietzman had just bought, and I was so hungover the next day there was no room in my pounding head for any anxiety about being caught. Bleary-eyed, I watched customs officials check and stamp our paperwork at the warehouse, and in a daze helped load our crate on to a trailer. We hitched the trailer to the El Camino we had bought to use while in the States, and towed it to a nearby rented warehouse where we unpacked the weed and got it ready for collection by Rod. We'd managed to cram the little Four X with three thousand pounds of dope, selling it on in the States at the established wholesale price of $2,000 per pound. The $600,000 we made on the shipment was then duly packed into the hiding places on the boat in which the weed had travelled, and the Four X was shipped straight back to Singapore, never once having sailed on American water.

Once the boat was back in Singapore I decided to stage a little race with some of the guys I had met around the marina. Really it was just a chance for me to show off our new toy and have some fun. While I had a fast boat but no real driving skills to speak of, my main opponent in the race, the only man there who could conceivably beat me, was just the opposite. His boat wasn't great but he could drive it like the devil.

We took off around Singapore harbour and soon the two of us had left the rest of the small pack behind as we battled for first place. When it became obvious that I was about to lose if I didn't take some drastic action I cut across the side of a barge at full speed in order to overtake my rival. But I'd mistimed and overshot and sent the boat crashing into the side of the barge and totalled it. As what was left of the Four X sank beneath the waters around Singapore my competitor gave me a lift back into the harbour and graciously allowed me to buy the drinks for the rest of the night.

One night in Singapore, while Lietzman was over in

America spending some time on his houseboat, I attended a party close to the hotel I was living in. While there my attention was immediately drawn to a group of four stunning Chinese girls on the other side of the room. One girl in particular caught my eye. She was exquisite, her jet-black hair cut into a bob that framed the most beautiful face I had ever seen. Transfixed if a little unnerved by her beauty, I summoned up the courage to approach her and strike up a conversation.

Her name was May, she said, she was eighteen years old and lived locally. I was struck at that first meeting by the effortless grace she exuded and soon got lost in her eyes, falling deeper as she laughed and told me of her large family and her traditional upbringing in the East. I was captivated by her looks and calmed by her presence, hit square-on by what the Sicilians call the Thunderbolt. I was sold.

By the time the party was drawing to a close I had obtained May's phone number and, as I pocketed it, the butterflies in my stomach told me I would definitely be calling. I didn't know it then, but I had just met the love of my life.

In the business of dope smuggling the most important asset to any enterprise, large or small, is trust, and nothing erodes that precious commodity like an out-of-whack pay-day. Trust is the glue that holds successful criminal enterprise together, as many of our contemporaries learned to their cost. The dope trade was full of whispers of the worm that turned, cautionary tales swapped by smugglers in the bars of Bangkok and Singapore. There was the story of a cokehead in America who was waiting rather impatiently for his share of the cash from a big pot deal, but his recent erratic behaviour and all-round coke-fuelled unreliability meant that his presence threatened to seriously fuck up the ongoing operation. In view of this, his partners elected to furnish him with fifty thousand dollars in an envelope and request he made himself scarce until all of the pot they were bringing in was offloaded and sold. They fully intended to pay him his full share when the back end of the deal was squared away but motivated as he was by uncut coke and knife-edge paranoia rather than anything like rational thinking, he suspected the worst and elected to take desperate measures. With the fifty grand still nestling in his inside pocket he marched straight into the nearest DEA office and gave chapter and verse on his partners in crime, taking out pre-emptive revenge and placing his compadres squarely in the firing line.

Unlike the horror stories of others, my partnership with Lietzman and our loose arrangement with Mark and George continued amicably for a couple of years. We were working hard, but while the loads were getting progressively larger (and in turn, of course, so were the profits) there was a ceiling to the amount a two-man operation could move. We soon realized that the key was to move the shipments in one operation, rather than the rolling scam of the fish tanks and minor one-offs like the picture frames and the Four X smuggle. If we wanted to expand, something would have to give.

It also became obvious to Lietzman and me that we needed a base, some secure headquarters to run the business from, somewhere safe to call home. Bangkok in

Thailand was then, as now, a magnet for a dubious kind of tourist, a place where the authorities were content not to ask too many questions as long as the bills got paid on time and the cash-rich Western holidaymakers kept the money rolling in. The city had benefited from the nation's quiet revolution of 1932 when it had converted to a system of constitutional monarchy, its eight million inhabitants witnessing the emergence of comforts and luxury so beloved of Western tourists and made evermore attractive to the new breed of casual international traveller by the welcoming, laid-back attitude of the indigenous people.

The anonymity offered by the city appealed to us. By now we were up to our necks in suitcases full of ready cash with no visible, legal means by which we'd earned it. It was only a question of time before someone noticed the unlikely pair of prosperous dilettantes, and if the prying eyes happened to be official, even in the casual atmosphere of Thailand, then our situation could become very sticky indeed.

'There's got to be something we can do with all this bloody money, Lietzman,' I grumbled. 'If you could have anything in the world, what would you pick?'

So we acquired a bar. Just like that, buying the lease for twenty thousand American dollars. Cash.

Owning a bar was the perfect cover. We may not have smoked the marijuana we dealt in but we were far from viceless. Despite agreeing early on that neither of us would touch the dope we smuggled, and that we would never move anything stronger than weed, we both enjoyed a drink and were already spending an awful lot of time in bars. Lietzman in particular was a fan of staying up all night, bourbon in hand, watching the action, so why not buy our own? And there were other good reasons for the acquisition: purchasing a bar meant we could remain private and sociable at the same time, create the impression of a healthy source of income and fill the long gaps between smuggling operations. And we could keep our eyes on the very private world we were building, we could keep it all under one roof, and we liked that.

The establishment we purchased was called the Charlie Superstar. It wasn't the flashiest joint on Bangkok's Patpong strip by any means, in fact when we moved in it was little more than a dive, but it had potential. Charlie Superstar had been decorated on a budget by the previous owners in bamboo and tired red velvet throughout but it was big enough to hold enough punters to turn a healthy profit. From day one the punters came and the project benefited from a sprinkling of the fairy dust that seemed to settle on everything we touched in the glory days.

To anyone entering the Charlie Superstar, Lietzman and I would have appeared to be no more than normal paying customers, regulars perhaps, who spent so much time in the place that we were on friendly terms with the bar staff and hostesses who worked there. Each of us had our favoured seat at the bar where we would put in many long hours drinking and surveying our small kingdom. We were as friendly to other paying customers as it was in our respective natures to be – I in particular enjoyed entertaining the journalists who began to frequent the place –

but we made sure never to discuss the dope business if there was ever the slightest chance of being overheard.

As was expected of any self-respecting Patpong bar, we filled the place with girls, the more beautiful the better, whose job it was to get the punters in and keep them drinking. We found them through Frank, a fun-loving local with a taste for the nightlife, who we brought in to front the business for us and manage the joint. It was a good piece of casting, and Frank soon turned out to be a real asset. He was a striking-looking guy, with an attractive mix of east and west that had earned him work as a model and a couple of appearances in TV commercials and marked him as a local celebrity. He provided the ideal counterpoint to the anonymity Lietzman and I actively sought and turned out to be a front-man par excellence. Not being Thai and the local laws regarding such things being what they are, we could not officially 'own' the bar, so to all official intents and purposes Frank was the boss.

Frank was married to a beautiful Thai girl, a fact which was well known in and around Patpong, and had great taste when it came to filling the bar with as many stunning local females as he could cram in. The girls smiled, shook and shimmied, they laughed at the punters' jokes and sang along to jukebox music with no real understanding of what the lyrics meant. They lent Charlie Superstar some class and the place was a roaring success from the get-go.

Owning the bar bought us freedom, we had the cash and the time to experiment and were constantly on the lookout for fresh ideas and ways to spend our time and money in addition to the new bar business. One afternoon, just as I returned to Charlie Superstar with my cigarettes, a carton of Benson and Hedges Gold to feed my three pack a day habit, Lietzman arrived and ordered himself a drink, taking the stool next to me at the bar.

'Hey, Michael, I just bought a barge.'

I blinked. 'You just bought a . . .'

'A barge, yeah. It's a big one too, Michael, big enough to live on, hell, this things so big you could fit a hotel on it.'

There had been no previous mention of his intention to make the purchase but, knowing him as I did, I took the news in my stride and wondered what on earth we would do with this addition to our assets. I needn't have worried though; once again, Bourbon had plans.

Lietzman had kept the *Diana* and still enjoyed sailing the trimaran, taking her on his many trips around the East and on up to Crete and the Greek islands. We both enjoyed the trips we had started making to Greece, spending long nights and wallets full of cash in bars and restaurants, nights that ended with a floor covered in smashed plates and a table strewn with empty bottles. We'd begun making a habit of sailing *Diana* there for rest and relaxation breaks as well as keeping an eye on the many boats that were constantly changing hands. Lietzman saw the *Diana* as a wasted asset, and insisted that our next smuggle would be the ideal chance to use the craft for the purpose for which she was originally intended.

'You want to load *Diana* with product and sail her to the States? Lietzman, even for you that's an outrageous idea.'

'No, man, you don't get it. We don't *sail* her there, we just fill her up and send her. We've done it before, we'll do it again. There's a lot of room on that boat, man. My *Diana*'s a girl who don't give up her secrets too easily.'

Diana, first and foremost, was a smuggler who, much like her owner, led a secret life. Despite a seemingly normal appearance the boat had been modified to make the most of the onboard space, which could be utilized to carry cargo undetected. She was going to be one big floating stash-box.

By loading the product into the specially hollowed out lateral struts that ran across the width of the boat, we could pack the *Diana* up with the six tons of weed Mark and George had picked up for us from Kamol without any real harm to the boat's performance or looks. Lietzman sailed the *Diana* from her mooring in Singapore to Phuket in Thailand, where the barge he had recently bought was moored, and we set about packing the dope into the trimaran for her voyage to America. At last Lietzman and I set sail together once again, but this time with a lot more at stake. We sailed the *Diana* up to Greece via the Suez Canal and then on to Crete. We got our act together properly in Crete, making sure that the weed was well hidden enough to make it through American customs checks undetected. Once in the port of Piraeus in Athens, busy with backpacking holidaymakers and loved-up honeymooners boarding ferries out to the islands, we oversaw *Diana* being packed onto a container and shipped to America as commercial freight.

While in Greece we did a little shopping and bought ourselves a pair of landing barges, the *Diver's Delight I* and *II*, which we thought would come in useful to load vehicles and stuff on and off the big barge that Lietzman had bought. Once *Diana* was well on her way to America we booked a couple of first-class tickets, and sent Mark and George on to America to pick up the Camino and drive her across country to meet the *Diana*. Lietzman and I headed back to Singapore to take delivery of the landing barges before we bought ourselves two more first-class air tickets to America. Rather than our usual port of San Francisco, we had this time elected to send the dope via Charleston in South Carolina. We reckoned Charleston was a quiet port, somewhere not usually associated with the dope game. Once the boat arrived in Charleston, we reasoned, our dogged self-belief fast turning the corner into full-blown arrogance, all we'd have to do was drive up to the dock at the bonded customs warehouse where the *Diana* was being stored, sign for the shipment under an assumed name and drive it away to offload and cash up.

Except that it wasn't quite that simple.

For some reason, customs at Charleston were suspicious of the *Diana* from the off. When we went to pick her up we were told by taciturn officials that she wouldn't be released for a while yet, there were checks that the authorities still wanted to carry out.

Charleston was a busy, scruffy port. Enquiring after the collection of the *Diana* involved reporting to the prefab site office and dealing with the officer who manned it. Over the next few weeks we started to hate his unsmiling face. Holed up in a nearby hotel overlooking the dock that was storing our boat and our dope, we began to get worried. We knew that the only way to deal with the situation was to keep cool and front it out; we were staring customs in the eye and neither side was prepared to blink first. We were making daily trips to the customs warehouse, frustrating excursions that always ended with our being told once again that our crate had not yet been cleared.

'Sorry to have to tell y'all but we're not quite ready to hand you fellas' boat over quite yet. But y'all keep in touch, shouldn't be too long now.'

A week and a half passed in this nerve-shredding manner and we all began to get a little twitchy. We passed the time drinking and trying not to imagine customs agents whooping as they began to pull hundreds of bricks of Thai weed from their hiding place. Over drinks in a bar close to the customs dock, Lietzman and I began to consider our options.

'We could walk away from it, Bourbon,' I said reluctantly. 'We could just fly home and leave it here. Chalk this one up to experience.'

'Michael, there are six tons of dope on that boat. Six tons. Do you even know how many millions of dollars that shipment is worth? Besides, those guys have got my *Diana*, and I want her back.'

Rather than just sit, drink and wait we decided to get proactive and see for ourselves what was going on. Lietzman and I hired a plane, a single-engine Cessna complete with pilot, and used it to fly over the customs compound and dock to look for a clue as to what was going on. It was worse than we thought. A small knot of officials had *Diana* surrounded, one crawled on all fours to see whether the bottom had been tampered with, others walked around the vessel, tapping away at her structure and listening out for the telltale echoing thud of a hollowed-out compartment or hidden space. The cockpit of the small plane was silent until Lietzman spoke and broke the increasing tension. 'The hell with this. Let's go get a drink.'

A week after *Diana*'s arrival Lietzman and I tried once again to collect the boat, painfully aware that the longer she stayed with customs, the more chance they had of stumbling across our weed.

'We still ain't quite ready to let y'all gentlemen have that boat back just yet,' the unsmiling customs officer told us. Then he sent my blood pressure rocketing. 'We're gonna let the sniffer dog take a look at it, see if Ol' Barney don't come across something we've all bin missin'.'

This was bad news. Very bad. We knew that the dope was too well hidden for anyone to find short of pulling the thing apart, but sniffer dogs were a different story. One well-trained wet nose coming within a foot of those hollowed-out lateral struts would have nailed the boat for what it was: a floating container full of tons of high-grade Thai dope.

By the start of the second week of the *Diana*'s captivity, my cohorts and I caught a much-needed break. It became apparent that there was a decided shortage of sniffer dogs in Charleston and that the particular canine the customs officials needed to check out the boat was elsewhere, no doubt putting paid to some other smuggler's best-laid plans. By now the American government were ploughing tens of millions annually into the war on drugs; luckily for our little cadre, they weren't spending the cash on dogs. It was now or never, Barney was a day away and could have arrived at any moment. It was time for action.

We seized the moment and headed for the warehouse to get pseudo tough. We feigned outrage and coughed and spluttered. At the customs office I exaggerated my English accent, puffed out my chest and acted my socks off, going for a cross between David Niven and my old Latin tutor, as I ringingly declared that enough was enough.

'Our boat has now been in your care for two weeks and no contraband or traces of contraband have been found anywhere in, on or around it. We want our boat back, and a refusal to release the craft will force us to resort to legal means to speed up the process and claim compensation through the courts for time wasted.'

Supervisors were called as I blustered through my impression of an aggrieved toff. Customs in Charleston had no choice but to begrudgingly let us have our boat back there and then.

As soon as the *Diana* was cleared we boarded her and sailed into Georgia. Lietzman seemed as relieved at having the *Diana* back as he was to have hold of the weed secreted aboard her. Happily passing his hip flask to and fro, he was talking to his boat. 'It'll take a lot more men than that to split me and you up, old girl, no doubt about it.'

I took a good hit from the flask and as the bourbon burned I tried not to think about how close we had just come to being caught. Again.

We sailed into a quiet backwoods swamp in which to retrieve the dope that customs had missed. The swamp was beautiful, lush and alive, providing this American Gothic backdrop complete with swirling mists and hungry alligators swimming around.

Every foreign noise screamed *Deliverance* as we unloaded *Diana* as speedily as we could manage, the bricks of dope piling up. That was when we started to get the first inkling that perhaps we hadn't thought the smuggle through quite as well as we should have.

The weed was expected in California, where Rod was waiting to pay cash on the nail, and the plan was to drive it cross-country in our 1965 flatbed El Camino pickup. We started loading the weed into the back, piling it up and up. All too soon the small truck was full, and we found ourselves having to secure the last of the dope to the roof of the driving compartment.

So now the weed in the back was a perilously high mound covered with moulded plastic, rendering the rear-view mirror as good as useless. The dope lashed to our makeshift roof rack was also covered by a scruffy sheet of tarpaulin. It looked bad enough but anyone coming within ten feet of the truck while it was stationary would have been in no doubt as to what was hidden under the covers. The shipment we had bought in hadn't been vacuum-packed or shrink-wrapped. It stank to high heaven.

Once the El Camino was loaded the four of us stood back and stared at the vehicle open-mouthed. Lietzman spoke first.

'Okay, guys, you know the plan. Two of us are gonna have to drive this thing over to California, the other two, including either me or Mike – no offence, guys, but Mike's the only other person in the world I'd trust with my boat – are gonna have to sail *Diana* out of here. Any volunteers?'

The silence that greeted the question was deafening. It took a full minute until I could answer my friend.

'So if I'm clear, what you're saying is that you're still expecting two of us to drive a car loaded down with tons of dope, dope that isn't even particularly well hidden, may I add, straight across America for about two days. There isn't a Plan B?'

'No need to panic, Mike,' Lietzman said, surprised. 'Shall we toss a coin for it?'

Mark and I lost. Minutes later we were on the road brazenly transporting tons of marijuana along the freeway. We took turns at the wheel, obsessively sticking to the speed limit. Before pulling into gas stations to refuel we had to ensure we were downwind of the other customers lest the sweet smell of success attract their attention. When we had to stop for food and drink we got into a comical routine involving me getting out of the truck as it was still rolling and buying our supplies as quickly as possible while Mark drove the El Camino and the dope around the block. He'd pause on the return journey just long enough to push open the door so I could dive in with our refreshments, spilling beer and burgers as I did so, and we could once again be on our merry way.

Somehow, two days later, the dope-stinking two-ton black-and-white El Camino pulled into the parking lot outside our warehouse in San Francisco. Mark and I fell bedraggled out of the car and began to learn to stand straight and walk again. Lietzman and George were there to meet us and as usual, Lietzman was somewhat disconcerting in his honesty.

'I gotta tell you, guys, driving that thing here is either the bravest or the dumbest thing I ever seen. How you ain't in jail is a mystery.'

I stared at Lietzman, unsure of whether or not he was serious. 'Well, we made it, Bourbon, and next time there's a suicide mission, we'll take it as read that you'll be undertaking it.'

'One thing's for sure, Mike, you won't have to buy another drink for a month.'

The dope was unloaded, reweighed, and the buyer contacted. We were invincible. What was beginning to be a normal day at work for me and my partners would have sent other, perhaps more sensible men, screaming for the dull routine of a simple nine to five.

CHAPTER FOUR

AND THEN THERE WERE THREE

Bobby Colflesh, Charlie Superstar and the ex-army connection.

Our bar, Charlie Superstar, was open for business during the heyday of the Patpong Road. At a time when air travel was becoming affordable and accessible, Patpong became the must-go destination for holidaying thrill-seekers keen to spend some time soaking up the danger that crackles through the air whenever nightlife and vice occupy the same small space. The strip had become popular with American soldiers during the nearby Vietnam War as the destination in which to leave the napalm behind and catch up with a little R & R, letting off steam at the many bars that were beginning to populate the area, all offering a heady mix of easy sex, strong liquor and cheap dope.

The road came alive at night, when the neon signs fizzed into life announcing the names of the bars in electric blues and shocking pinks. Punters, GIs, sex-tourists and travellers jostled shoulder to shoulder, still sweating in their civilian T-shirts, shorts and flip-flops. Thai bargirls were bussed in from outlying villages in halternecks, hotpants, miniskirts and clicky-clicky heels and hung out on the street near the open-air market plying their trade, calling out over the non-stop mix of music and tuk-tuk traffic to passers-by, inviting them to come and sample whatever was on offer in the particular establishment they worked for.

'You wahn see dancing girls? Most beautiful in all world.'

'You handsome man, wahn come meet me and my friend?'

'You like it here best . . . special show . . . just for you.'

In the midst of all this was the building housing the Charlie Superstar, narrow but tall, reaching up for four storeys, the uppermost of which had been converted into a small but comfortable two-bedroom apartment that we fitted out with a couple of beds to provide amenable, private living accommodation. The apartment was little more than a crash-pad. Most of our time in Thailand was spent in Charlie Superstar or touring the other Patpong bars, listening to gossip and plotting moves. It was a fun time and a fun place. Rather than looking seedy to us, Patpong felt vibrant and alive, pulsing with the promise and opportunity that we fully intended to capitalize on. Lietzman and I ran the business together at management meetings comprised of the two of us sitting around planning, talking and drinking, always thinking up new ways to spend the suitcases full of cash we were accruing.

We began to assess everything and everyone we came

across with an eye to the smuggle. We became experts in the second-hand boat market, checking out the vessels we found for sale in ports or classified ads in trade magazines for their potential to undergo the renovations required to hide and move serious quantities of dope.

We soon found that not only was the weed business flourishing but that we had a natural aptitude for the bar business too. We did so well as managers and hosts that the business end of the Charlie Superstar grew from its initial first-floor bar to the second, which we opened as an after-hours illegal nightclub and discothèque accessed by its clientele via a second, more private door. Even Bangkok, lax as it was in many respects, still had strict drinking laws, laws that were occasionally even enforced. The second-floor nightclub soon became a haven for those who, like Lietzman, weren't quite ready to go home when the rest of the bars on the strip officially closed.

One night, Mark and George had some news for us. George returned from the men's room edgy and animated, taking great long sniffs and talking in machine-gun bursts full of enthusiasm and freshly powdered vigour.

'Guys, it's been great, it's been great working with you. And thanks and everything [sniff], thanks for everything, thanks, but we're gonna go it alone, y'know? We're gonna set up our own thing, take our own loads over [sniff]. We've got a buyer over in the States, Mark met this guy at the yacht club who says he'll be able to move as much as we can send over so we're gonna, y'know [sniff], we're gonna go for it.'

We couldn't blame them for wanting to make the big

money by landing the dope in America and selling it on to the buyers there.

'Well, Mark, George, it's been a pleasure working with you both and there's no hard feelings,' I said truthfully. 'We completely understand why you'd want to strike out on your own, I'd probably do the same in your position. Best of luck, boys, and may Customs and Excise never come calling.'

As a parting gesture they asked Lietzman to score them a load from his supplier, which he duly did, waiving any kind of commission on the deal as a gesture of good faith. There was more than enough business for everybody and their setting up on their own in no way threatened our enterprise.

But their leaving did present us with a problem. By covering transportation in Thailand, Mark and George had assumed most of the risk for us at the South East Asian end, where drug smuggling, though a huge industry, was frowned upon to say the least. Their involvement had meant that Lietzman and I didn't even need to touch the dope until it was ready to send or ship and would therefore never be in possession of the weed until the last possible moment.

Not long after we'd said goodbye, I sat at the bar in Patpong nursing a tall one and a hangover when I ran into an English mutual acquaintance of ours, one of the many unpredictable bit-part players with big mouths who occasionally found their way into Charlie Superstar.

'Those two guys, Mark and George, you and Lietzman knew those guys, right?'

This was shaky ground; after all, I hardly really knew this guy, but my curiosity as to how our friends were doing got the better of me and I threw caution to the wind.

'Yes, I knew Mark and George, quite a pair of characters. Haven't seen them in the bar for a while, though. How are they?'

The Englishman began laughing, doubling over and gasping, getting to the point where he was soon starting to choke. 'Seems they wanted to try their hand at smuggling, saw themselves moving a weight of whatever into America. They'd been helping some guys out in the trade for a while apparently, then they thought they'd go it alone.'

'Really? I had no idea they were involved . . .'

'Yeah . . . So they bought themselves a shit-load of weed and packed their boat with it, hid it away so's customs wouldn't get a sniff of it then sent it off as cargo freight.'

Mark and George, it seemed, had decided to use one of our tried and tested smuggling methods.

'But they lost it at the last minute, bottled out by all accounts. George has been hammering the coke, paranoid as hell, the boat's been shipped to America, all fine and above board but they've convinced themselves that they're being watched by the feds, customs, whoever, that they've been rumbled. So in the end they've just left it! A boat full of Thailand's finest sitting in a customs dock somewhere with no one to claim it.'

Not only had Mark and George lost the first load they had tried to get into America, the enterprise had cost them their boat too. It was the last I ever heard of them. Shame.

Before we knew it, the 1980s were just around the corner. Up in space NASA were doing flybys of Saturn and down on earth Michael Jackson had released his *Off The Wall* album. Over in Thailand, Lietzman and I had a succession of money-spinning tropical-fish runs and one-off scams under our belts and were actively looking for more. Sipping bourbon and Cokes one night in Charlie Superstar, we discussed the problem,

'Trouble is, Mike, most of the guys out here working in the business, they just ain't careful enough. Most of them will hook up with anyone, doesn't matter who, if there's a chance of getting a load through.'

Lietzman was right. We had a personnel problem but so far had failed to find any suitable new recruits. Then Robert Colflesh, an ex-Special Forces soldier with time on his hands, walked up to the bar.

Bobby's timing was great. In the dope game, finding people to work with can be a very tricky business indeed. There are no temp agencies to call, nowhere to advertise for help. Recruitment relies upon a delicate mix of good timing, the ability to read people, and old fashioned luck. The skills required to make it in the weed business are very specific; potential players need talents not possessed by the average Joe. A certain moral flexibility is a must, creativity, organizational aptitude and the ability to think on your feet are also vital. And balls, you need balls.

Robert Colflesh, Bobby to his friends, was Pennsylvania born and Special Forces trained. He was one half of a pair of American twins born on the November day in 1957 when Eisenhower was re-elected to the White House and the day after Elvis showed the world his sensitive side by releasing 'Love Me Tender'. He, along with his twin brother Sam, had joined the army upon leaving school and both finished up their short but illustrious four-and-a-half-year military careers as Green Berets. His time in the army had introduced Robert Colflesh to Asia and the East, and he soon fell in love with the life and culture on offer in Thailand to the extent that he was ready to call the country home. It was while exploring the myriad delights on offer in Patpong that Robert Colflesh stopped in at one of its many go-go joints, leaned against the bar sipping his drink and watched the crowd throw Travolta shapes to the Bee Gees' 'Stayin' Alive'.

Looking around Charlie Superstar, Colflesh suspected there was more to the story than met the eye, that the pair who owned the place were up to something special. If he was right, he wanted in. He kept coming back, taking a stool next to us at the bar, striking up a conversation. For our part, Lietzman and I liked Bobby immediately. He was a nice guy, he was humble, he seemed typically all-American, squared jawed as a cartoon character and buzzing with infectious energy and enthusiasm. But still, Lietzman was cautious about the repeat visits.

'The only people with that much time on their hands out here who ain't just visiting on vacation are either DEA or smugglers,' he said with a shrug. 'I don't have Bobby down as an agent.'

The more we got to know Bobby, the more we believed

he could keep a secret. Bobby was in good shape too, as a result of his training at the hardcore end of the American military. On finishing up his extensive training on the American government's dollar he had spent some time learning the fine art of deep-sea diving while working out on the oil fields. Bobby knew the sea and he knew boats. Most impressively, as far as we were concerned, he was learning to speak Thai, a valuable skill that neither Lietzman nor I possessed. Bobby was becoming so proficient in the language that he could pass as local over the phone and any Thais he came in contact with face to face were charmed and impressed by his ability to communicate in the local tongue. Yes, Bobby Colflesh fit the bill, and he'd do just fine.

We spoke around the subject with Bobby for a while, talking vaguely of our interests in the export business, the need for secrecy in our line of work. We probably weren't as subtle as we thought.

I put it to him over drinks one night in Charlie Superstar. 'Bobby, Bourbon and I have been talking and we have a proposition to put to you, along the lines of a job offer.'

Bobby smiled, and motioned for me to continue. I took a deep breath. 'Aside from the bar here we run loads of dope into the States, and we're talking tons of the stuff. We buy it here and send it from Singapore. We need some help at this end of the operation and over in America. The money's good and the hours are flexible. You'd be involved in buying, packing and sending the dope. Would work of that kind be of interest to you?'

'I have to say, Michael, I thought you'd never ask!'

With the deal done there and then on a handshake, we offered Bobby, by way of an introduction to the game, a 12 per cent share of the take from both the bar and the dope, still leaving Lietzman and me with a respectable 44 per cent each. Now things could really move up a gear.

The few people who got close to Lietzman often didn't know how to take him; I wasn't so great at dealing with people either, but everybody liked Bobby. Through the connections he built up in Bangkok and the friends he had made while diving on the oil fields Bobby quickly earned himself a discreet cadre of local talent ready to help us in our endeavours. Our thirst for the adrenalin rush of the successful smuggle was growing faster than the smuggles themselves, and the limitations on what we could achieve were turning the scene to boring black and white. But Bobby's involvement in the more nefarious side of the business would soon switch the whole thing back to glorious Technicolor.

But we still erred on the side of caution for a while, holding back on introducing our newest partner to our smiling weed supplier.

As middleman, Kamol had seen his own fortunes grow with those of our organization. The deal he had negotiated with the farmer was that he would take up-front money at the start of every operation, to cover expenses, then twice as much at the back-end of the deal. With the wholesale price from Kamol at $150 per pound of weed, it meant that Lietzman and I were paying $50 per pound up front, then making up the $100 balance at the back end, once we had been paid. It was a nice set-up for all concerned. Kamol easily paid his farmer in full out of the first payment then sat back and waited for us to return from America with our cut, and his profit.

Paying people from the back-end of the deal ensured that we weren't the only ones with a vested interest in our dope getting out of Thailand and over to America safely. Okay, so we weren't venturing into the country and buying direct from the source, but we were still getting our dope at bargain-basement prices and not paying for the bulk of the weed until it had been sold on in California. Kamol was just as concerned about the possibility of getting busted as we were and as a result took security very seriously, which did a lot for peace of mind over at Charlie Superstar.

And we had hit upon a method of keeping the brotherhood of hippies over in California happy and loyal too. In order to do this, we always delivered slightly over the agreed weight. Not enough to significantly hurt our profit, of course, but just enough free dope to keep the customer satisfied and put them off the idea of looking elsewhere for their supply of illegal green, a smart business practice we kept up for over a decade until our career was brought to an abrupt and official end. We may not have known where to buy the dope at the source in those early days, but our smiling middleman had no idea how to pack, move or sell the product, so the wheels turned smoothly and the money rolled in.

Bobby Colflesh made himself useful in the bar and helped out with the overhaul of the scruffy flat-top barge Lietzman had bought. Lietzman and I had decided we would live aboard the 200-foot barge, which we named *Dari Laut*, translated from the Malay as 'from the sea'.

Once the renovations were completed, we planned to tow it to Phuket in Thailand where we had found an idyllic spot just off one of the area's beautiful white beaches.

Lietzman and I travelled up to the barge during the renovations and took our new toys with us. We had elected to treat ourselves to a pair of 30-foot cigarette boats, the high-performance vessel that was fast becoming a favourite with smugglers across the globe. The tanned young men of the dope trade with their expensive watches and loose-fit Brioni shirts soon caught on to the cigarette boat as the offload vessel of choice, reassured by the fact that they could outrun anything the Coast Guard had to offer. In the Miami of the time they were all the rage, the ideal smuggler vessel for work and play.

Renowned for both its speed and stealth, the boats were roomy and quick, designed by Donald Aronow with 1,000 horsepower engines to be capable of speeds of up to 90 knots (150 km per hour) on smooth seas, dropping to around 80 in choppy waters. Cigarette boats are something else. The name apparently derived from one of the first uses they were put to, smuggling tons of cigarettes into Canada in order to avoid paying that country's tax on tobacco. Moving tons of cartons of cigarettes was only the beginning of the boat's smuggling career though and they soon graduated to harder stuff.

Opening one of Aronow's babies up and driving it at full pelt produces a sensation somewhere between sailing, dreaming and flying. At high speeds on smooth waters with the speedometer needle edging into the red, just four inches of the boat will be in contact with the water at any one time, skimming the surface like a stone and bouncing off the smallest ripple as you hang on for dear life, while the warm wind whips and the sun beats down. Like I said, cigarette boats are something else.

The transformation of our barge in Singapore began when four Portakabins were winched up on to its flat deck, two forming the lower deck and two the upper. The Portakabins were squat, even ugly perhaps, but they were effective and ideally suited to the purpose. Two of the cabins were equipped as living quarters for myself and Lietzman, each taking up half of the newly fashioned upper deck. The rough and ready living quarters were sparsely furnished, they contained beds, somewhere to put our clothes, a table, and a couple of ashtrays. Life aboard the *Dari Laut* was an outdoor affair; the sleeping/living quarters on the boat filled the same function as the apartment we kept above Charlie Superstar – somewhere to crash out after a long night's drinking and to emerge from mid-morning for the day's first coffee and a cigarette before jumping on a jet ski, firing up a speed-boat or smuggling some dope.

Next door to my living quarters a smaller cabin was installed to serve as an office, and we saw to it that none of the extra deck or hull space on the barge went unused. Anchor winches were installed at either end of the floating structure and what was left of its floor space was left as an open deck area, covered merely by tarpaulin held in place on a makeshift frame. This area was intended to house our Land Rover and the *Diver's Delight I & II*, the two heavy landing craft we had recently bought. As well as the landing craft, intended to allow the Land Rover to drive straight off the barge and onto the nearest beach, Lietzman and I had got hold of a pair of Zodiac dinghies, two US army-issue jet-black inflatables, nineteen feet long and fitted with outboard motors, which were tethered to the side of the fast expanding barge. Favoured above all of the extras acquired for the *Dari Laut*, though, was the pair of cigarette boats we had invested in.

To accommodate the speed boats two huge arms were built out from the sides of the barge so that we could winch the cigarette boats up to the level of our living quarters. As they were situated at either side of the newly constructed top deck of the barge, winching the speedboats up to first-floor level meant that should we so desire, Lietzman and I could wake in our respective cabins, climb aboard our boats and drop fifteen feet down into the surf for a morning burn across flat, open ocean to blow away the cobwebs and ease the hangover we'd worked so hard to earn the night before.

Behind the apartments, at the back of the boat, we installed a fully stocked bar, complete with open veranda and seating upon which to sip drinks, admire our matching speedboats and enjoy the spectacular local sunsets. With Bobby's help, we had let the inner child within each of us run riot and built the biggest den in the world, creating another quiet corner in the growing secret empire.

Once the renovations to the barge were complete it was loaded up and towed to its new home in Phuket. As the barge made its way to Thailand and passed the hippie colonies that flourished on the beaches in that part of the world, Lietzman and I would each jump into our cigarette boats and floor it, driving the boats up on to the beaches where we would sit for a while and enjoy the girls and the sights with a drink in one hand and a Benson and Hedges in the other. We'd buy rounds of cocktails for everybody on the beach from the makeshift bars and catch some shade beneath a palm tree while we took in the white sand and clear ocean, waiting until the barge was a dot on the horizon before getting back into our cigarettes and racing one another to catch up with the convoy.

We took our time with the tow, being in no real hurry to get to Phuket, and our journey took us by way of Penang. Negotiating that part of the world involves heading through the strait that separates Penang from mainland Malaysia. The waterway there is famously narrow and plagued by fierce currents. It's also a busy port of call, providing a stop-off point for the nearby Royal Air Force base and the local Malaysian prison where among the inmates they kept those poor unfortunates convicted of drug smuggling. It was no joke. The lucky ones were looking at being in there for life while all the less fortunate had to look forward to was the opposite. The Penang port authority allocated us a mooring not far from the bridge that separated the island from the mainland, so we had the tug tow us into position, weighed anchor and looked forward to spending some time in the Malaysian sun.

Once *Dari Laut* was in position near the bridge and the tug had taken off and left us to it, we hit the onboard bar and set about drinking. There was a full moon that night. For a while, none of us realized the significance of that salient little fact, choosing instead to merely stare at it, drink in hand, before heading off to our cabins to catch some sleep. But the full moon raised the tides and speeded up the currents around Penang, lifting the water level to such an extent that the anchor tethering our barge to the bottom of the sea was pulled out and we were soon at the mercy of the tides and travelling at a hell of a speed. Backwards.

The first I knew of our predicament was when a raised voice, which turned out to be Lietzman's, roused me from my peaceful slumber.

'Why the fuck are we moving?'

As I shook myself awake up and got my bearings I realized that Lietzman was right, the barge was most definitely in motion. I put my head outside the door of my cabin and saw just how perilous our situation was. This was no fucking way to wake up.

The *Dari Laut* had no engine, no power of its own, which was no problem while it was moored or being towed but definitely provided one or two challenges when the barge was, as now, being blown around all over the place in a narrow waterway and likely to smash into at least one of the other nearby ships at any moment. Our cigarette boats were hanging off the side of the barge on their winches and if we hit anything side-on, they would have been the first to go, reduced to splinters. We had to do something and fast.

There was a splash off the side of the barge as one of the landing barges we had bought in Greece was dispatched with Lietzman at the helm.

'Mike, throw me a fuckin' line. I'm gonna see if I can't pull us out of trouble.'

I tossed a line from the barge down to Lietzman, but compared to *Dari Laut* the landing barge was pathetic, a mouse trying to tow an elephant. At night.

'I can't see for shit,' he yelled. 'Which way should I head, Mike?'

My view from the barge wasn't much better. 'Any way you want, but try to avoid that fucking huge ship behind you.'

As Lietzman looked to see what I meant, that his face turned as white as the moon that had caused all this trouble in the first place. Somehow the landing barge with its weedy stern-drive engine sounding as though it would give up the ghost any moment moved us just enough to prevent collision with the nearby cargo ship. The current had a firmer hold of the barge though, and took it where it would until the white-knuckle ride eventually ran out of steam some miles later where the water level dropped enough for the anchor to once more take hold of the seabed.

For the entire length of our freeform excursion the anchor had been dragged along the ocean floor. Our panic levels rose again as we realized we were about to sail over the main power line that ran from the mainland to the island. With Lietzman now back on board the barge we stared helplessly at the point where the anchor line disappeared beneath the ocean,

'If we cut that power line we're fried,' he said helpfully. 'Been nice knowing you, Mike.'

Happily, the God of Dumb Luck and the Patron Saint of Outrageous Fortune had chosen to smile on us once more that night and it seemed we were going too fast to gain enough purchase to pull up the cable from the seabed. If we had, we could well have plunged the whole area into darkness and made ourselves exceedingly unpopular with the locals.

When we eventually came to rest we called the port authority and had them come and tow us back to a less crowded spot. Rather than hang around, we sheepishly left the area as soon as the sun came up next morning.

Many tales have been told of *Dari Laut,* mostly by people who were never there, stories which have somehow transformed the barge from a scruffy, ramshackle floating collection of rag-tag elements (which it was) into a gilded palace of extravagance and excess (which it most certainly wasn't). What it was for a while, though, was a home away from home. With its creature comforts, toys and fully stocked bar, it was always a fun place to be. As well as the European barge-master employed to oversee the upkeep and maintenance of the barge, and a permanent cook, we also employed locals when we needed extra help.

Excited about the possibilities it offered, not least the chance of further legitimizing our enterprise, we constructed eight smaller cabins in the hull, with the intention of renting them out to watersport-loving holidaymakers. I'm pretty sure it was me who coined the word 'boatel' to describe the barge and its amenities. We even went so far as to print up brochures with swirling far-out graphics to lure potential paying guests. The brochure sold the barge as a floating private club, going on to state that anyone staying on it would have access to the boats we'd begun collecting. Anyone wishing to spend time on the barge but unsure of what to bring with them on their visit was advised that '*Dari Laut* is best approached with the smallest suitcase. Proper dressing amongst our international members is generally swimsuits. For accessories, sunglasses will do fine.'

The brochures looked great and made the *Dari Laut* sound like a fun place to take a holiday. If we had distributed them once we had them delivered from the printers, rather than leave them in a box in a corner of the office, we may even have had a few takers.

The arrival of new personnel within the organization we had built together had done nothing to affect Lietzman's and my friendship. We never articulated the bond, never said it out loud as it was not in our nature to do so, but we found other ways to let each other know how much the friendship meant to us. We bought each other gifts. We were two grown men who'd just built the biggest den in the world and filled it with toys and distractions, we had money to burn and relished the fact. We bought two of everything, spurred on by our matching love of thrills and speed, always upping the ante in the chase for kicks with speedboats, seaplanes, fast cars.

Not long after we moored the *Dari Laut* in Phuket, Robert Lietzman presented me with a very odd gift indeed. He boarded the barge one evening and joined me in the bar where I sat alone, watching the sunset and enjoying a long cool one.

'I bought you these,' Lietzman told me, and offered me a beautiful inlaid wooden box about a foot long and ten inches wide. He put it down on the table next to my drink and headed over to the bar to pour himself a bourbon and Coke, three cubes of ice, quarter slice of lemon. I looked up at my friend, then down at the box.

Lietzman smiled. 'Go ahead man . . . open it . . .' I undid the small filigreed latch and there, nestled in velvet, were two pearl-handled chrome pistols, Berettas, gleaming up at me and catching the last rays of the dying sun. I had never owned guns like them, I hadn't even fired one since I was a kid, and never wanted to. I looked up at Lietzman unsure quite what to make of it but touched by the gesture and told him, 'Thanks'.

We carried on drinking on deck as night fell. There were the usual voices of the crew, the cries of birds swooping down to the water's surface, the sound of the ocean lapping at the side of the barge. I twirled the guns like they do in the movies; they arced clumsily around my fingers as I gauged their weight. They were heavy, those guns; they didn't look it, but the size of the things threw me. They looked small and weighed big. Too big. I didn't like them. I appreciated the gift, the workmanship, the thought, and knew that Lietzman having given them to me meant they were probably the finest quality that money could buy, but nothing could assuage the feeling that I was uncomfortable around them. Just being found with them in my possession would have landed me in an awful lot of trouble.

For the next two weeks, the guns moved through the barge. They sat in the office for a while, hidden in a drawer, they followed me to my cabin and sat atop the table next to my bed, the last thing I saw at night, the sight that greeted me in the morning. They began to haunt me. Weeks later the weight of the guns finally got me down. I couldn't have them around, they boded ill to me and had to go. We'd had the local army on board the barge, they were friendly enough but they'd been asking a lot of questions and didn't always seem too impressed with how we answered them. If they had decided to search us and found those guns we could have wound up in an awful lot of trouble and garnered exactly the kind of attention we spent our lives attempting to avoid. As I sat in the bar and yet another sun set before me, I took the Berettas and launched them over the back of the barge, listening to the dull splash they made and watching spritzes of spray jump as the water claimed them, raising my glass in a salute as the matching set of pistols sank quick and hard to the bottom of the ocean.

A month later, while on a trip collecting a briefcase full of cash from one of Hippie Rod's partners in California, Lietzman and I once again decided to dip into our cash reserves and treat ourselves. We bought a pair of matching seaplanes, small, fast and fun with buzzy overhead engines. I was my father's son and fell in love with flying the moment I took off from the water on my first test run. Once I had bought the plane I made my way to Texas, to the factory that built them, and enrolled in a course to learn to fly for real. I passed and finished up my flight training in California where I obtained my Private Pilot's Licence. Being awarded the licence meant that I had been trained to fly the seaplane, but wasn't qualified to do so at night or through heavy cloud. Not that that ever stopped me. We then had the planes crated up and shipped to Singapore, where we signed for them and flew them to the barge in Thailand. We made the most of the trip by flying the long way round, via Malaysia and Penang before landing on the water alongside the *Dari Laut* in Phuket.

The planes were fun, and for a while I got my kicks by taking off after a drink or two and swooping over the neighbours, buzzing treetops with a Benson and Hedges clamped between my teeth and testing just what my newest toy was capable of. It's a miracle I wasn't shot down for taking such liberties in Thai airspace. Presumably the officials manning the local control tower decided to turn a blind eye to a half-drunk Englishman playing Biggles.

The coastline at Phuket at the time was in the early stages of being turned into what would later become a tourist hotspot. Some of the landscape around us was still jungle, wild and unspoiled, but here and there resorts were growing up and beginning to dot the coastline as a taste of things to come. One night, alone aboard the *Dari Laut,* I felt the urge to visit one of these hotspots. There was no one else on the barge and it wouldn't be until much later in adult life that I was comfortable for long stretches in my own company. The spot I had in mind had lately become a bit of a favourite with Lietzman, Bobby and me, and I chose a little blue motorboat that we had tethered to the side of the barge as my mode of transport. It was the middle of the night and dark, and I was slightly, though not totally, drunk. I took no charts or maps with me, nothing but the pig-headed, half-pissed belief that I would find my way to the nearest populated bar through the use of some kind of God-given sixth sense of cosmic celestial navigation. I didn't.

The reef I hit ten minutes later was hidden just below the surface of the water. It stopped me dead in my tracks and from the unhappy noise the boat was making I knew I'd done it some serious damage. Judging by the lights in the distance I could see that I was still a fair way from land but the waters where I had hit the reef were shallow. I had to get the boat moving quickly so I stepped over the side and stood atop the sharp reef, ripping the soles of my shoes as I pushed the boat off the coral and towards the deeper water. For a moment there, just a second or two, when I stepped out of that boat and on to the coral, that I felt utterly unbeatable, able to walk on water by the light of the moon. My already healthy current account at the Bank of Arrogance had received yet another hefty deposit. The boat I was on wasn't in such good shape though. The propeller had been trashed by the crash and was now operating apologetically with just one functioning blade, and that one sounded as though it was ready to give up the ghost at any moment. I made it to the beach resort just as the boat finally gave out and set myself up at the bar, ordering a drink, lighting a cigarette, and waiting until Lietzman or Bobby passed through and offered me a ride home.

CHAPTER FIVE

SUPERSTAR

Long hot nights on the Patpong Road.

With Bobby part of the organization the bottom line numbers on the balance sheet began rising sharply. With his contribution to the refit of the barge and the running of the bar he had proved himself an asset and was on his way to earning a third of the full take. The new recruit may not have brought money with him to the table, there was plenty of that floating around by now anyway, but his youthful enthusiasm and energy were worth their weight in weed. Six months after Bobby came on board, we decided to upgrade the bar. We wanted bigger, we wanted better. We scouted the local area and soon found the perfect location a few hundred yards along the street.

The new bar had potential, offering larger premises in a slightly better location. Bobby in particular loved the place, seeing past the grim shell to the garden of earthly delights it could become. We set about turning a dark, depressing space used to drink whisky in low light into the flashiest, trashiest, most successful go-go joint on the strip.

To begin the transformation we ripped out every cubicle in the place. The maze of plaster grottos installed by the previous Japanese owners were sacrificed to make way for five new bars and three discothèques over four floors. We added a multicoloured dance floor made up of squares that would light up underfoot, de rigueur at the time for that *Night Fever*, Euro jet-set vibe. We built an island bar and installed brass poles everywhere for the in-house dancing girls to shake and shimmy round. Booths were installed that frilled the edges of the club for those who wanted a little privacy in order to get to know the legions of pretty local hostesses who frequented the place. Finally came the flashing lights, a pounding Bose sound system and box-fresh twin decks, often manned by me or one or other of my partners whenever we felt the urge to play DJ for the night. I'd learned my way around DJ decks during my time working at the radio station in Sydney and passed many happy hours in the bar playing records from the vast collection of disco twelve-inches that I would buy in bulk on shopping trips to New York. Blondie's 'Heart of Glass' was a big tune that year, played back to back with Donna Summer and 'Le Freak'.

We'd had the DJ booth made far bigger than was strictly necessary. The result was more like a small room, which could, and often did, happily accommodate up to ten of us, drunkenly taking turns to select records and elbowing each other out of the way to attempt to line up the next tune. We were Superstar DJs in name only – luckily our audience were as refreshed as we were and didn't offer too many objections when we dropped the needle halfway through 'Funkytown' rather than play the intro. Murray Head's 'One Night In Bangkok' was a big hit in the club; a signed photo of Murray hung over the bar.

Bobby and I had tested the club's sound system while the renovations to the place were being completed. We'd waited one night until the workmen had left, turned the volume on the club's PA up as high as it would go and sat down square in the middle of the illuminated dance floor as the red, blue, orange and white squares lit up in haphazard sequence beneath us. Passing a bottle of Scotch back and forth, nodding to one another at the quality of the sound raging around us, we burst out laughing as the alcohol kicked in and we took a moment to realize how we must have looked, two grown men in an empty nightclub with the music turned up full, giggling like children.

On the ground floor, the fully equipped kitchen employed a chef, an English guy who hung out on *Dari Laut* on his days off and began his daily duties preparing breakfast in the club's kitchen for those who'd just arrived or the previous night's stragglers who'd failed yet to make it home. As well as serving local cuisine, the bar, with our chef's help, turned the humble British chip into a must-have local delicacy served both inside the club and out from a hatch which opened on to Patpong. Such was my naiveté around the harsh realities of hard drugs that the chef's taste for the pokey local smack was hardly noticed until I found myself aboard the *Dari Laut* reviving him from his second overdose.

We dropped the Charlie and named the new bar simply

Superstar, announcing ourselves open for business via a huge baby-blue and soft-pink neon that spelled out the name, loud, brash and bright, with a flashing white star between the words Super and Star. Our bar was unmissable by potential punters making their way along the Patpong Road looking for somewhere to drink and watch pretty girls dance.

Full-colour beer mats were printed up to our design featuring a naked female reclining across the neon Superstar logo, and for extra decoration we hung a few vintage Triumph and Harley Davidson motorcycles from the walls, their chrome engines and exhausts reflecting the red and green lights that pulsed in time to 'I Feel Love'. In the late afternoons the television sets would be playing pirate Betamax copies of Hollywood's latest big-budget offerings, *The Deer Hunter* maybe, or *Rocky II*, to the handfuls of the curious and the hardcore who had already hit the bar. By seven in the evening the televisions would be muted, the sound system turned up in order for Gloria Gaynor to announce that yes, she would survive, and that the disco bar was open for business proper. We had it all covered; any local Thais not wishing to be seen entering the club were catered for by the entrance to the second-storey nightclub accessed via a multi-level car park.

Superstar lived up to its name, and was big in every sense. The club could easily accommodate two thousand paying customers on its four floors, and often did. As well as the members of the foreign press who frequented the establishment, local law-enforcement officers and Thai army personnel took advantage of the pleasures on offer at the bar. We stood them drinks and welcomed the presence of these obvious representatives of authority, which ensured that no trouble ever broke out in the club. Not that Lietzman, Bobby or I would have worried if it did. Security at Superstar was as unconventional as you'd expect, courtesy of Bobby. Through his local connections, Bobby had befriended members of a retired circus troupe who acted as the club's bouncers when they weren't busy performing their balancing act atop a brass dancing pole to the accompanying *Oohs* and *Aahs* of the massed punters.

And we had the best girls on the strip. Up to two hundred dancing girls worked the Superstar, giving it that essential leopard-skin bikini and high heels early lap-dance vibe, charming customers out of their holiday dollar with their honed shimmy skills and the artful pretence that they actually cared what these men were saying to them. The girls were free to make their own arrangements with anyone they met in the club, but strict rules were enforced on the premises: the girls at Superstar were employed as dancers, not hookers; their job was to get the punters to drink; they had to remain covered at all times – we were running a go-go joint not a strip club – and while occasionally things would perhaps get a little boisterous and clothes would get shed, on the whole we ran what we considered a clean house. If a girl should decide to leave the premises for a while, perhaps for an assignation with someone she had met in the bar, then on her return she would be fined, the amount deducted from her wages. Often, if the girls did disappear to one of the local hotels that rented out rooms by the hour, any money she had made in that time would more than cover the fine. Compared with other clubs on the Patpong Road, the rules we enforced as far as the girls were concerned marked Superstar out as positively demure. Anyone wishing to experience the more hardcore end of the Thai floor show, ping-pong balls and all, would have to drink elsewhere.

The top floor of the building housed the club's office where our overworked but well-paid European accountant did his best just to keep up as the waves of cash rolled in.

Near Superstar was a smaller, sleazier establishment, currently being run by a shady, slimy American whom none of us were particularly fond of. Something about the man was just unutterably, undeniably, wrong. When we heard the whisper that he was heavily involved in smuggling heroin our suspicions about him were confirmed and we made a point from that moment on of steering well clear, refusing even to acknowledge him with a hello. It may seem hypocritical given that we smuggled drugs as well, but we saw the effects of heroin addiction all around us and the price paid in human misery. Smoking dope, on the other hand, seemed no more risky to the health than drinking alcohol.

At the time we were operating, the dope trade, although by definition a wholly criminal enterprise, was not yet run solely by a typically criminal element. American soldiers who had been introduced to the delights of Thai weed during tours of duty in nearby Vietnam operated alongside the evangelical stoners who had travelled to the source of the infamous Thai stick in order to spread the word of the weed. Pilots and boat captains from the four corners of the world formed alliances in order to move dope into Europe, Australia and America, loose affiliations of smugglers grew up in and around bars like Charlie Superstar whose members would float between deals in an attempt to muster the contacts and experience which would mark them as the *man*. The idea of joining a confederation of smugglers was anathema to us; it was just not the way we did business.

Nevertheless, dope smuggling in late seventies and early eighties Thailand was becoming a boom business, getting bigger by the year, with ever-growing numbers prepared to travel east and take the unnecessary risks that joint ventures with virtual strangers could throw up. Many of them passed through the doors of Superstar, some even used the place as a base while they were in town, meeting partners there and spending nights and early mornings watching the girls and planning their shipments. Howard Marks visited, introduced to the bar by his friend Jim Hobbs, whom who was at the time working out of Bangkok. While drinking at Superstar, Howard hatched plans to import loads to London, Canada and Amsterdam. Phil Sparrowhawk would pass through, another ducker and diver whose interests outside of smuggling with Howard Marks and others included local massage parlours.

We heard rumours about the secret of our success being swapped around the booths that lined the dance floor. But rumours they remained. We were as ever self-contained and wary of outsiders, we never shared confidences with the other smugglers doing the rounds of the Patpong Road and would refuse even to socialize with some of them.

The longer we spent on the Patpong Road the more acquaintances we made among its denizens. Many of the bar owners there had secrets and were either actively involved in the drug trade in one way or other or had quit while they were ahead and opened their establishments with the proceeds from it. We knew that one bar, a little further along the street, was owned by an ex-CIA agent so any ambassadors of American law and order in town for work or business would always drop in there as a matter of course. In doing so they unwittingly announced their presence to the ever watchful eyes of the Patpong Road.

Any trouble that broke out in the clubs or on the streets was, more often than not, alcohol fuelled. Heat, action and cheap booze combined to ensure that on any given night there were as many people staggering along the street outside our club as there were walking. Drunken policemen were a common sight and often far more unstable and dangerous than any tourist. It was always solvable though. If a sozzled policeman began waving his gun around then we simply sought out one of his more sober partners from the local force, preferably one with a bigger gun, and left it to him. The contacts we made through the bar ensured that in the structured Thai society of the time, if we found we were the target for local troublemakers then we simply went over their heads to appeal for help and the trouble would end as swiftly as it had begun. It didn't happen often, but it was nice to know that we were covered by the insurance our local friendships bought.

The dope game was seasonal, which meant that as far as smuggling timetables went, nature made the rules. The local crop earmarked for our little gang could only be harvested during the summer, so we fell into a steady routine around the preparations for collecting and moving the weed, which meant we could devote much of our time to hanging out on the barge, travelling to our homes in Hong Kong, Singapore and America and running and enjoying the bar. We would place our order with Kamol in the early part of the year, pick up our product around July and usually aim to smuggle it into America around September. It was all very civilized.

And all very hidden. The language of the dope smuggler is not that of the end user. When discussing matters pertaining to business, marijuana becomes 'product', smuggling becomes 'shipping' and cash becomes 'capital'. Anyone eavesdropping on one of our conversations might easily think they were listening in on legitimate directors of a shipping company discussing an impressive order of fridges. Of course, fridges would be far less profitable.

Orders were placed with Kamol face to face. As always, phones were used as little as possible. Even early on there was the ever-present concern over security: the fewer links in the chain, the less chance that it would be compromised. If we had to use a phone to arrange a meeting, then we would make sure it was a public phone box, one off the beaten track. If the local call boxes were deemed too busy we would simply purchase a cell phone.

Cell phones at the outset of the eighties were heavy, expensive and bulky, and the privacy they offered then, as now, was limited. But one advantage of the new mobile technology was that once the call was made, the battery and handsets were so heavy and unwieldy that they sank quickly to the bottom of the nearest ocean. Somewhere just off the Thai coast is a school of brightly coloured tropical fish darting in and out of barely used vintage mobile phones.

Kamol had diversified his interests a little too, by getting into the fish business. The fish farm he'd recently bought with his cut of the dope money proved a good place for us to rendezvous and discuss business, away from prying eyes, save those of the fish happily swimming in their giant oblong pools. The fish farm even once played host to the annual packing of the weed, a laborious process that required space and time.

As time went on we proved our reliability to our supplier, the mystery farmer contacted by Kamol, and were separating ourselves by reputation from the hordes of get-rich-quick fly-by-nights who inhabit any business where the work-to-profit ratio is so unequally balanced. The quality of the weed he provided started going up, even I could see that. As we begin to work our way through the pecking order of who got what, we saw our product turning from brittle dry brown bush to vibrant moist green weed, fresh from the fields. Not being smokers ourselves, it wasn't until we heard Rod's overjoyed reaction that we realized that the farmer was now supplying us with the cream of his crop. In a hotel car park Rod bent so low to inhale the weed that he almost lost his lavender turban, but the suntanned Californian came up smiling.

'My good, good friends, may God's light shine ever upon you and may you continue to supply ever increasing amounts of this most righteous crop.'

'You keep buying it, Rod, and we'll keep sending it,' I assured him.

And we were always more than ready to pass on any changes in the marketplace to our supplier. When the taste changed from Buddha sticks to the more recognizable Sensimelia, that's what we asked for, and that's what we got. The taste for the seedless Sensimelia didn't last for long though, and after smuggling one load of it through, we were asked by Rod to go back to supplying the trusty Thai stick.

Once the weed was delivered we needed to pack it. Traditionally it would arrive in black bin bags, often hundreds of them. In a million houses all over the world right now are people who will attest to the fact that the small amount of weed they keep for personal use smells somewhat. The odour is sweet, a little sickly and, to those who know it, unique and instantly recognizable. In the amounts we were dealing with, it stank to high heaven. To combat the problem, we began vacuum-packing the weed, a process that could take place anywhere from a quiet beach or Kamol's fish farm to the middle of the Thai jungle.

Depending on the quantity, packing a shipment of weed into manageable slabs usually took us from three to five days; continuous privacy for the duration of the process was paramount. When Bobby and I decided to pack the weed in the jungle, we took with us all the necessary machinery, the vacuum press (then the size of a small table), an electric generator and gas bottles. We set up a camp in a clearing, unloaded the necessary, and got to work. Vacuum-packing is an efficient method of preparing weed for shipment for a number of reasons. First, by sucking out the air from the bags of weed it reduces their size and allows more to travel. Second, replacing the air in the packages with inert gas means that any bacteria in the shipment are neutralized, ensuring the plants will arrive at their final destination as healthy as the day they left Thailand. Third, vacuum-packing virtually eliminates any odour from the shipment that would otherwise be a dead giveaway.

There's a story that did the rounds of a gang operating around the same time who hit upon the ingenious idea of smuggling dope into England in miniature replicas of London landmarks. Boxes of Tower Bridges, Big Bens, black cabs, and Buckingham Palaces arrived at a customs warehouse unchecked, leaving the goods inside essentially free and clear. But fate sometimes has a sense of humour. The shipment was mixed up with another batch of more innocent tourist trinkets, destined for souvenir shops all over the capital who, unbeknownst to them, soon began dealing drugs to tourists who wanted a reminder of their time in the great city. Next time you see one of these things, gathering dust maybe on the mantelpiece of a relative, pick it up, see if it feels a little heavier than it should or has a familiar smell.

CHAPTER SIX

THE EIGHTIES

Here comes success. 1980. The arrival of Samuel Colflesh and the gang's all here, with special thanks to the Coast Guard.

I eventually worked up the courage to ask May, the girl I'd met at the party in Singapore a couple of years previously, to marry me. We had seen as much of each other as my hectic schedule would allow and I knew she was the one for me. We married in San Francisco in a quiet ceremony on 13 February. During our relationship thus far May had watched her erstwhile suitor go from successful tropical-fish exporter to prosperous Patpong Road club owner. Even with May, I kept the true nature of my business to myself, as we all did where the women in our lives were concerned. Lietzman's occasional local girlfriend Elsie and Carolyn, the wife he had married in 1973 but by now rarely saw, were kept as in the dark about our illegal importation business as was May, and throughout our career we never saw any need to invite them into our very private gentlemen's club. There was more than a whiff of chauvinism involved. We saw smuggling as a man's world.

Marriage wasn't the only big change to my life that 1980 brought with it. The smuggling gang was altered too, its ranks swelled by the arrival on the scene of one Samuel Colflesh.

Sammy was Bobby's twin brother and the pair had had a lifelong running argument, occasionally reignited by alcohol, over who had been birthed first. The striking physical likeness the two shared was where their similarities ended. Where Bobby was more laid-back and open, his brother Sam was dyed-in-the-wool army all the way. Far more ready to follow orders than his brother, despite no longer being enlisted, Sammy was still happiest when he was working within an established chain of command. He impressed us by his ability to break down any challenge into a series of practical problems, problems that were never insurmountable and that, with a little lateral thinking and some dogged determination, could always be overcome.

Despite the good-natured sibling rivalry the Colfleshes indulged in, the brothers were tight. Sammy, who was learning to fly over in America, would travel out to Thailand to visit his brother and was soon introduced to Bobby's new partners, myself and Lietzman. During his visits, Sammy would make himself useful, helping out at Superstar and, eventually, with smuggling dope, albeit initially as a hired hand.

I wasn't sure about Sammy at first; something I couldn't quite put my finger on bothered me about the new Colflesh. Perhaps it was that Sammy's dogged practical approach was somewhat at odds with the way I dealt with things. But I liked Bobby enough to trust his judgement and saw the sense in recruiting a fourth member to our elite team, particularly one who was related to one of our number and had so many valuable skills to offer. Sammy didn't come on board with a full cut at first though, taking 10 per cent while Lietzman, Bobby and I each earned 30 per cent of the take from the bar and smuggling. But Sammy was patient, prepared to prove himself to us. He didn't have long to wait.

I was sitting in the bar one afternoon in early 1980 when Lietzman strolled in, back from spending some time in Kamol. He was looking pretty pleased with himself.

'The shopping was fine,' he said, 'bought us a great new boat.'

I shook my head and smiled. This was becoming a habit. The vessel in question was the *Yellow Bull*, a forty-foot Thai fishing boat that Lietzman wanted to fill with dope and sail to America. He was enthusiastic about the vessel's potential but I wasn't at all convinced.

'A Thai fishing boat? You want to sail from here to Washington in a Thai fishing boat?'

'It's not as dumb as it sounds, Mike, trust me.'

Hmmm. The boat was certainly sturdy enough to get us from Thailand to America and roomy enough to make the trip with four tons of dope hidden in the bows and front section. But there was a problem. Thai fishing boats are not designed with round the world trips in mind. A journey covering thousands of miles and lasting for anything up to three months aboard *Yellow Bull* would soon become very uncomfortable indeed. Obviously there was only one thing to do. We began to remodel the boat, making renovations that went far beyond those needed to hide and disguise the weed. We ripped open the centre of the craft and installed a cabin large enough for us to relax in and outfitted the new space with all the creature comforts of a well-appointed sitting room – couches, tables and unnecessary odds and ends. The alterations to the boat were completed over six months while she was moored in Singapore. Once the changes were made to the structure we outfitted the bridge of *Yellow Bull* with a few choice pieces of kit to help us navigate the boat halfway around the world: the latest radar, speedometer and radio communications equipment.

Once the cabin was outfitted for the journey we sailed to Thailand where we loaded on the last and most important of our supplies: enough cartons of Benson and Hedges to see us through months at sea, a few cases of Lietzman's favourite bourbon – oh, and four tons of Thai marijuana.

The night before we were due to set sail, I broke the news to May that I was off on a trip. 'I've got to go away and do some business. I could be gone for a while.'

She didn't look overjoyed at the news, her countenance falling as the conversation proceeded.'Michael, you're hardly ever here as it is. How long will you be gone?'

'Not too long,' I said, 'maybe three months.'

May was hurt by the news, and my matter-of-fact delivery of it. For what would not be the last time in our marriage, she prepared to carry on without her new husband. As we kissed each other farewell the next morning, I was tempted to tell her the truth behind my voyage but decided against it at the last minute, figuring that divulging to my new wife that I was in fact a marijuana smuggler would cause more problems than it solved.

I soon forgot any lingering guilt as we set off in bright Asian sunshine on glassy seas, plain sailing. To cool off from the heat on deck we dived off the side of the boat and swam in the ocean, never straying too far from *Yellow Bull* though, just in case those left aboard had forgotten that one of their number had elected to take a dip and carried on without him. Another worry while swimming was the possibility that our progress through the ocean had attracted attention from below, the sharks that were not unheard of in the area could well have decided that that day, they fancied a smuggler for lunch. The weather as we left the East and sailed towards California seemed to be on our side and boat and crew sailed along happily.

The first order of business, once a case of bourbon had been cracked open and a toast raised to the success of our newest venture, was to disguise our vessel. If the *Yellow Bull* mission had been compromised in any way, if we'd been ratted out in Thailand and anyone at the American end was waiting for us, then they would be looking for the distinctive white boat that had left Asia and not the rather poorly painted yellow one that would shortly be sailing proudly into San Francisco harbour.

While the sea remained calm and weather warm we began the task of repainting the vessel, covering the white with a coat of bright canary yellow. The facelift was achieved by hanging off the hull of the *Yellow Bull* sitting on planks supported at each side by ropes secured on deck, like window cleaners on a skyscraper. With paintbrushes and bourbons in hand and cigarettes clamped between our teeth we spent a happy week or so covering ourselves and the boat in an even-ish coat of yellow paint. At the time, ideas like that seemed normal, sensible even. The plan to repaint the boat while at sea was not seen as dangerous or foolhardy, but rather as an example of our forward thinking. It's the kind of arrogance that can kill.

In order to make the journey to the States we needed to take on more fuel and had chosen the Marshall Islands in the Pacific as the perfect spot to fill up. We weren't the only customers shopping for gas that day, and as we took on board the fuel we needed, we met a band of fresh faced young smugglers coming the opposite way. Not one of these guys could have been more than twenty-five years old. They were heading for Thailand in order to fill their small boat with dope and sail it back to America. Eight shaggy-haired American kids in Adidas sneakers, faded jeans and skinny T-shirts on their merry way to make their first million. The boat the young men were sailing east was completely sterile, clean as a whistle, not a rope, net or fishing rod offered even the pretence of its being a working boat. To trained eyes their whole operation screamed out smuggler, and inexperienced ones at that.

We wished the gang the best of luck and watched them head off.

'Fucking amateurs,' Bobby said, shaking his head pityingly. We all laughed at the idea of being so unprepared.

But there was one thing *we* hadn't counted on: the weather. Nor had we counted on the fact that the extensive renovations we had made to *Yellow Bull* had dramatically weakened the structure of the boat. In order to install our living quarters we had ripped out many of the large wooden bulk heads that kept *Yellow Bull* rigid. That oversight was almost about to sink us. Literally.

As Hawaii, our next fuel stop, approached the weather began to turn nasty, fierce storms blowing up. The boat began to sway at first, pitching slightly more than was comfortable, the smooth rock and roll we had been experiencing since leaving the Thai coast giving way to something far more worrying. Then the weather worsened and suddenly we were being thrown around inside the hull of the boat, fear leaking into our bourbon-soaked brains. The waves started to touch ten feet, the boat pitching dramatically. We were drinking now to keep us brave in the face of increasingly unsettling odds. This was no time to be sober.

Then *Yellow Bull* began to make noises we hadn't heard from her before, noises you really don't want to hear from the only thing separating you from a mile or so of who-knows-what-infested watery depths. She came alive with a series of drawn out horror-movie creaks and shudders, the sudden loud cracks and low long moans audible even above the fury of the storm. The bow became progressively weaker under the incessant pound-ing. To my horror and bemusement, I saw a crack appear halfway along the deck in the middle of the boat.

'Guys,' I yelled, pointing a shaking finger, 'this doesn't look good, this doesn't look good at all.'

The crack grew in front of our eyes, getting very bad very quick as *Yellow Bull* rocked through the open sea. Soon it looked as though the bow of the boat was threatened, like it was getting ready to snap and send our band of drunken sailors and our six tons of dope into the dark fathoms below. No joke. By now, with rain lashing the vessel and waves crashing into her from all sides, the only thing holding the boat together was the keel, and wishful thinking.

Thai fishing boats are traditionally built of wood and corking. As *Yellow Bull* fought her way through the storm some of the corking had worked itself loose and as a consequence the boat had sprung a series of leaks, taking on so much water that the pumps we carried were struggling to contain the problem. Lietzman's mechanical fix-anything skills came to the fore as he battled desperately to fix the pumps, drenched from head to foot. Soon we were ankle deep everywhere. It was then that the journey went from bad to worse, and everything on the boat that possibly could go wrong did.

Lietzman was flying by the seat of his pants, making repairs that would have been difficult enough in a shipyard under the most unholy of circumstances and, I suspected, rather enjoying himself while he did it. We stood by and tried to make ourselves useful while he worked, handing him the tools he would scream out for while trying to save the boat, our lives, and the dope.

'The wrench! Someone get me the fucking wrench . . . And while you're at it, get me another drink.'

At one point, above the noise of the storm, I thought I heard him singing. We were repairing the boat as we sailed, high on bourbon nerve and bravado. Somehow we managed to navigate *Yellow Bull*, barely still in one piece and as ragged and tired as its small crew, into Kona, near Hawaii.

Once in Kona the weather settled and our hangovers cleared a little. Lietzman took off for a little much needed rest and relaxation while Bobby, Terry the deckhand and I enjoyed the brief respite from our ordeal. As it happened, the seas around the Kona coast of Hawaii where we had elected to stop awhile and take on supplies were playing host to a fishing competition, a big one, with a fleet of boats of all different shapes and sizes taking part, all trying to hook marlin. I was still a keen fisherman and brought along my new rods and reels, upgraded to the best that money could buy. So we cast off and started fishing.

We weren't enrolled in the competition, we hadn't registered or paid the nominal entry fee but didn't see minor details like that as excluding us from the fun. We cast off our lines and began to fish. Since arriving in the area, the radio aboard *Yellow Bull* had been tuned to Channel 16, the international distress channel, which meant that we could keep up with any sudden news concerning the area we were sailing. We also knew that as a matter of course the Coast Guard would also have their radio tuned into Channel 16 on the lookout for any maritime emergency that required their immediate attention.

Before long we began to attract unwanted attention, one of our fellow competitors taking exception to what he assumed was a Mexican fishing boat plying its trade in American waters. He put in a call to the Coast Guard and ratted us out. Fortunately for us he made the call on Channel 16 and we could listen in to every word. The last thing we needed after the trials of our journey so far was unwelcome attention from the authorities, with six tons of dope still on the boat. We reeled in our lines quick time and headed out for the safety of the open sea until things had cooled off a little, not returning until later when we could safely pick up Lietzman for the final leg of the journey.

I disembarked in Hawaii and made my way by air to San Francisco to finalize arrangements for the offload. We were the lucky ones as the *Yellow Bull*'s problems weren't over. The boat still had two thousand miles to go before she reached the safety of San Francisco harbour and on the way there the crew, now reduced to Lietzman, Bobby Colflesh and Terry, were hit by yet more storms. By now the boat simply couldn't take the constant battering it was being subjected to by the elements and the leaks were getting progressively worse. The two pumps on board were clearing water for all they were worth but were simply not up to the job. If the shipment was to get through and the crew were to survive then something had to be done. Desperate times were calling for desperate measures.

As soon as they were within radio range of the California coast they called the Coast Guard on Channel 16 and reported themselves as a vessel in distress, supplied their coordinates and waited. Before too long a Coast Guard helicopter battled its way through the storm and lowered a pump down on to the deck of *Yellow Bull*. Once the pump was safely on deck the Coast Guard wished the crew good luck and went on their way, blissfully unaware that they had just helped four tons of dope make the final stretch of a long and tiring journey.

The new pump worked a treat, able to evacuate more water than the two we already had on board combined. *Yellow Bull* finally limped into San Francisco harbour where Sam and I were waiting to meet her. The once proud vessel had all but given up. Its crew, doused in bourbon and tired to their bones, under cover of night offloaded the dope into the warehouse we still kept on a long-term let, then loaded the Coast Guard's pump aboard the trusty Camino and returned it to them, with sincere and heartfelt thanks.

Yellow Bull ended her journey abandoned on the mud-flats of San Francisco, battered and bruised by the trip, but having served us admirably.

A lot of dope had been brought into America that year, so much that the two thousand dollars a pound we could usually expect had dropped by almost half. We weren't pleased by the news to put it mildly, but even at a reduced selling price the four ton load had still grossed us close to ten million dollars, ensuring that the cost of buying, fitting out and abandoning the fishing boat was hardly noticed when we got to the bottom line.

Delivering such a large amount to Rod and the hippie connection meant that we would have to hand the weed over to them at a series of different pick-up points. Over the next four days we met with Rod or members of his commune at car parks dotted around the city. Payment for the load was received piecemeal too, with hundred-thousand-dollar Halliburton suitcases handed over to us in twos and threes once or twice a day for the next three weeks. Once the money had all been collected we moved it back to Thailand and Singapore, sent as hand luggage in Halliburton cases on a number of expensive but luxurious first-class flights. I bought May a necklace, a peace offering to make up for my prolonged absence, and presented it to her as soon as I returned home.

'Michael, it's beautiful,' she smiled.

'It's no less than you deserve. It's just a little something to make up for all of the time I've spent away.'

'You didn't need to. Does this mean that you're here to stay for a while now?'

'Well, actually, no,' I said uncomfortably. 'I've got a flight booked back to Thailand this evening.'

I told myself there was nothing I could do, I had to get back to the gang. By midnight I was at Superstar, drinking with Lietzman and the Colflesh brothers.

Because we had no truck with outsiders the four of us socialized and worked together exclusively, and as a consequence our family lives began to suffer. Our wives and partners were never privy to the more shadowy aspects of our ever-growing business, and were never invited on our long drinking sprees. We would book ourselves hotel suites – Hong Kong's Mandarin Oriental was a particular favourite – and hole up for weeks on end, planning, drinking and growing more convinced of our invincibility. The women in our lives were treated well materially but no amount of money can compensate for the levels of secrecy and absence necessary when you're related or even married to a smuggler, even one living the supposed 'clean' life of a prosperous ex-pat bar owner.

CHAPTER SEVEN

MILLIONS OF DOLLARS AND TOMBSTONE NAMES

High jinks in the East.

Belgian Jimmy was a military man, ex-Foreign Legion who had since become a mercenary by trade. Jimmy hung out at the bar, and occasionally acted as our de facto bodyguard or bouncer. It wasn't that we needed a bodyguard, we had no enemies and no intentions of making any, but having muscle like Jimmy on hand appealed to our growing sense of ourselves as smuggling masterminds, a sense fuelled by the arrogance of illegal success.

Everybody liked Jimmy, he was a big man who'd seen awful things in the course of his work yet was always ready to lift his trademark bushy black moustache into a broad infectious grin. The shared experience of military life gave Jimmy much in common with the Colflesh brothers, who both held their new Belgian friend in very high regard. Being a soldier for hire meant that Jimmy would often take off at a moment's notice, leaving no word of when we could expect to see him again. Sure enough though, once his job was complete, you could expect a hearty slap on the back as you sat at the bar in Superstar, accompanied by a resounding, 'Right then, whose round is it?'

Jimmy was never in on the dope business, we never formally employed him in a professional capacity, but we loved having him around nonetheless. He never paid for drinks at Superstar and was often included when we took our little cocktail sabbaticals elsewhere, a weekend in Rome perhaps, taking in the sights, sampling the local wine and covering Jimmy's share of the huge bar tabs we accrued wherever we hung out.

People like Jimmy were part of the reason Superstar was such a hit. Our punters went there to meet them, to hear stories of a life led far from the beaten track and touch base with a world they would never know. As well as those attracted by the girls and the atmosphere, the place acted as a magnet to characters far removed from the everyday, people with a story to tell and a willingness to listen.

We also attracted men like Eddie. The first time I saw him he was sporting the salmon-pink sunburn tan of the recent arrival and dressed in a Coors Light T-shirt, fishing hat, khaki shorts, and flip-flops. He was of medium build and maybe thirty years old. He was typical of the would-be *narco-trafficante*, lured into Asia by the promise of easy cash and a whiff of danger, buying huge rounds at the bar and making the most of the little gangster movies they were writing themselves into.

He first came to my attention when Li, one of the girls

who danced at the club, introduced me to him, her body wrapped around his.

'Mike, this Eddie; Eddie, this my boss, Mike.'

Li was new and hadn't yet got to grips with the fact that I didn't want to be introduced to anyone as the boss, particularly not someone like Eddie. He chewed a cigar and had his hands all over Li's ass.

'Me and Li here are gonna take off for a little while, Mike. She's gonna . . . show me the sights.'

This character winked as he spoke, and pulled Li closer. I couldn't wait to get away from him.

'Well, enjoy yourselves then, and Li, I'll see you back at work.'

I ordered a drink as I watched them leave and wondered what it was that had so irked me about him. I didn't have to decide straight away, as Eddie became a regular visitor at the club. He came to meet up with a group of three men, one of whom I'd seen around and heard had been pretty successful smuggling fair-sized amounts of weed into England and France.

The meetings took place in one the booths on the edge of the dance floor. I watched over the coming weeks as Eddie and his associates become increasingly animated and involved as their big day approached. They'd surround themselves with champagne buckets and dancing girls, partying long and hard as a prelude to what they saw as their inevitable success. Eddie dominated Li's time now, and got angry with her if she so much as approached another customer. He insisted that she dress the way he liked, in a tiny mini-skirt, vest-top and heels, and I heard her refer to Johnson on at least one occasion as her 'boyfriend'. Eddie's monopolization of Li's time wasn't cool and, were it not for the big money he and his friends were spending at the bar, it would not usually have been tolerated.

A month or so after our initial meeting, Eddie came into the bar alone one night, a defeated look in his eyes, his gangster bravado depleted. I watched him call Li over and his favourite dancer duly made her way to him. He didn't order drinks for either of them, nor did he make his usual grab for the girl. Instead their conversation became more and more heated until finally Li turned her back on Eddie and made to walk away. He grabbed her by the wrist and turned her back round to face him. It was an ugly scene. By the time I reached them he had let go of Li's wrist, and she was furious.

'Fuck you, Eddie, fuck you! I no give you nothing.'

I looked at Li, then at Eddie.

'Problem?' I asked.

Eddie wasn't happy. 'No problem, no fucking problem at all. Shouldn't have expected anything less from a hooker, I guess. Fuck you all.'

And with that, Eddie turned on his heels and left Superstar, never to be seen again. At the end of the night I asked Li what had caused the final argument between them.

'Eddie have some business here, with the Falangs he meet in bar. They spend all their money and fill up a boat with Thai stick. Eddie always tell me he make two million dollar when it land. But they lose boat, men with guns come, take everything. Tonight Eddie ask me for money for plane back to America. I no have it, he get angry. He got nothing left.'

The history of the Thai dope trade at that time is littered with accounts of busts and rip-offs. Boatloads of dope were routinely intercepted and held for ransom and the danger of double-cross was everywhere. There were stories of pirates operating off the coast of Thailand believed to be responsible for the half-dozen yachts that had gone missing in that stretch of water in 1978 alone. In nearby Cambodia the Khmer Rouge were constantly on the lookout for foreign spies, their paranoid vigilance bringing them into contact with smugglers who had strayed into their waters and whose ugly destiny at their hands was one of slow torture and eventual murder.

Unlike the scams of some of our contemporaries, ours were all working, all of our weed was getting through. Our 100 per cent success rate may have made us over-confident but it didn't mean we grew slipshod. Lietzman and I had always kept our dealings to ourselves. And the Colflesh brothers were ex-Special Forces and both knew well the importance of secrecy and a strong, authored chain of command. Loose lips bust ships.

As far as the illegal side of the business was concerned we had completely assimilated a clandestine approach into our working practices. As far as possible we carved up the duties in preparing and moving shipments between the four of us. On the occasions when we had to take on extra hands, for loading and offloading the dope and crewing the *Yellow Bull* voyage to America, we employed the same old faces; western workers Bobby knew from the nearby oilfields supplementing their wages, or Thai locals, also sourced and recruited by Bobby. All were well paid for their efforts, they were put on salary and we gave fat bonuses to one and all when loads got through. Any staff employed were made aware of the premium we put on absolute secrecy and loyalty as a matter of course.

Operating from a permanent base in the form of the nightclub meant that we had the luxury of getting to know people gradually, watching potential employees in action before deciding whether or not to employ them. Bobby had taken up Thai boxing; he was good at it and eventually reaching competition level, and his sparring sessions and gym workouts offered another ideal opportunity to get to know potential help. But no matter how many auxiliary staff we employed, only the four of us had an overall picture of how the scams worked, so we stuck together like glue and kept our mouths shut. No outsiders.

As a further security precaution, the various sides of our business were each kept strictly autonomous. We never brought dope or the cash it earned through the bar. And despite having homes in different countries we were officially registered nowhere, which had the added bonus that we paid no taxes.

Dari Laut, which still provided an occasional home to Lietzman and me, was never used for the packing or storage of weed and never played any part in any of our smuggling operations throughout the time we owned it. The one Thai hired hand who worked on the barge and was known to enjoy smoking weed was taken aside and politely warned never to do so on *Dari Laut* if he wanted to keep his job. Even if anyone was watching, and we were sure that they weren't, our constant travelling between our numerous homes and bases would have made us very hard men to keep track of.

So when the rumour spread through Superstar that there was an American investigator in town by the name of Jack Palladino who was asking awkward questions about the dope trade, we wanted to know more. Jack was a gregarious character and made no attempt to hide his presence. The first time I saw him he was leaning against the bar in the club, surveying the scene and pronouncing 'Hi' to anyone who'd listen, 'I'm Jack . . .'

Palladino was an interesting guy, a good example of the strange cast of characters beginning to gravitate towards the weed trade. When he first arrived we heard conflicting stories about who he was and what he was doing in our club. He was a private eye with a law degree and a history of hanging out on the periphery of the dope business. Or he was a DEA agent with his own way of working. Or he was in town doing research for some American smugglers. The list went on and on. All the stories were equally unnerving.

Luckily, the hotel Palladino was staying in was staffed by 'friends' of ours, people we called on to help us with the heave-ho of the on and offload of dope. They were always well reimbursed for their efforts, and were more than ready to help out the generous Falangs at Superstar, supplying us with an itemized log of all of Jack's calls and a detailed record of his comings and goings in the city of sin. We didn't know who he was after, but it clearly wasn't us.

For someone whose main income was supposedly derived from a go-go joint on the Patpong Road, I was moving around an awful lot in Asia, Europe and America. When we divided up the duties involved in a particular scam I would push myself forward to take on any that involved travel, flying into America to pick up cash or secure the vehicles or boats we needed at that end. In order to travel and remain safe I needed a new identity to hide behind. Just to be on the safe side, I got four.

First I became Michael Charles Young, an alias I would use on and off for years and for which I eventually acquired a full suite of supporting documentation that helped to flesh out the identity and add a fictional back-story. Michael Young was a tombstone name, that is to say the name of someone of roughly your own age who had died young, usually as a child, before ever applying for a passport. Once you'd found the name – in my case through a a guy I met in a bar who had some useful connections – you could obtain a birth certificate by filling in a form and sending it to the local registrar. The birth certificate could be used to apply for a passport, which could then be used to begin a collection of credit cards and memberships. Voilà, one new identity.

As well as the Young identity, which was British, I also used the tombstone method to turn myself into Rodney Wayne Boggs, an American identity for which I collected another full suite of supporting documentation. The Boggs identity, though, needed a back-story. Although I tried to tone down my English accent when using it, it would have been obvious to anyone spending more than five minutes in my company that I was not an American. I made Rodney Wayne Boggs an antiques dealer who had spent the last ten years working in England, loving the country so much that he'd picked up the accent. Though not quite as well supported as the Young identity, the Boggs name proved real enough for me to use it to buy a house in San Francisco, a modest family dwelling on the outside but inside an extensively remodelled luxury pad.

The Young and Boggs identities were the most well rounded but I used other names to a lesser extent. I was also Michael Escreet and Michael Leslie Stocks, each identity having enough supporting documentation to be plausible. Wherever possible I would create new identities using my real first name and a fictitious surname. Sometimes, just remembering who I was supposed to be proved a full-time job.

As a nickname, my three partners had crowned me 'Fox', a reference to the fact that my real surname, the one I was using less and less, began with the letter F. As a nod to my newly secured alias I occasionally signed in and out of hotels under the name Michael Reynard, after the French for Fox.

I soon became very adept at altering passports. I experimented long into the night, listening to the sound of the street while curlicues and question marks of smoke rose up from the tip of my Benson and Hedges as I trained myself in the fine and ancient art of forgery. I worked at faking the passports alone, in my office at home in Singapore or in the office above the club, at tables strewn with bottles, visa stamps, passport photographs and blank pages. It was trial and error at first and many early attempts ended up in the wastepaper bin. But I kept going, because altering passports and travel documents was thrilling: it harked back to the spy stories

I had enjoyed as a boy and appealed to the watch-maker within.

Through tireless application I found that when I used the steam from a boiling kettle to heat a passport I could, very slowly and very carefully, remove the document's hard cover, which would in turn expose the spine of the document's inner pages.

Once I had access to these pages I noticed that they were stitched together rather than glued. I set about sourcing the thread used to bind the pages and practised, practised, practised, honing my sewing skills until I was confident that I could replace or swap pages, lose a travel stamp here or add one there, with no sign the passport had been tampered with. I had a collection of entry and exit visa stamps for all of the countries I visited on business and pleasure, thanks to the services of a local Thai forger Bobby had found and enlisted.

A passport stamped with multiple visas in and out of Thailand would have been guaranteed an unwanted pull in Europe or America by customs officials who were by now wising up to the Thai dope trade. Once a page in any particular passport began to appear overburdened with entry and exit visas it was simply removed and replaced with one which recorded a far less hectic travel schedule. By replacing pages I could make my passport, in whichever alias I was travelling under, read like that of a first-time tourist or a businessman whose work took him to the East once or twice a year. My passports became pure fiction.

In the days before the war on terror and the shrine to government-sponsored paranoia that modern air travel has since become, you could, if you desired, board a plane under one name and disembark in another country as someone else entirely. All you needed was the passports and the balls, and I had both. I began carrying at least two passports with me at all times and was soon slipping effortlessly between my growing collection of bought-and-paid-for identities. On one memorable occasion preparations for a smuggle called for me to visit five countries in a single day. Beginning the mammoth journey in Singapore at 8 a.m., I flew to Hong Kong to collect the cash to pay Kamol for that year's weed, and from there straight to Thailand where I handed the money over to our supplier in the early afternoon. Once Kamol was paid I flew to Jakarta in Indonesia to finalize arrangements for the onload of the dope shipment. Once my business was complete in Indonesia I flew back to Superstar to deliver the news that the crew were prepped and ready to go. Finally, as midnight approached, I boarded my last plane of the day to take me back to Singapore. Throughout the whistle-stop tour of South East Asia I used all of my fake names and began to wonder once I arrived home exhausted, if I couldn't do with a few more besides.

I made the most of a world in transition. On the one hand the world was moving towards a bright new technological age – progress, they called it – on the other it was still run without the use of high-speed accessible international communications and full cooperation between nations. With my passports in hand, I slipped through the gaps between the old world and the new.

I loved to travel, whoever I was. Michael Young,

Rodney Boggs, Michael Escreet, all of my aliases had in common a growing affection for the luxury afforded while flying first class on the world's premier airlines. Boarding planes to America to pick up cash or meet with our buyer became an exercise in self-amusement, part method acting, part subterfuge. Walking through customs with the trusty Halliburton stuffed to the gills with used dollar bills was a kick in itself. On top of the cash, I'd lay a couple of T-shirts, a sweater maybe, as a token attempt at concealing the fact that I was carrying up to a quarter of a million dollars out of America and back to the East. Quite how I thought a layer of cashmere would disguise the money should customs decide to take a look is an issue I chose never to fully explore.

We'd taken Samuel Colflesh on board as a full partner after the *Yellow Bull* smuggle, which meant Lietzman and I could take a step back from the logistical side of the smuggling scams. Logistics were Sam's forte, a legacy of his military days, and he soon nailed down a disciplined approach to every aspect of the operations. Nothing was ever left to chance, no detail was too small to garner his attention, no warehouse floor or boat deck was left unswept and unchecked for the telltale detritus of sticks, seeds and stems. No smuggle was initiated without a full rundown prepared in advance of everything we could possibly need to move our dope successfully from here to there.

In view of this, Lietzman and I were kicking back a little. Lietzman was spending more time in the States with Carolyn, the Australian girl he had married back in

1973. And I was spending more time with May at the new apartment I had bought in Singapore, in swanky Draycott Towers. Each thousand-square-foot apartment in this newly built shrine to luxury ex-pat living featured a circular living room, large and comfortable with a killer view of the city through its floor-to-ceiling windows, revolving around the centrepiece of a well-stocked bar. As with almost everything I was buying at the time, I wasn't happy until I'd altered the place to fit my own needs. I hired an interior designer to do a number on the apartment, installed mirrored walls, kitted it out with black Japanese lacquered furniture and had the place accented throughout with red, green and gold buddhas mounted on gold plinths. There was fitted purple carpet throughout, circular white leather sofas and gold lights. As a final touch I got my hands dirty building a water feature for the living room.

Lietzman, the Colflesh brothers and I spent many long nights at Draycott Towers, talking, drinking and laughing until the early hours. If it were just the four of us, if there were no drinking buddies or hangers-on around then we sometimes discussed the dope there. I kept a few maps at the apartment, and we'd occasionally pull them out and plan possible smuggling routes and look for new points at which to perform the on-load.

One night, as we drank and planned, with a couple of maps spread out before us over the purple carpet, May came into the room and became embroiled in what she believed was an innocuous conversation. We'd been planning routes and dreaming up names for the front companies we'd need for the next smuggle. Then we got to discussing the new graphics I was planning on having added to my newly acquired cigarette boat *Kim Ono*. I wanted big numbers so through a fug of Jack Daniel's and cigarette smoke I asked May what the luckiest Chinese number was, knowing how much store her native culture set by providence. Eighty-eight, she told me, sitting with us for a while and explaining the numbers and symbols associated with good fortune. The conversation was over as quickly as it had begun and May once again left us to it.

The event would have passed and gone, blown into nothing by the Singapore breeze, were it not for the fact that one of our number was logging it on to his onboard files for later use and would one day recount the event with devastating consequences.

By the time 1981 rolled around, we were ready to go again with another scam and, having learned our lesson the previous year, this time we had something more substantial than the *Yellow Bull* to rely on to help us achieve our objectives. We had the *Cape Elizabeth*.

Cape Elizabeth had begun life in the sixties as a cargo vessel. Lietzman had found the boat in England the year before and gladly paid the $100,000 asking price. Once he and a friend of his had got drunk aboard the new boat and sailed her around for a few days, he was sure she was just what we needed.

One of the plus points of the vessel, apart from its size and durability, was the heavy-duty winch installed to lift cargo on and off the main deck. We intended to use the winch to lift and drop our two new cigarette boats. This time Lietzman and I had gone top of the range, buying forty-foot speedboats, *Kim Ono* and *Mariposa*, rather than the twenty-eight-footers we'd started with. Cigarette boats weren't cheap, each one setting us back $250,000, even though *Mariposa* wasn't a true cigarette; owning four meant that we had almost a million dollars tied up in speedboats alone. Things were edging towards crazy but, as yet, no one had noticed.

The back end of *Kim Ono* had been ripped out and replaced. The decking which covered the back end of the boat would usually be short enough to allow two rows of seats, much like the front and back seats of a car. I had the decking on my boat lengthened until it was brought up flush with the back of the first row of seats, nudging the driver's shoulders. This gave me a 40-foot hull where I could secrete up to three tons of dope. No one watching it speed by would be any the wiser. I had the boat decorated with the number 88 at May's suggestion, go-faster stripes and decals. I'd even invented the *Kim Ono* logo, featuring an oriental Geisha in traditional dress, which decorated the sides. As a final touch, I went so far as to have a bomber jacket made up featuring the same logo which I wore to drive the boat. Lietzman's *Mariposa,* though not a true cigarette, had been built to our exacting specifications and was able to hide as much dope as *Kim Ono*, between the pair of them they could hold six tons without any trouble whatsoever.

The smuggle started with the *Cape Elizabeth*, captained by Samuel Colflesh, sitting off the coast of Phuket. The weed was packed and pressed in Thailand. Bobby had rented a local warehouse in which to get the shipment ready and it became a hive of activity as we toiled, vacuum-packing and baling machines working day and night to turn the two tons of marijuana into waterproof bricks. They had to be compact enough to be hidden in twelve-inch PVC piping, the kind seen running down the sides of houses all over the world as rainwater pipes, the same type we had used to store the fish-tank dope in at the bottom of the ocean. The pipes measured eight feet in length and again came complete with waterproof endcaps which ensured that nothing secreted inside the tubing was visible.

Once the pipes were packed with weed they were painted yellow up to the mid-point, the words THIS WAY UP and FLOATING LEVEL HERE were carefully added with stencils and, as a final touch, an aerial was added, left dangling uselessly from the endcap at the top of this curious item.

Ten days of hard work later and, hey presto, one shipment of electronic marine buoys, destined for California. The 'buoys' were then loaded into the speedboats and driven out to the *Cape Elizabeth*.

The buoys were packed four to a crate and stacked in the far corner of the hold, which was then covered with wooden slats and a sheet of tarpaulin, secured by lengths of rope and ready to be transported to Singapore, from where they would complete their journey to America as normal freight.

The shipping lanes around South East Asia, those we shadowed but never stuck to completely, were often awash with hidden obstacles that meant our onboard forward-looking radar system became a necessity rather than a luxury. Huge cargo ships sailed the area, picking up and dropping off hundreds of tons of freight at a time in steel containers. Often the containers were stored on deck, loosely secured as they made their way around the world. It was not unheard of, in bad weather, with the cargo ships tossed this way and that by the huge waves that could blow up, for one of the containers to simply slide off the deck and into the sea. Because airtight containers were sealed and often not completely full, they held enough air to keep them afloat. Even if the crew of the ship that had lost the container knew it had gone overboard their tight schedules would not allow them to turn back and retrieve it, so these small steel icebergs were simply left bobbing in the ocean. The forward-looking radar system we had fitted on the boat gave us enough prior warning to divert us from any potential hazards, though it could not tell us whether those hazards were a large school of migrating fish, a whale making its slow heavy way from here to there, or a container full of training shoes and tractor parts, waiting to sink us.

The other major hazard of our journey was the other ships we would encounter en route. As soon as another boat appeared on our radar or line of sight we immediately began to speculate. Who are they? Where are they from? And what do we look like to them? We always purposely stayed just far enough off the major shipping lanes to avoid such run-ins and most of the other boats that appeared in the twelve miles between us and the horizon were probably there for the very same reason as us.

Cape Elizabeth sailed into Singapore harbouring her illicit bounty. Once there we arranged for the buoys to be shipped into America as commercial freight using one of our spurious company fronts. When the paperwork was signed and the waybills needed to collect the product at the other end were in order it was simply a case of flying to America to meet the ship carrying our dope, signing for it, and selling it on. Happy days.

By 1981 the American dope market had stabilized and the price of Thai weed was back up to between $1,200 and $1,700 per pound, ensuring that our overall gross receipts from the *Cape Elizabeth* smuggle nudged a very respectable nine million dollars.

Once you're counting money in hundreds of thousands, in million-dollar increments, it becomes something abstract. Dollars in Disneyworld amounts, Mickey Mouse money. We had so much that some of it was left collecting dust in boxes stored in our various homes around the world. (I certainly always had a million or so in cash handy in a suitcase under the bed, should I need it.) Most of the cash was deposited at the Singapore branch of an international bank, giving us access to our money in that city and also, should we need it, at their branch in the Far East Trading Centre in Hong Kong (also favoured by Howard Marks). Luckily we had found a bank that was content to take suitcases full of cash from us and not ask any questions whatsoever. Perhaps we weren't so out of the ordinary, maybe they were used to dealing with millions of dollars handed over by half-hungover nightclub owners in sandals and jeans with brand-new Jags parked out front; perhaps they had us marked out as respectable businessmen with an unconventional approach.

In 1982 we remodelled the *Diver's Delight* landing barges, cutting the decks open and taking out the foam that lined them. The space left in each could easily accommodate the two tons of dope we had ordered from Kamol. Once the dope was packed and hidden the craft were crated up and shipped to San Francisco. The crates travelled as normal freight with the accompanying paperwork filled out in fictitious names representing non-existent companies. I picked them up from the customs clearing at dockside and moved them to the warehouse to unload.

We made another nine millions dollars, cash. It was that easy. Of course the money wasn't pure profit; the costs of running the operation were big, and getting bigger. We had the rent on the warehouse in San Francisco. A journey from Thailand to America and back on a vessel like *Cape Elizabeth* could cost half a million dollars in fuel and crew alone. We'd put our casual team of helpers on salary and were routinely paying them huge cash bonuses, as much as a hundred thousand dollars per man, when the money from another successful shipment rolled in. But still we were left with roughly two million dollars each. Cash.

As if that wasn't enough, Superstar's popularity was such that on a bad day we could reasonably expect to take thousands of dollars in cash. And that was on a bad day. Annually, the bar was turning over a huge amount of money. We were charging to get into the place and our drinks weren't cheap. Of course, the money going through the bar wasn't all profit, there were running and staff costs, but, even so, selling legal intoxicants was definitely giving the weed business a run for its money. In cash.

With that kind of money in such large and endless supply, the best thing to do is spend it, because the next smuggle will bring in more.

Lietzman indulged his love of the wide-open spaces and bought himself a ranch, the O-Bar-O, in New Mexico. On my first visit he proudly showed me the helicopter pad he'd recently had installed. We climbed aboard Lietzman's new Enstrom helicopter, drinks in hand, took off and, with Lietzman at the controls, climbed high, inspecting from the air his newly acquired spread overlooked by mountains and a clear blue sky, his own little piece of America.

Bobby built a house, from the ground up, for his new Thai wife. He'd met and fallen in love with a local girl and eventually married her in a traditional Thai ceremony, a fantastic affair attended by the girl's family as well as Lietzman, Sam and me. His wife had a son from a previous marriage and Bobby elected to bring up the boy as his own. He was a good man.

Bobby's affection for the Thai way of life had earned him the nickname JT, a reference to the ex-military American Jim Thompson who had famously gone native to the extent that he had eschewed all things Western. Thompson had virtually single-handedly created a world market for the quality Thai silk he produced and traded in. By running his Thai Silk Company as a cooperative, Thompson made millionaires and friends out of a handful of the Thais who worked with him in the endeavour. Like Bobby Colflesh, Thompson had felt so at home in South East Asia that he melted into it and became one with the landscape. The nickname JT fitted Bobby well, and we ignored any possible ill omen in Thompson's eventual fate: he went missing on Easter Sunday in 1967 while walking in the Malaysian Cameron Highlands.

Sam bought himself a yacht, the *Hoopoe III*, and moored it in Hong Kong's exclusive Aberdeen Marina. It was a nice yacht. Not as nice as mine though.

I was an avid reader of boating magazines, keen to keep up to date with technical advances in the nautical world. With my mind on the smuggle, I always made sure to check out the classified section, seeing which boats were for sale and where. I was always looking for new ways to make the operation more efficient and the loads bigger while shortening the odds on the risk factor. It was while staying with friends in New York, relaxing with a tall one and a Benson and Hedges after a shopping trip to Bleeker Street for a box of new twelve-inches for the club (the extended mix of 'Don't You Want Me' and Michael Jackson's 'Thriller'), that I saw an advertisement in *Boating* magazine.

There in a grainy black and white photo was a yacht called *Delfino II*, currently moored in Miami and up for sale at a price of 1.2 million dollars. The yacht wouldn't be so useful as far as the smuggling operation went, but as an addition to my personal stock of toys and property, *Delfino II* was irresistible. I picked up one of my fake passports and flew straight down to Miami to take a closer look. I wasn't disappointed.

Delfino II was beautiful. As soon as I saw the yacht up close and personal, I knew I had to have her. *Delfino II* was one hundred and thirty feet of pure hand-crafted, expertly fashioned, no expense spared, state-of-the-art seagoing luxury. She was graceful, elegant and powerful with enough room on board to hold the party to end all parties. *Delfino* had originally been built in 1971 with no other purpose in mind than to offer all the unnecessary extras of a five-star hotel on the ocean. I was in love.

And there were practical considerations for the acquisition too, bubbling just beneath the surface and, to my mind, justifying the huge expense. Although my partners and I had not yet had any kind of run-in with the forces of law and order, in the murkier recesses of my consciousness I was aware of the amount of trouble we would be in should things ever go seriously wrong. We were buying our dope in Asia where the death penalty was not unheard of for trafficking offences and shipping it to and selling it in America where sentences for narcotics smuggling were seemingly ever on the up. This, coupled with the imminent arrival of our first child (my beautiful daughter Nicole was born a few months later in September) meant that I needed to think of the long-term safety and security of my young family. Once fully loaded with supplies and fuel, *Delfino II* was potentially capable of spending up to six months out at sea without ever having to come in to dock on dry land. Should questions of extradition or arrest ever arise, with enough money behind me, I figured I would be able to live aboard the yacht indefinitely and stay out of reach of official hands.

I talked myself into the purchase in three seconds flat. Using the tried and tested cover story that I was a very wealthy international dealer in oriental antiques, buying in the East and selling in the West, I bought the yacht, writing a cheque for the full amount there and then.

CHAPTER EIGHT

1983. MORE MONEY THAN SENSE

Stormy weather and trouble at sea.

'No, listen!' Indignant, I flourished the long black-and-gold cigarette holder I'd taken to using, an affectation like my jade ring and diamond-and-jade Buddha necklace. 'Listen! What we need is a submarine. We'll pick up an ex-navy submarine at auction, paint it yellow, fill the missile silos with dope. Once we get in range we'll shoot the dope into San Francisco harbour.'

Sammy wasn't impressed with my idea at all. 'They'll pick us up on radar three days out of America, think we're Russian and blow us out of the fucking water. Think again, Fox.'

Most of the ideas we came up with seemed brilliant at the time, inspired Eureka flashes courtesy of Jack Daniel's. By the sober light of day they often seemed more like the wild drunken ramblings of crazed madmen.

We decided instead that for our next smuggle we would re-employ *Cape Elizabeth*, the ship that had served us so well two years earlier. This time we would import a four-ton load and in the process earn ourselves around $13.5 million, more than enough to keep the home fires burning for a while.

It was such a beautiful day that loading the dope on board *Cape Elizabeth* was a lot of fun. She was moored off the coast of Phuket, far enough out that she could not be seen from the mainland. We were surrounded by islands too small to be inhabited, tiny beach oases poking their golden sandy shoulders out of the water. The sun beat down from a clear blue sky and there wasn't another living soul for miles around.

Bobby arrived with a small fleet of Thai fishing boats laden with dope, the delivery organized by Kamol. The crews helped with the onload, which consisted of a few hours' huffing and puffing beneath an Asian sun, dragging the heavy bales on to the waiting ship and stowing them away in a container. As we wished Sam bon voyage we felt secure in the knowledge that fate, luck and everything else we could possibly need to get our dope safely into America was on our side.

Sammy was to take on the task of captaining the *Cape Elizabeth* on her month-long journey to America. Once there, Bobby and I would meet him offshore in the cigarette boats which had been sent as freight to America. We'd transfer the dope to the two smaller craft and sail them into San Francisco harbour where they'd be hitched to a trailer on the back of the truck and driven the short distance to the warehouse.

The journey to America went without a hitch; Sammy was a more than competent captain and made the trip in good time. However, off the coast of San Francisco we ran into trouble. Lietzman had sailed his houseboat out into the open ocean and remained nearby, not close enough that he could be seen by *Cape Elizabeth* but near enough that he could be contacted and called in via VHF radio should his assistance be required. But once again the forces of nature were lined up against us and Lietzman's boat would be in no position to help.

Cape Elizabeth arrived off the coast in September, in the middle of a horrendous storm. Bobby and I sped out to meet the ship in the cigarette boats, fighting to control them as they launched into heart-stopping jumps every time they hit one of the huge waves the storm was throwing up. The wind howled, the rain lashed down on us, and what on paper looked to be a relatively simple exercise in illegal importation took on a rather more epic character than we had first envisaged over drinks in the bar at the Mandarin Oriental. The storm was so loud that the hand-held radios we had bought along to communicate with Sam were useless. It was pitch black, visibility down to zero but for ineffectual shrugs of torch and lamplight as we attempted once, twice, then three times to manoeuvre the two speedboats into position to have the dope lowered down to them as Sam yelled warnings to us from the deck of the boat.

'Easy there, Fox, any nearer and you're gonna hit me. JT, you too. Any one of these swells could take us all down, so easy does it.'

Bringing the speedboats too close to the body of the *Cape Elizabeth* opened them up to the very real danger of being smashed to pieces against the side of her. But we still tried, for a couple of exhausting hours. Finally I looked over at Bobby as another giant swell caught and lifted him in his speedboat.

'JT, we're just gonna have to forget it,' I yelled, straining to be heard above the noise of the storm. 'There's no way we're unloading tonight, won't happen and we'll kill ourselves trying. We'll have to head back to shore. Haig, we're calling it a night. We'll radio in when we hit land.'

Bobby and I made our way back to San Francisco as Sammy turned the *Cape Elizabeth* round and headed once more out into open sea to await further instructions. Back on dry land, Bobby's frustrations were apparent. 'We're going to have to try again, Fox. *My brother's out there in a boat full of weed.*'

'I know, JT, I know, but if we go straight back out now it'll just be the same story. Let's turn on the TV, see if the weather's got any better.'

The weather forecasters doling out their predictions on the local channel needn't have bothered manoeuvring the cardboard cut-out clouds and storm fronts over their facsimile of the California coastline; a simple 'Forget it boys, there's no way you can offload your dope today' would have sufficed.

Two days later, with Sammy still out at sea, the storm was showing no signs of letting up. But the offload would have to go ahead, Sammy could not float out there indefinitely with a boat full of dope at his command. Coast Guard ships and helicopters were heading out hourly in search of vessels in distress and it was only a matter of time before *Cape Elizabeth* attracted unwanted official attention. So we radioed through to the boat, arranged to meet up at the same spot, and tried again.

This time, once again under cover of darkness, we tried a new plan. Rather than attempt to offload the dope from *Cape Elizabeth* straight into the speedboats, we lowered the two nineteen-foot Zodiac dinghies down from the ship and into the raging ocean, securing them to the *Cape Elizabeth* by a line and in turn securing the speedboats to the dinghies. Rain lashed down on us as bales of weed were heaved off *Cape Elizabeth*'s deck, tossed down into the dinghies and then dragged manually into the specially designed and renovated hulls of the cigarette boats. We worked for hours in the most inhospitable of conditions, wet through, tired and scared as we fought to keep our balance in the teeth of the winds blowing in from all sides. Conditions were so severe that any man overboard would have most certainly been lost.

The chain of boats were tethered together but the swells thrown up by the storm were touching ten feet, meaning that we would have to wait for the few seconds that the sea levelled off to resume the exercise. Bales thrown down into the waiting Zodiacs were in real danger of simply bouncing off the rubber floor of the dinghies straight to the floor of the waiting ocean. It was a long, hard night, but eventually, somehow, the offload was complete. The small crew aboard the *Cape Elizabeth* had more than earned their generous bonuses.

Racing back to San Francisco in a cigarette boat full of dope still buffeted by huge waves and howling winds, I had never felt so alive.

Back at the warehouse, a quick inventory revealed that a number of our bales had got soaked through during the offload and had to spend a day drying, convection heaters on full. The warehouse soon began to smell like a pot-smokers' convention.

The second trip had worn the *Cape Elizabeth* out. Like the *Yellow Bull* in the previous year, she had proved herself reliable, but ultimately unable to take the strain of international smuggling. What little was left of the boat when Sam finally edged her into Los Angeles was sold for scrap for a single American dollar, which hung proudly from then on behind the bar at Superstar.

As soon as the dope had been sold on to Hippie Rod and his friends and arrangements made for the money to be carried back to Singapore, I headed to Miami.

The gateway between North and South America, Miami in the eighties was built in no small part by the profits of the drug business. In the mid-seventies Miami established itself as the distribution point for an estimated 95 per cent of the dope smoked in America. The town became so saturated with weed that it shifted its focus to the cocaine business. While the rest of early eighties America buckled under Reaganomic recession, Miami saw a construction boom. Its wealth of shiny new skyscrapers, hotels, nightclubs and high-end car dealerships were all financed by the millions of dollars that flooded in from the cocaine trade.

I loved the electric atmosphere of Miami but I was there primarily because that's where I decided to leave *Delfino II*. In Miami she was just another yacht, easily missed among the large numbers of luxury boats. In Thailand she would have stuck out like a sore thumb and been as effective an advertisement of what I did for a living as taking an ad out in the local paper.

I'd hired an interior designer to remodel the boat and the final result was Miami meets Art Deco, with some extra dope-smuggler chic supplied by me.

The yacht was air-conditioned throughout, with thick pile carpet everywhere. The main saloon was big enough to host a business conference. The walls of the master bedroom were covered in mirrors, its shelves fully loaded with a state-of-the-art entertainment system, easily controlled by the remotes that sat on the table next to the king-size bed.

All of the dolphin-shaped taps in the bathrooms were gold plated, and the en-suite leading off the master bedroom contained an oversize bath with jacuzzi taps, which could comfortably sit five. Examples of antique and contemporary oriental art were hung and mounted throughout the boat, some sourced by the interior designer and some from my own collection of oriental china, which was growing at a steady rate. What had begun as a few pieces that caught my eye on my travels through Asia and the East was soon a serious collection, a million dollars' worth of the stuff.

What we couldn't buy off the shelf, I had made. I became obsessed with the detail, and would skimp on nothing to achieve the effect I was after. On the lower deck of *Delfino II* I had one cabin refitted as two with a sliding interconnecting door. Rather than just have my on-site carpenters rustle up and fit a new door, I decided that I wanted something special. We hired a local artist, a native American, and gave him carte blanche to follow the lead of his muse and create a one-off. The man covered the door in a 3-D dope-inspired collage of bird feather and paint, each individual feather painstakingly cut to size and glued on, in a process that took months to complete.

I lived aboard most of the time while the work was being completed, but when conditions got too difficult I simply moved aboard *L'Archipel* for a while, a beautiful game-fishing boat I'd bought for fun and sport.

Soon after buying the yacht I'd hired my first crew members, Jim and Moira Griffiths. They had met and fallen in love while serving as officers in the RAF. Jim was twenty years Moira's senior and had joined the RAF as aircrew just before the outbreak of war, seeing action on the huge Sunderland flying boats and completing several tours of duty with Bomber Command prior to being picked for the elite VIP squadron, the same squadron that had accompanied Winston Churchill to Casablanca and Yalta. Captain Jim, as he would later become known, was every inch the boy's own hero and cut from the very same cloth as my father.

Since leaving the Air Force, Jim and Moira had travelled the world working as crew on a succession of luxury yachts. They were not the first people I interviewed for the crew positions aboard *Delfino,* but as soon as I met them, I knew my search was over. Where the other applicants had turned up in jeans and flip-flops for jobs aboard a million-dollar yacht, Jim and Moira arrived looking and sounding the part. I employed them on the spot as skipper and cook.

I'd also installed a helipad, and bought a Bell helicopter, which seated five and had a flying range of three hundred miles. The next step was to employ a pilot, who was to wear the uniform I supplied at all times, even while on standby. The pilot's gig was a breeze. Most of his time aboard *Delfino II* was spent polishing the helicopter, which had of course been painted up to match the yacht, and waiting around lest his new boss should feel the urge to take to the skies.

By the time the work was done, even I was happy, so much so that I commissioned a video made in order to entice potential clients who may wish to spend the $50,000 dollar a week charge to hire the yacht out. The video wasn't cheap to produce but then again, nor would *Delfino* be for anyone who wanted to hire her out.

During the years that I owned the yacht we hired her out twice, for a week at a time. The hundred thousand dollars earned in fees just about covered the cost of the taps in the master bathroom.

Two years after buying *Delfino* the yacht was ready to to cruise. I took my pride and joy on a jaunt around the Caribbean and the Bahamas, relaxing on deck and taking some time to cast off and indulge my love of fishing. When I fancied the idea of a picnic I asked Moira to make me up a basket, sandwiches, chilled champagne, fresh fruit, the best. I picked a nearby uninhabited island and flew there, landing on the deserted beach of pure white sand, and had the helicopter pilot stand by while Captain Jim, Moira and I enjoyed the excellent lunch and a beach barbecue in the idyllic surroundings.

Driving *Delfino* was a joy. The engine overhaul had left her a delight to handle, easily manoeuvrable and capable of twelve knots in comfort. Against his better judgement, Captain Jim let me take control of the yacht on a number of memorable occasions – mostly when we were far enough out at sea to ensure that there was nothing I could hit. Even so I managed to run her aground on sandbanks on a few occasions, before sheepishly handing control of the boat back to my not-at-all amused skipper. The euphoria that comes from being in control of something as big and as beautiful as *Delfino II* was immense, and made the money I was spending on her seem worth every penny – in fact, at times like those it felt like a bargain.

Although I never sat Jim and Moira down and told them that the twelve million or so I had sunk into buying, renovating and running the boat thus far had come from the dope business, they soon sussed out that I was not the dealer in Eastern objets d'art and antiquities that had become my main cover. I was not on board the day that the US Coast Guard boarded the yacht and began to ask questions about its absent owner, but was relieved and grateful when I heard Captain Jim describe how he'd convinced them I was just another harmless European millionaire with more money than sense.

As if to prove his point I also began flying the Bell helicopter I'd bought for the yacht, despite having no formal training in flying a chopper whatsoever. The ride in that thing was pure thrill from start to finish, hitting 120 knots fifty feet above the surface of the ocean with nothing but my cigarette between me and the horizon, taking advantage of the three-dimensional ride the helicopter offered by taking it backwards, forwards, side to side, up, down and back again while the pilot sat next

Ernest Forwell, bomber pilot, war hero.

Mum, Dad and me.

Me as a young man. London, 1958.

As a teenager with my parents in Australia.

With May in my bar, the Charlie Superstar.
Bangkok, 1978.

Draycott Towers, Singapore. Eighties dope-smuggler chic.

Long nights. Singapore, mid eighties.
L–R: Unknown, unknown, Robert Lietzman, Elsie, me, Samuel Colflesh.

'Hello, I see you've got a boat for sale?' Hard at it, mid eighties.

Above and right
Cigarettes and alcohol. South East Asia.

The *Delfino II*, Miami.

Sailing with Nicole.
Hong Kong, 1986.

Have jacket, will smuggle. Specially made for driving *Kim Ono*.

On the run. Australia, 1990.

With the family. St John's Wood, 1990.

Dream Street, Camden Stables Market, in the early nineties.

Prisoner number 25299-086. Terminal Island Prison, San Pedro, California, 1996.

FEDERAL CORRECTIONAL INSTITUTION

INMATE INFORMATION HANDBOOK
1995
FEDERAL BUREAU OF PRISONS

TERMINAL ISLAND, CAL.

Below Lee Bullman, left, and me. Kent, 2008.

to me praying for the moment I handed the controls back to him.

We spent many happy months aboard *Delfino* cruising between her home in the Merrill Stevens dockyard in Miami and the Bahamas. We noticed on these trips that evidence of drug smuggling between the Bahamas and Florida was rife. You only had to view the perimeter end of the small Bahamian runway in Bimini to see the large number of crashed aircraft that had been used for drug running, evidence of loads that had not quite made it, having been caught up in heavy weather or intercepted and chased down by the Coast Guard, or product that had got through and made so much money for the smugglers bringing it in that it made sense to sacrifice the plane that had got them there as they sped off in their fully loaded cigarette boats to an awaiting small fortune.

Often while we were at anchor off Bimini at night we would amuse ourselves by watching on the ship's radar the fast blips of the cigarette boats used by smugglers shooting across the gulfstream from the Bahamas into the Everglades in Florida. Watching with drinks in hand, the radar show became better than TV as millions were made and lost on that busy stretch of water.

As they are in smuggling hotspots around the world, pay-offs and backhanders were common in the area at the time. One particular customs official we met seemed to be doing exceptionally well for a man earning a government salary. His vast collection of gold and diamond jewellery, worn all at once and glinting ferociously in the Caribbean sun, made him a dead ringer for Mr T.

Although not a fan of guns myself, yacht piracy was

such a problem in the seas *Delfino II* regularly sailed that I insisted the crew kept an onboard cache of firearms just in case anyone decided to attempt to take what I had broken so many laws to earn. We stocked up with a legal supply of handguns and rifles, which were kept safely under lock and key aboard the yacht, but instantly accessible should the need to resort to firepower ever arise.

I was proud of the yacht, and keen to show her off to my friends. Bobby and Sammy visited while May and I entertained them lavishly. I was expecting Lietzman and his wife but in the end Carolyn came on her own. I realized then that I hadn't spoken to Robert in a while.

CHAPTER NINE

SO LONG, DELFINO

A secret habit, and some very bad news.

By now I was based between my homes in San Francisco, Miami and South East Asia with occasional shopping trips to London or New York thrown in to break the routine, while Lietzman was spending more and more time holed up in New Mexico at the O-Bar-O and aboard his San Francisco houseboat. On the increasingly rare occasions when we did hang out, it was far less fun.

'I've seen a boat for sale, Bourbon, it's right up your street,' I said, when unusually we were at the Superstar together. 'The guy who's selling it reckons it'll outrun a cigarette, says we're welcome to take it out for a test run.'

'I'll give that a miss. Don't we have enough boats?'

Lietzman's dismissal of my idea seemed out of character, it smarted, so I tried another tack. 'Okay then, what say we head over to Singapore, book a couple rooms at the Oriental and drink ourselves silly for a few days? I'm buying, see if we can't go through every bottle of Scotch in the place.'

'I'm gonna take a pass on that, too many pairs of ears

in that place for my liking and I've got plenty enough Scotch at home. While I'm here though, anything I should know about?'

There was. In Thailand at the tail end of 1984, trouble was brewing on *Dari Laut*. Two of the members of staff who worked on the barge had got into an argument, a petty squabble that had got way out of hand and ended in murder when one of the men involved shot the other to death. None of us was implicated in the homicide – it was established early on that the killing was the result of a feud between the two workers – and the barge-master actually dealt with the police, but still we felt we could do without the official attention the crime bought.

Lietzman and I decided we should get rid of the barge and cut loose the bad karma. Privacy and secrets. No outsiders.

I felt a pang for old times but Lietzman didn't seem to care when *Dari Laut* was stripped down and sold on for use as a diving platform to a buyer in the Philippines, finally used as we had originally intended when we'd bought and renovated it years previously. The ancillary boats, vehicles and equipment that had been attached to the barge, the Land Rovers and Zodiac dinghies, and the winches, were all crated up and shipped to the San Francisco warehouse where they would work for the smuggling operation at the American end.

I'd been aware for a while now that something was not quite right with my old partner and friend. Whatever was with Lietzman had only been captured at first in my peripheral vision, but something was most definitely up and the dark cloud that had been slowly gathering over his personality was now fully formed. He was spending more and more time on his ranch, breaking all contact with us in Thailand while we planned the next smuggle and unwilling to talk to me about his absence on his return.

'Nice of you to join us, Bourbon,' I joked. 'We've missed you.'

'You can drop the thinly veiled English sarcasm, Fox, I'm here now. Just tell me what we're doing and let's get on with it.'

'Well, we were discussing the next load. Any ideas?'

'You guys seem to be getting on pretty well here without me, so why don't you just cut to the chase and fill me in on what you've come up with.'

Lietzman was becoming truculent, antsy, paranoid, ever ready to criticize the way the operation was being run but lacking the patience to suggest means of improvement. He was becoming a pain in the arse to the point that I no longer recognized my partner in crime. Where once he had come on like James Dean with a hangover, his overall mood now took on a more brittle character.

For the first time since we started working together, money became an issue. Lietzman was beginning to hint that he wanted out, and that he expected a golden handshake upon leaving the organization he had helped to create.

There was, as always, cash around. The previous year I had hired a lock-up garage in San Francisco and used it to store boxes full of used bills, in case any unexpected business expenses should arise at the American end of the operation. There was close to a million dollars sitting in boxes in the garage, and Lietzman wanted it.

As the vague talk of his leaving turned to hard figures, the news reached me at Superstar that someone had driven into the door of the San Francisco garage and left it hanging off its hinges. A million in cash was out in the open and anybody's for the taking. I made a few calls and had the money moved, finally agreeing that if Robert Lietzman wanted it, then he should have it. We discussed details of how he would pick up the money.

'There's almost a million waiting for you, Bourbon. It's all yours.'

'Seems fair. I'll go pick it up, and leave you to it. It'll be like none of this ever happened.'

'No, Bourbon, it won't be like that at all. A drink before you go? One for the road?'

'Not right now, Fox, I've got things I need to be getting on with. Maybe next time.'

I never saw my friend again.

Lietzman's abrupt departure spelled the end of an era. I had always assumed we'd remain friends long after our dope business together was done but my American ally had left under a cloud. Things that should have been said weren't. Over the years we'd spent endless hours together in bars and on boats all around the world, knocking back bourbon and discussing legit ways we could earn on a similar scale without smuggling, dreaming dreams of businesses we could set up. But talk is all it ever was, and dreams, like talk, come cheap.

Somehow, remaining with the Colflesh brothers while

Lietzman headed out to wherever he headed out to felt disloyal. The perceived betrayal nagged at me even as I faced the harsh financial reality of my friend's leaving. Although the gang were earning millions every year from the dope we were moving, we were spending hard and fast too. On paper we were millionaires over and over, but much of our wealth was tied up in the assets we had accrued in the course of our career.

I had traded in my Draycott Towers pad in Singapore and moved to the more upmarket Chancery Lane. The new abode was twice the size of the old, measuring in at a roomy two thousand square feet of chic wall-to-wall opulence. There was a very practical reason for the house move: on 28 June my son Nicholas was born, and Nicole was by then two years old and an active toddler. We needed the space.

Lietzman's pay-off had left us short of cash for the first time. We needed cash to operate – not many people in our business took cheques – and suddenly that commodity, usually so abundant as to not warrant a second thought, was very thin on the ground. All our impulse purchases in pursuit of the good life were stretching the purse strings to breaking point. Something had to give, and though I hated to admit it, I knew what it was.

Delfino II was a money pit. In the few short years I had owned the yacht I had spent millions on its refurbishment and upkeep. Just keeping the thing moored and staffed was costing a small fortune. It was a luxury I could no longer afford. For the sake of the team I had to let my beloved yacht go. My dream of a safe haven for me, my family and my partners in crime, away from the threat of extradition, would have to go on ice for a while.

The super-rich enjoy their playthings, and Captain Jim soon found one of their number who was ready to take *Delfino II* off my hands for the bargain price of two million dollars. The buyer was a rich big shot involved in the American booze trade. Despite the man being worth untold millions he drove a hard bargain and I found myself being beaten down from my original asking price by a cool half million dollars. The new buyer kept Jim and Moira on, as well as a few other members of the crew who had, for the time we'd been together, felt like family. I stayed in touch with Captain Jim and Moira, hoping the day would come when our paths would cross again.

With Lietzman gone the dynamic between myself and my two remaining partners, Bobby and Sam Colflesh, shifted somewhat. For his part, Bobby remained pretty much the same, as reliable and mellow as ever. I was shaken by my friend's departure, but it was Samuel Colflesh who was most radically changed. Lietzman's leaving created something of a vacuum that Sammy stepped up to fill.

On first meeting Sam, nothing about his appearance or demeanour marked him as a potential member of a gang of multi-ton marijuana smugglers. He dressed fastidiously – there was nothing off the peg about Sam's wardrobe choices – and when travelling, the good-looking blond guy with his complete set of matching Louis Vuitton luggage looked like the CEO of some world-beating multinational conglomerate.

Although still nominally the 'leader' of the now three-man gang since Lietzman had left, I watched as Samuel Colflesh gradually took on more and more of the responsibility of running the dope operation. Sam loved to organize, and he was good at it, gifted in fact, but sometimes he would take it just a little too far. One night, with a few drinks inside of us, at that point in the evening when good-natured ribbing had started to replace intelligent conversation, the fact that Sam had booked us a limousine to ferry us from bar to bar, a journey of fifty yards or so, caused us to howl at his efficiency and zeal. His codes too would often be the cause of much hilarity at our planning and strategy meetings, still conducted in hotel bars across South East Asia.

'Where the fuck is CCN again?' Bobby asked.

'Central Control North. It's Bangkok, CCN is fucking Bangkok!'

'Right, okay. And where is CCS?'

'Singapore! Central Control South. CCS is Singapore!'

For his part, Sam took the chiding in good humour, as we all did when our turn as the butt of the night's jokes came round.

We'd been organized before but now the smuggles we planned as a trio moved with military precision. No detail of any job was too small to warrant Sam's undivided attention.

The Thai marijuana trade was undergoing radical changes in the mid-eighties and many of the changes were down to the hard work and vision of one man. Brian Daniels was an American smuggler who had, ironically, once been a partner of Robert Lietzman's. The trouble with the Australian authorities that Lietzman had been so keen to avoid when he and I had first met was the direct result of his work with Daniels, the pair having been caught up in the sting operation that had very nearly cost Lietzman his freedom.

A decade later in Thailand, Daniels had moved onwards and upwards. He was a true believer in the product, one of the breed of smugglers who had an eye on the glorious day when the social hypocrisy surrounding marijuana was faced down and the weed was legalized. For some in the business it seemed inevitable that that day would come, and as soon as it did they would be ready to cash in. Column inches in newspapers and magazines were being devoted to the fact that far from being detrimental to the health of the user, there were certain diseases and afflictions which marijuana actually eased, an argument that gained credence when respected medical professionals joined the ranks of those calling for the plant's legalization. Marijuana had become so ubiquitous that it was enjoyed by people at every level of society, whether they admitted to inhaling or not, and was the one activity which often turned productive, hard-working, tax-paying members of society into criminals two or three nights a week.

Unlike me, Daniels was a true child of the sixties, witnessing first hand the trials and tribulations of the Love Generation. He'd found himself slap bang in the centre of hippie counter-culture and immediately felt at home there.

There are two types of ex-hippie. The first is the one

we hear so much about, victims of their search for the nirvana of psychedelic enlightenment, the poor unfortunates who took one toke too many and never found their way back.

The second type don't get mentioned so much, which is odd, as they are the cultural generation who carried hippie ideals over into their working lives and gave us the Internet and the protest movement, while laying the foundations for virtually every cultural movement worth a damn that has grown up since. Like our buyers in California, Daniels belonged to the latter. Far from being some caricature stoner making the peace sign in tea shades and nodding out to Jefferson Airplane, Daniels was an activist with a plan.

By the mid-eighties he was in the process of making his dream of a huge smuggling conglomerate operating between Thailand and America come true. Daniels had gone up-country to the source of the weed. Thanks to contacts he made through his Thai wife's extended family he'd sat down with the farmers who grew and harvested much of the dope in Thailand and began to convince many of them to work to a synchronized schedule. He'd organized them into a money-spinning collective, and he'd made himself a fortune doing it. With the farmers now aiming to harvest their crop at the same time, the potential was there for a buyer to buy loads from all of them at the same time, rather than purchase piecemeal loads from a single outlet, and ship the massive multi-ton loads into America. Brian had connections not just with the farmers who grew and harvested the weed but had made friends in the Thai military and within its government.

Despite the ambitiousness of his plans, Daniels was making admirable headway. Many people, both farmers and smugglers alike, saw the advantages that combining resources in this way could bring. It was really just an extension of the syndicate idea, tried and tested by groups operating out of Thailand at the same time as we were, but the scale of Daniels's imaginings would, if he could pull it all together, make smuggling history.

Rumours about what Daniels was up to spread along the Patpong Road, but my own involvement with him was still a long way off. In the meantime I had news to deal with, news that would shake and change me. News that signalled a warning I chose not to hear.

Since leaving Thailand and his life with us behind, Lietzman had slipped off the radar. We believed he was spending his retirement out in New Mexico at his ranch up in the hills, but details of where he was and who he was with were sketchy at best. It turned out that since leaving Thailand, Lietzman had begun attracting unwanted attention back home in the States.

The Internal Revenue Service were poking around, curious as to where all the money for Lietzman's ranch had come from. In the grand tradition of American law enforcement, it was starting to look likely that if they caught up with Lietzman at all it would be the same way they eventually got Al Capone: on a tax beef. I found out later they had slapped him with a tax bill for over six million dollars in the previous year.

I was in the Superstar when I heard the news. Bobby walked over to me one May afternoon with a look I hadn't seen on my partner's face before and sat down next to me. For the first time since I had met him, Bobby was freaked. His voice was as soft as ever, but tinged now with something else as he said the words out loud, perhaps as much for his own benefit as mine.

'Lietzman's dead.'

His words didn't register at first. If this was some kind of a joke then it was in supremely bad taste and totally out of character for Bobby. But somewhere deep down I knew that that wasn't Bobby's style. This wasn't a joke. This was real.

Bobby, himself still in shock, explained the reason for Lietzman's increasingly erratic behaviour when I had last seen him. It was cocaine. Of all the things in the world that it could have been, it was cocaine. Somewhere along the way, during the increasing amount of time we had spent apart, Robert Lietzman had found himself new playmates and a new playground and starting spending some of that hard-earned on South America's finest. He'd crossed a white line he'd never come back from.

Perhaps Lietzman's high tolerance to the booze had led him to search out his kicks elsewhere, and that search had led him to coke. Or maybe the thrill ride of smuggling was no longer enough, so he'd turned to powders for a new shot of illicit kicks. Or maybe it was the tax bill, maybe Lietzman used coke to block out the trouble he was in with the American authorities. Though seemingly scared of nothing and used to running gauntlets, the bill must have got to Lietzman; its arrival chimed with the changes I had noticed in my friend, which feels now like far more than coincidence.

He'd never once mentioned cocaine to me. And even if

I had been able to talk to him about his problem, I had no experience whatsoever with hard drugs, I'd got stoned from a bong hit back in my travelling days and slapped an ODing chef in Superstar until he coughed and spluttered back to life, and those disparate events made up the sum total of my experience of drug use.

Over the following weeks the details of Lietzman's demise came through hazy, second-hand Chinese whispers, crisis-junky guesswork and paranoid summation fleshing out the thin facts available. Lietzman had taken his Enstrom helicopter, the same helicopter he and I had flown laughing and drunk, and ploughed it into one of the mountains that ringed his ranch. The impact had thrown him from the pilot seat of the chopper and he'd bled to death while attempting to crawl back to the radio in his cockpit to call in for help. It had taken search and rescue days to find him. When Lietzman's body was eventually discovered they found his pockets stuffed with cash and a suitcase in the wreckage containing a weight of cocaine.

It didn't take long for the rumours to start flying. The conspiracy theorists had a field day as the ice melted in their drinks: it was murder, it was suicide, he'd turned state's evidence and someone wanted to stop him testifying. It was all bullshit, the inane chattering of monkeys.

I sat back and let the rumours flow as the news of my friend's demise embedded itself into my consciousness. I knew Lietzman better than any of them, and I was certain from the off that his death was nothing more than a sad, tragic, wasteful accident. It brought home to me all of the things I should have said. I wished I'd been able to give him help with his drug problem. I wished we'd been more open with one another, but knew that in reality our long friendship had not depended on openness and communication – that was not in our natures.

Lietzman's death hurt like hell and I missed him. I still do.

CHAPTER TEN

ENCOUNTER BAY

The re-emergence of ingenious Bullshit, losing someone else's ship and the case of the empty spools.

I was determined that the money from the sale of *Delfino II* should be put to good use, and looked around for a new ship to invest in, something that could work for the smuggling business on a grand scale. And I found exactly what I was looking for moored in Singapore, in the shape of *Encounter Bay*, an oil supply ship for sale at an asking price of just over one million dollars.

Encounter Bay was perfect. She was huge and solid, built with the capability of completing the arduous pan-oceanic voyages that were becoming our stock in trade. The ship had recently come out of class, meaning that she was no longer considered able to perform the tasks which had earned her living thus far. Rather than carry out the expensive modifications required to bring *Encounter Bay* up to speed, her owners had instead elected to sell her on. She was durable, sturdy and reliable. She was perfect.

Signing the ownership papers and handing over the

money order to seal the deal was completed in the London office of the seller's lawyers. I went alone to the meeting to be met by a conference table of suits and ties who must have wondered more than once through the course of the transaction who exactly I was and what the hell I really wanted with their boat. As soon as the paperwork was completed in London, in Singapore the captain of the ship handed over control of *Encounter Bay* to our man, Jeffrey Press, a qualified captain in between jobs.

Encounter Bay was big and beautiful, a vision of grace on the water. She was 190 feet long, weighing in at over 200 tons with an icebreaker hull painted bright red. The deck area alone could have accommodated a skateboard park and when you were out at sea, standing on that open back deck it felt like you were the only person left in the world, floating around on your very own mobile island.

I had bought *Encounter Bay* using a front company I had registered by the name of Royalville Ltd. The European point of contact for Royalville was our 'office' at 15a Norfolk Place, London W2, a good address situated close to Hyde Park. In reality, 15a Norfolk Place was a business services company, an outfit that offered phone lines for hire that would be answered by the onsite skeleton staff. What that meant in effect was that should anyone wish to contact one of the various companies we were beginning to incorporate, they simply called the number on the letterheads and faxes we were sending out and had their call answered by our 'secretary' who would announce that we were out of the office at present but could she please take a message. The secretary would then contact me, halfway round the world, and I'd return the original call as though I had just stepped back into the office from a long boozy lunch.

As well as the phone service, using the Norfolk Place address also meant we had somewhere neutral from which to send and receive mail and offered a wash of respectability over an enterprise that was anything but. Like the other front companies we were setting up, Royalville only really existed on paper and was created specifically for this kind of work, acting as a buffer between us and the rest of the world.

Although bought via the London address, *Encounter Bay* was registered in Panama. The relationship between America and Panama was tempestuous and delicate at the time, and I figured anything flying that country's flag would be less likely to be stopped and searched. The country was at the time offering a one-stop shop for all of your dope-smuggling, cash-laundering needs courtesy of its infamous leader General Manuel Noriega. This despot, once trained by the Americans at Fort Bragg, had since turned his back on the US and seemed not to care who knew it. Because of the come-one come-all, no-questions-asked economic policy currently prevalent in the country, the banks in Panama were overflowing with cocaine money from Miami, flown over especially on the same planes that were bringing the powder from Colombia and landing it in America. Bank of Panama cheques were used regularly to buy convertible sports Mercedes and BMWs from the car lots of Fort Lauderdale and Tampa, boosting the ego of the drug trade and lining the pockets of the car dealers. At a street level, the cocaine trade there was by now policed by an army of dealers and enforcers who took their orders straight from Colombia, or from people like Griselda Blanco, *La Madrina*, the freebasing, throat-cutting, bisexual Godmother of the Miami dope trade who had settled in Florida with her four sons (the youngest of whom she had christened Michael Corleone Blanco. How wild is that?). New buildings were still going up all over the state, their real foundation not concrete but cocaine. Sometimes I missed Miami.

In order to start earning back the money I'd paid for her, *Encounter Bay* had to be put to work for the gang immediately. We contacted Kamol, put in an order for weed and began to plot how exactly we would get that year's shipment into America. While we waited for our consignment of dope to be delivered, *Encounter Bay* went through the necessary shipyard alterations which would turn her from a working oil supply ship to a state-of-the-art smuggler's vessel. High-tech radio and communications systems were installed, allowing us to monitor radio traffic as well as send it, to give us a head start over anyone who might be following the ship. The engine was overhauled and tuned up and within six months she was ready to begin work in the illegal importation business.

While work was being completed on *Encounter Bay* it struck me that we had two cigarette boats each capable of carrying three tons of dope, which would be ideal to offload the shipment that year. Once we'd loaded our six tons on to the ship and sailed it off the coast of San

Francisco we could smuggle the dope into the city aboard the cigarettes. And here's the clever bit: we'd catapult the boats off the deck at the back of the *Encounter Bay*. And that is exactly what we did.

There were simpler, safer ways to complete our proposed offload, but none that seemed quite as exciting. We packed the weed straight into the cigarettes, which travelled hidden in containers on deck, and by the time we reached America we were all set for the dramatic offload. Although the plan was simple, the means we had chosen to get the cigarette boats into the water left absolutely no margin for error – and no chance of a rehearsal. If it didn't work first time we lost our speed-boats and our dope. If that wasn't pressure enough, we were working at night so the whole process, which had to be completed quickly, was illuminated throughout by nothing more than the lamps on the deck of *Encounter Bay* and the light of the Pacific moon. Luckily, it was a clear night.

Bobby, Sam and I opened the containers and pulled the cigarettes out on to the deck of the ship. The boats had no wheels so dragging them out and into position was hard work, but before long the two forty-foot cigarette boats stood present, correct and ready to rock. As soon as the boats were on deck we started their engines, warming them up and making sure that they would be ready to go the moment they hit the water. Once we were happy the engines were warm and purring nicely we turned them off and began loading the boats, one at a time, into the specially constructed cradles. They were winched up and lifted out over the back of the ship and above the ocean. By adjusting the ballast at the back end of the *Encounter Bay*, we had bought her stern down until it was almost at water level.

Although not stormy the night was a little choppy as I readied myself to be dropped into the ocean aboard *Kim Ono*. The boat would be hitting the sea ass first so it was vital that the exhaust was covered so no water could run up it and flood the engine. *Kim Ono* slid over the huge roller at the back of the ship and once gravity kicked in and there was no turning back, the quick-release snaps keeping the boat in the cradle were opened. She half-fell, half-flew into the water. The whole process seemed to happen in slow motion as my stomach made its way up to somewhere around my throat, which was at the time attempting to vocalize a long drawn out 'Ohhhhhh ffffuuuuuccccckkkkkk.'

The second she hit the sea I started the engine, the small plastic bucket we had placed over the exhaust was kicked off by the exhaust pressure and the boat roared into life. It had worked!

The greatest danger in getting the cigarettes off the back of *Encounter Bay,* backwards, at night, was the angle at which the quarter-million-dollar speedboats hit the water. If the angle were too severe then water would cover the back end of the boat and it would just keep going down, taking our dope with it. Luck and judgement combined to equal the perfect angle that night, and the plan went like a dream.

Once I had the first boat in the water I headed back to the side of *Encounter Bay* to swap places with Bobby, who clambered down to join me. We each had to drive one boat into San Francisco but I was to be on both as they were spat into the ocean – I didn't trust anyone else to handle this delicate task. With Bobby at the controls of *Kim Ono* I had him keep steady alongside the ship so I could repeat the process with *Mariposa*. Bobby pulled up next to the ship but when I tried to board her I missed somehow and had to be dragged from where I had ended up, hanging on for dear life from one of the tyres than ran around *Encounter Bay*.

Launching the second cigarette boat went as smoothly as it had the first time, and was just as exciting.

With *Kim Ono* and *Mariposa* both loaded to the gills, Bobby and I drove under Golden Gate Bridge as the sun came up, high on fear, speed and adrenalin, my all-time favourite cocktail. The tons of dope hidden in my *Kim Ono* cigarette slowed her performance a little over that hundred-mile journey, but not enough to get in the way of the fun I was having. Soon we were back at the warehouse and wondering whether we should go out to eat that night or call for a takeout. We retrieved the dope from the cigarette boats and packed and stacked it neatly in the corner of the warehouse to await delivery to Rod and the hippie connection. The fact that I later hired a helicopter and a cameraman to take pictures of us while we fired into Frisco on a cigarette, just as if we were speeding the weed into the harbour, is a perfect illustration of just how arrogant ten years of successful smuggling had made me.

We were now dealing with a new buyer for our hippie connection. At home in his well-cut pin-striped suit, with short hair and shiny shoes, Alfred looked like a preppy accountant and was unlike the other buyers I had met, who had seemed permanently stoned but somehow still on the ball. Where Rod and his friends always seemed to be freaks operating in the straight world, Alfred was just the opposite. Where money and dope handovers with Rod and his friends had become friendly affairs over the years, suddenly our car park rendezvous was all business.

'You have the product with you?' Alfred asked, unsmiling.

'I've got the first trunk full. We can let you have the rest wherever you need it, anywhere in Frisco, same as always. Just say the word.'

'Then I'll call you as soon as we've checked the quality of this batch and arrange another pickup.'

'The weed's as good as ever,' I said, surprised.

'If it's all the same with you I'll call once I'm confident of that.'

'Your decision. You have the money?'

Alfred walked to his car and returned with a sports bag containing the money for the first handover, $750,000. Once we'd unloaded the dope from my car to his, Alfred offered to wait around while I counted the cash. I told him not to bother, that we would work as we always had, on trust. It seemed that things were changing at both ends of the operation.

I'd enjoyed every minute of *Encounter Bay*'s first importation; it had been my favourite so far. The only thing missing from the smuggle was Robert Lietzman. If anyone in the world could have appreciated the utter ridiculousness of a plan to launch speedboats from the back of a ship, and understood that that very ridiculousness was the reason it had to be attempted, it was Bourbon. I like to think he was along for the ride, if only in spirit. When it came in, the millions of dollars from the six tons we had imported were duly packed into suitcases and went some way to alleviating our recent cashflow problems.

A year on from her smuggling debut in 1985, *Encounter Bay* was again heading out to America carrying a multi-ton cargo of Thailand's finest. We had loaded the dope on to the ship in the seas around Phuket, using smaller fishing boats to transfer the bales of weed from the beach to *Encounter Bay.* As before Sam captained the boat on our trip to the US and once again the trip went as smoothly as we had hoped. Well, almost.

Encounter Bay had taken on board her fuel for the trip in Singapore, where it was warm. Because of the weather and the time of year we were leaving Asia to sail our dope into America we had bought a 'summer mix' fuel, which is heavy on additives such as paraffin wax. As we sailed north towards America, we were navigating through colder seas, dropping at points to a temperature well below zero degrees. Because the fuel tanks were situated on the outside of the boat, underneath the hull and therefore below the waterline, the paraffin wax in the fuel began to freeze. Before very long the fuel pipes and filters were blocked, the engine was left with nothing to run on and conked out. Suddenly we were floating at the mercy of the elements in a freezing storm somewhere a thousand miles off the coast of Japan. We were tossed about by the waves and drifting further off course for a couple of days while we tried to work out what the problem was.

'What the hell is wrong with this fucking thing,' I said with frustration.

'What's wrong is that you seem to have acquired a somewhat decrepit vessel,' Sam deadpanned.

'Remind me, Fox, how much did you pay for it?' Bobby chipped in, grinning.

Examining the engine, I noticed the build-up of wax that was accumulating at the edge of the filter seals and was convinced that we'd found the problem, and the way to deal with it. We needed to heat up the fuel in the tanks and to do so brought everything we could find on board that produced any heat down into the engine room and began the slow process of thawing out the fuel in the ship's tanks. The paraffin wax began to melt and the engine groaned back to life again to a rousing cheer of celebratory relief, and we continued our journey, heading for warmer seas.

During 1986 we had been discussing possible new ways of getting our product into America and, for a while, Canada had looked like a good option. We had heard whispers in Superstar of the methods employed by the smugglers working out of Canada, my favourite of which was the log scam. Timber and logs are routinely sailed from Canada to America in huge, heavy shipments, and what some enterprising groups and individuals had begun doing was sending their weed in with the logs. They would set up false company fronts, just as we were doing in London, America and Asia, in order to make their load of timber look on the up and up. What the purchase orders and way-bills neglected to mention was that a number of the huge logs in the shipments had been sawn in half, hollowed out, filled with weed and glued back together again. Once the timber landed in America the marked logs were then cracked open and emptied. You can fit an awful lot of weed in a log.

As soon as *Encounter Bay* had dropped off the 1986 consignment of weed in California we sailed her up to Canada where we had arranged some meetings in which we would tentatively check out the possibility of moving part of our operation to that part of the world. We moored *Encounter Bay* at Vancouver and set off for a series of meetings with legitimate players in the local logging and shipping industries. We also looked into the possibility of buying another boat there that we could use to ship our logs full of dope into the States.

I was travelling into the country on my Michael Forwell passport for another meeting, waiting for my passport to be stamped, when I heard the phrase every smuggler dreads.

'Are you travelling to Canada for business or pleasure, sir?'

'For business.'

'Right, Mr Forwell, if you'll just follow me, please.'

Sam, who'd travelled in with me, looked on helplessly as I was escorted to a small room and asked to take a seat. The officer who had pulled me in was soon joined by another. In absolute silence they set about going through my briefcase and belongings with a fine-tooth comb, looking over at me occasionally and ignoring my repeated requests to be told exactly what was going on.

As I sat there watching the two customs agents examining my luggage I began running over everything in my head, all of my recent moves and destinations, everyone I'd spoken to and seen, trying to remember anything out of the ordinary, trying to find a reason to explain the random search, which at that moment felt like anything but. I knew that all of the paperwork I had with me related to my role as an employee of one or other of the front companies we had formed and was confident the officers' search was coming to nothing – until they began to examine the clothes I was wearing, starting with my pockets.

'Okay, sir, can you explain these?'

Shit. They had found a couple of tabs of Valium in my Brioni suit jacket, freely available in Thailand but subject to drug laws in much of the rest of the world. The worst part was, I'd forgotten they were there.

'It's Valium, it helps me get some sleep on long-haul flights.'

'Please wait there while we check it out.'

The officers were gone for what seemed like hours. They came back satisfied that the pills were in fact only Valium, but that wasn't the end of it.

'What precisely is it that you do, Mr Forwell, and what brings you to Canada?'

Luckily, on my previous trips into the country I had travelled under one of my assumed identities, so as far as they were concerned this was my first visit, but it was all beginning to feel a little uncomfortable and I wanted out as soon as possible.

'I work for Royalville, a shipping company, and I'm

here for meetings with prospective clients, looking to open up new markets. One of our ships is currently moored in Canada.'

Something in the way the customs officers were interrogating me, something in their tone and their eyes and their refusal to accept what I was saying started alarm bells ringing, but I somehow managed to keep my cool. Eventually, after enjoying hours of their suspicious hospitality, I was allowed into the country.

Sam, who was waiting for me while I was being 'interviewed', was as shaken as I was over the affair. Back at the hotel bar we went over and over the possibilities. Was it a routine stop or the telltale signs of something more sinister? Were they on to us or had they picked me out at random? Had they let me through in order to follow me, were they watching me even then? Whatever the answers – and to this day I don't know – we packed our bags and sailed *Encounter Bay* out of there. Our plans to work in Canada were put on permanent hold.

The inspiration for our next smuggle came from the guys Bobby knew from the oil rigs. They were still hanging out at Superstar and helping us out occasionally when we needed some muscle to assist with the loading of our dope on and off boats in Thailand. When there was no work to do we'd sit around drinking with them, and they'd describe life out on the rigs and the machinery they routinely used as they did battle with the elements in order to procure oil. The conversations got me thinking and formed the basis of the plan we would use to smuggle our next load of dope into America.

The idea was to hide as much dope as possible in something that you would never ever think could be used for smuggling. That's harder than it sounds. Take the most outlandish idea you've ever had, double it, and you can bet your bottom dollar that somebody somewhere has already tried it. We needed something so big, so heavy and so apparently technical and expensive that the very thought of opening it up and checking it out would seem both a waste of time and a complete nightmare for customs. We needed a monster, so we built one.

We decided we would invent and build a piece of pseudo-maritime machinery, one that would not look out of place aboard an oil rig and was big and well made enough to easily hold the six tons of weed we intended to move without giving the game away. The idea, vague at first, started to crystallize over many long nights in hotel bars and nightclubs. One morning in Superstar, when the sun had come up and the girls had all gone home, we came up with the spools, or, to give them their full and proper name, the Halcyon Motorized Spooling Reels.

There were two of them, almost fifteen feet tall and weighing about five tons apiece. To anyone who asked, they were high-power winches capable of pulling, lifting and lowering great weights on the rolls of thick steel cable that wound about their midriff. They were highly durable, weather resistant and capable of sustaining the battering they would receive from the elements as they pulled tons of material at a time on and off oil rigs.

Except that they weren't. What the spools were in reality was a very big, very well-made, very heavy, very impressive-looking lie.

The design specs began life as drunken 3 a.m. scrawls on soaking beer mats, which eventually became the highly technical line drawings that were included in the full-colour, all-complete-bullshit brochures we had printed up to send with them on their journey to America. In addition to the spurious specifications and doctored photographs showing the spools at work on the rigs, the brochures purported to show the technical specs of the spools, including line drawings of the machinery, side elevations and promises the machinery itself just could not keep. The spools were also assigned the completely random model number 2909a, to add a further spurious realism.

The design of the spools was essentially that of a cotton reel turned on its side, with a motor and chain attached at one end in order to reel in and out the thick metal cable wrapped around the central arm. The whole contraption was then welded into place on a base made out of the same heavy steel as the spools themselves. It was inside the central arm, which was covered by the length of cable, that we intended to hide our dope. According to the drawings in the brochure, the arm that ran across the middle of the spool and held the cable in place was around a foot in diameter. In reality it was far thicker, hollow and filled with Thai weed. The arm was hidden behind the steel cable, so without unravelling the cable it was impossible to see just where the spools on the ground differed from those in the brochure.

The cable we used was ordered specially from a company in Scotland and that alone cost us $100,000. Other parts of the frame and machinery were sourced from various specialist outlets around the world. Ordering the component parts for our folly from genuine specialist suppliers brought with it a handy raft of documentation, which went towards legitimizing the spools. Soon, even I believed in them.

Once the spools were built and painted, in a Singapore warehouse Bobby had rented, we added a few finishing touches ourselves, such as the rope. They looked the part completely, and were an awe-inspiring sight, hundreds of thousands of dollars' worth of complete and utter uselessness.

In order to move the spools we created yet another front company, again based at 15a Norfolk Place. This one we had elected to call Halcyon Ocean Ltd. I designed a logo for the fictitious company featuring a kingfisher in full flight, which featured heavily on the brochures. The Kingfisher logo was highly appropriate: the spools couldn't have lifted a feather.

The spools were crated up and carried by *Encounter Bay* to Sri Lanka where we trans-shipped them, passing the load on to a well-known shipping company that sent them on as commercial freight first to Hamburg, where Bobby Colflesh and I visited them at the dock, and then on to Newark in New Jersey. The fact that we were operating under the local Mafia's noses didn't even cross our minds; the world of organized crime in America was so far removed from our own it might as well have been another planet.

Once the spools had landed at the docks we had them delivered on trucks to a rented lot nearby. Along with some help from members of the *Encounter Bay* crew, the

Colflesh brothers and I set about stripping down the machinery and emptying out the weed. There was a small shed which provided some welcome shade after midday, and a kettle with which we could make tea. Once emptied of their treasure the spools themselves were simply left abandoned in the warehouse, $200,000 worth of heavy, useless machinery collecting New Jersey dust.

The camper van we were using to take the dope to San Francisco had weed secreted in the trunk, in the door panels, under the seats and behind the dashboard, but to look at it you would never even have known it was there. Once the weed was all packed away, I started laughing.

'What's so funny?' Bobby asked.

'Nothing, nothing. It's just that I drove a load across America once before, and it wasn't quite as well hidden as this.'

Once safely in San Francisco we met up with Alfred and received some rather bad news.

'The quality's good as always, better maybe,' he said, 'but we're just not in a position to move the product right now. There's a lot of weed around and no one's buying. Anyone who is buying just wants to pay bargain basement prices. We can take it off your hands, but we're not gonna be able to pay anything like what you're expecting.'

The market that was usually so welcoming of our product had just taken delivery of forty-two tons of Thai stick, courtesy of one Brian Daniels and his confederates. Because the market was so saturated with Daniels' dope the law of supply and demand had kicked in and we found that our marijuana was worth just half of what we usually got for it. Rod and his friends were prepared to take the dope but would have to store it until such a time as the massive load that Daniels had brought into the country had been smoked, a fact that increased the costs to our buyer, which were in turn passed on to us.

This was a financial blow. Not only would we be receiving less for our dope, we would have to wait longer for our money. We were still a long way from being broke, but we were closer than we'd been for years.

The nature of the Thai dope trade was changing, and we needed a fresh approach if we were to stay ahead of the game.

Although it had been Royalville Ltd that had bought the *Encounter Bay* and indeed sold *Delfino* in order to do so, the ship was administered by another front company, TradeMax, which was run out of the office we were renting in Hong Kong harbour. The idea behind TradeMax was the same as that behind all of our front companies, to offer a veneer of respectability and provide a facade for our merry band of smugglers to hide behind. Astonishingly, once we bought *Encounter Bay*, Trade-Max actually began to be taken seriously as a shipping and haulage firm and some potential offers of legitimate work had come in. The most interesting and potentially profitable of these offers came from an unlikely source, a firm of Taiwanese scrap metal merchants working on a huge scale who needed a tow. They had heard of a warship and tug boat recently decommissioned by the Chilean Navy and were interested in buying the vessels to break down and sell on. All the scrap dealers needed was someone to pick up the warship and tug in Chile and tow it across to their facility in Taiwan. With Sam dealing with the details and Lloyd's of London insuring the job we got the contract as soon as we had dropped off that year's weed.

Sam was running the operation. Taking the necessary meetings with Chilean Navy officials and squaring away the details of the cross-continental tow were duties right up his alley as he ably took on the newly acquired role of ambassador for TradeMax in South America. He sailed *Encounter Bay* down to Chile and moored her in the naval dockyards there while any potential problems were ironed out and the details finalized. Sam made the most of the waiting time at the naval dockyard by covering the *Encounter Bay*'s distinctive flame-red paint job in gun-metal grey – very military, very Sam.

The warship and tug were tethered to the stern of *Encounter Bay*, warship in first place, with the tug then secured to it but so far away from *Encounter Bay* that it wasn't always visible. Far from being the straightforward exercise we had imagined, the job was a complete nightmare from the word go. Because the warship had been decommissioned and out of action for so long its huge rudder had seized up. What this meant in effect was that the crewless boat was virtually impossible to control and the *Encounter Bay* had to work twice as hard as it should have to keep the beast travelling roughly in a straight line.

Worse still, somewhere around the Philippine Islands, disaster struck. The line connecting the warship to the tug at the back of the rag-tag convoy had snapped somehow during the dead of night. The tug was so far away that it was hard enough for Sam to see during the day, so losing it at night gave him no chance. Sam blithely sailed on, not realizing until much later that what had been a line of three boats had now been reduced to two. As soon as Sammy contacted us and told us the news we knew that our customers in Taiwan would not be happy.

'Fox, we've hit something of a problem here.'

'What is it, Haig, what's happened?'

'We've lost the third boat, the tug, it's gone.'

Having us tow their boats halfway around the world was an expensive business that the money they made for scrapping the warship would only just cover. Their profit, the only real reason they had bought the pair of boats for scrap in the first place, was in the tug that was now floating wherever the tides took it and bumping into things somewhere around the Philippines. Our first foray into the world of legitimate shipping was definitely not going as planned; it was turning into Laurel and Hardy on a grand scale. But it wasn't funny.

Bobby and I flew to meet Sam and the two remaining ships in New Guinea to decide on the best course of action. The rudder on the warship was still resolutely locked solid so we decided to at least see if we could fix that and make the final leg of the journey a little easier. We dived on the ship to get a better look at the problem but soon saw that there was nothing we could do. We wandered through the warship's huge, deserted engine room filled with immaculate, beautifully maintained machinery and equipment but found there was no solution there either. We had no choice, *Encounter Bay* would have to continue dragging the huge stubborn warship onto its final destination.

The buyers in Taiwan were getting increasingly irate. Because of the warship's rudder problem the tow was taking far longer than we had expected. That, coupled with the fact that we had mislaid one of their boats somewhere around the Philippines, meant we were not exactly flavour of the month. Turning around and looking for the tug would have been a complete waste of time; we didn't know exactly where we had lost the boat and by now, at the mercy of the tides, it could be anywhere.

The owners were less than over the moon when I called them with an update on how the job was proceeding.

'Because the warship has offered such resistance to the tow we have been forced to use more fuel and will in turn be forced to charge you more money.'

As I put down the phone, I filled Bobby in on how our client had reacted to the news. 'They're not happy, JT, not happy at all.'

The request for extra cash for the job was the straw that broke the camel's back, so they called in the harbour authorities, who would be waiting to arrest us and impound *Encounter Bay* on her arrival in Taiwan. The situation resulted in a Mexican standoff: we had their boat and they had our money. Now we had reason to be glad that Sam had insisted we take out maritime insurance, and we hatched a plan. Once Sammy had towed the warship close to where we were due to drop it and the tug off, we called the insurers to come and verify that the warship was in fact where it should be. As soon as this was done Sam quickly sailed *Encounter Bay* to the safety of Singapore. Once the insurers were happy with the fact that the warship had arrived they released the payment for the job that they were currently holding in escrow. With the warship in Taiwan and the bulk of our payment safely deposited in our account we then contacted the buyer and informed them that without the balance of payment due for the excess fuel we had used we would not tell them where we had left the boat. They kicked, screamed and threatened but soon came to realize that we had them over a barrel. The outstanding money, some fifty thousand dollars or so, was duly delivered by a severe-looking courier to our Hong Kong office. In cash.

Despite the fact that we hadn't done so well from the smuggle and that towing the Chilean warship had gone less successfully than we might have hoped, 1987 finished on a high. On 7 December in Singapore, May gave birth to our third child, Nigel, and I chose to mark the happy occasion by quitting smoking. By then I'd forgone my brand loyalty to Benson and Hedges and had switched to Merits, but whatever the brand I had still been smoking up to two packs a day and that was two too many, so I stubbed out my last to celebrate my son.

CHAPTER ELEVEN

MUST BE THE SEASON OF THE WITCH

Spring/Summer 1988. No outsiders.

April

It was happening.

There had been talk for a while and, as dope deals generally do, it had begun in a whisper and ended in a handshake.

It was probably only a question of time before Bobby Colflesh came into contact with Brian Daniels since both were married to Thai women and had friends among the more powerful echelons of Thai society. In fact, Daniels and Bobby were introduced by a mutual friend called Thai Tony who had over the last few years become a major fix-it man and supplier for smugglers working out of the area. Thai Tony's real name was Thanong Siripreechapong and he was fast making a name for himself within the local dope trade. So good was the service offered by Thai Tony that even we had ceased buying from Kamol and now went to Tony with our orders. Everyone knew Tony and Tony knew everything. His weed was that little bit cheaper and the quality was primo. There was barely a dope deal that went down in Thailand at the time that he didn't have a hand in somewhere along the line.

At first, hearing the name Thai Tony at the end of the eighties in relation to the buying and selling of weed was odd to say the least. We had heard on the grapevine, as far back as 1983, that the man was dead. And he was. That is, the original Thai Tony, whose real name was Sunthorn Kraithamjitkul, had indeed died in the early eighties but Siripreechapong had risen to prominence, using the other man's nickname and taking over his business.

Towards the end of 1987, Brian Daniels had shown up at Superstar in search of Bobby. Pretty soon after, Bobby had met up with Daniels to discuss the possibility of moving a shipment of dope Daniels was planning to send into America, and during that discussion it became obvious that his organization and ours were in a position to work together. Daniels was planning the biggest shipment ever attempted, and we had a huge boat.

Bobby put the idea of working with Daniels to Sam and me one night at Superstar. 'It'd mean paying out less money up front. Daniels has pretty much raised the cash.'

I wasn't so sure. 'What, we wouldn't have to put up anything? Sounds too good to be true.'

'We'd be expected to invest some money, sure. Maybe half a million dollars to help buy the weed, but everything else is covered, and once the load gets through we're looking at making twenty-five, maybe thirty million dollars. That's not a bad return.'

Sammy whistled as his brother broke down the deal and how it would work. He was as impressed as I was with the potential return for so little outlay,

'I say we do it. If we don't, then chances are we'll miss out on moving anything this year.'

Sam was right. The truth was that we spent so long discussing the whys and wherefores of the proposal that we missed the window for ordering dope for our own smuggle. The opportunity of simply moving what was essentially someone else's weed and earning more from the venture than we would were we to do it ourselves was very inviting. Laziness and greed both played a big part in our agreeing to move those tons of dope to America.

The load under discussion was huge. The first weight we were quoted was forty-something tons and it seemed to grow every time the subject came up. And the subject came up a lot. Our cut of the deal was agreed at 20 per cent of the sale price, which meant that even at the lowest projected haul we would each have enough money to retire from the dope game for ever. The thought of retiring was hugely appealing. I now had three kids between the ages of one and seven and could see that the marijuana business was changing for the worse, the syndicates were growing and so was the risk of capture as the US government started to clamp down. The trade was heading down roads where I wasn't prepared to follow.

However, as soon as we embarked on the project with Brian Daniels it became clear that this wasn't the kind of operation we were used to. There were lots of new people around all of a sudden, lots of names I didn't know and faces I didn't recognize, and that unnerved me a little.

The smuggle was fast taking on a life of its own, running completely out of our control and turning into Robert Lietzman's idea of hell.

It was a big job, huge, but at the same time it was just what we normally did just on a much grander scale. This one was lining up to be an epic. The original figures had it that Daniels was planning to move between forty and sixty tons of dope into the US from Vietnam, to land it in Washington and distribute to his buyers from there. Our job would be to transport the dope from the seas around Da Nang in Vietnam to a point around 500 miles off the Washington coast where it would then be picked up and transported ashore by a contact of Daniels' called the Fisherman.

In order to facilitate this series of events, on 10 April Bobby went to meet Brian Daniels in Thailand, along with two of his confederates in the operation, Jack Corman and Phillip B. Christensen. The four men at the meeting talked through the logistics of moving the dope and decided that it definitely could, and probably should, be done.

Four days later in Hong Kong, after Bobby had filled Sam and me in on his meeting, the three of us went to the harbour to meet the Fisherman, and a friend of his called Henry who would be help with the offload of *Encounter Bay* for us in America. Over a drink aboard the yacht we had hired for the purpose the Fisherman, Larry, told us he had a small fleet of fishing boats and knew the coastline in Washington well. He went so far as to show us pictures of his boats and then assured us he was more than capable of carrying out what was required.

At the meeting I was introduced to our new partners in crime by Sam, who was conducting proceedings, as Mike Forwell. Sam went through specifics with Larry, quizzing him about the engine size and storage capacity of the boats he would use for the offload and Larry answered every single question to Sam's satisfaction.

I tried not to say much at the meeting, but I did have a query regarding security of the offload.

'As far as I can see, the biggest potential major problem at the Washington end is the Coast Guard. And it won't just be the Americans, we'll have the Canadians to look out for too. You're confident that neither will be a problem?'

'Don't sweat it,' the Fisherman said. 'We'll make sure we stay well clear of anyone who's not invited.'

Sam then explained to the two men how the offload would work. 'I'll arrive on the *Encounter Bay* to meet up with you guys. With enough men to do the work – and it'll be hard work – I'm estimating that offloading the product on to your fleet of fishing boats and sailing it into Washington should take about two full days.'

The Fisherman seemed unfazed by the undertaking. Sam, Bobby and I left that meeting satisfied that the offload in Washington was feasible and that the man charged with the venture could handle it.

We all met up again the following day to go over more details and finalize arrangements, sailing around Hong Kong harbour. The smuggle was definitely happening now and the Fisherman was in. He told us he had his own private dock, which would offer discretion and provide perfect cover for the offload. The Fisherman was ready, he understood what he needed to do and was happy with the instructions as laid out by Sam.

Unbeknownst to us, the Fisherman was Special Agent Larry Brant of the DEA.

Brant was forty-four at the time we met him. He was brave, cool-headed and smart, and had by that point served in law enforcement for over twenty years since he began studying police science and criminology at the age of eighteen. His keen interest in sailing mixed with his ability to talk convincingly on the subject marked him as the ideal man to infiltrate a smuggling organization like ours, which specialized in bringing its dope in in boats. Not only that, but as a boy Brant had sailed the very coast we were planning to use to offload; he really did know the area well, as he told us, and was therefore able to allay any fears we had regarding the American end of the job.

Prior to meeting us Brant had been stationed at Blaine, Washington, where he had been assigned to investigate Brian Daniels. Although he'd been known to them since 1977, Daniels had only recently begun to attract very close scrutiny from the DEA. He was strongly suspected of bringing increasingly large loads into America. Months previously the DEA had arrested a small-time pot dealer in America who had, as a way of cutting a deal on the charges facing him, given them chapter and verse on Daniels' newest venture. As a result, Brant had been in South East Asia, building up his cover story and steadily infiltrating Daniels', and thereby our, organization. The man accompanying the Fisherman who was introduced as Henry was in fact Helmut Witt, another DEA agent.

Brant had previous experience in taking down groups of smugglers, having recently feigned smuggling a shipment of weed from Thailand to Vancouver Island in British Columbia. Working with the Canadian Mounted Police and a SWAT team, Brant had helped to arrest the fourteen men who came to unload and distribute his fictitious cargo.

We should have checked up on him. One simple flight to America and a stroll along the Washington coastline would have showed us that Brant had no boats where he said he did. We could even have called friends in America, we wouldn't have had to make the trip ourselves, and had them check out Brant's story for us. But we didn't. As far as we were concerned, Brant had come with the job, recommended by the very people who were putting the load together. Surely they knew him? Surely they'd checked him out? But they didn't and they hadn't, and nor had we. The word was that Daniels had enough contacts in the right places to ensure that people like Brant couldn't get close; apparently he'd met the mysterious Jack Paladino in February to discuss the names of possible DEA informants and check that we were clean. He'd received a list of names, but still Agent Brant had slipped through the net.

Before Sam introduced me as Mike Forwell to Brant at that fateful meeting, my name wasn't flagged anywhere. But since Brant had now heard it and no doubt related it immediately back to his superiors, they started checking. That grilling by Canadian customs caught up with me: I'd travelled as Forwell that day.

A day after our second meeting with Brant, on

15 April, I showed that we were serious about taking part in the planned caper and handed over the $400,000 good faith money to be passed on to Brian Daniels. The cash I gave to Daniels was a drop in the ocean – the costs of setting up and running the operation, and paying for the weed, were immense – but it was financial proof that we were dedicated to the task in hand.

I put cash in with strangers for dope that wasn't mine. I did what I had avoided doing in the Thai dope trade for the last twelve years: I joined a syndicate.

I'd just brought the money over from California. It was a part payment for last year's weed, the money for which was still trickling through. I'd travelled over to Asia with $600,000 in a brown and gold Louis Vuitton trunk that had then been transferred to a cardboard box hidden under my bed. We had switched allegiance from the Halliburton after many years and nowadays favoured customizing Louis Vuitton travel trunks. They were roomy anyway, and with a couple of minor alterations here and there they could carry an awful lot of cash and still appear innocent, merely stuffed with clothes. The clothes themselves also had all available pocket space filled with cash.

The next two weeks in the life of a doomed dope deal were taken up with the details and side deals which I was not privy to. The arrangements were made for money to be paid to the supplier, suitcases full of cash got on planes in America and off in Thailand, were handed over in airports and nondescript hotel bars. International coded phone calls were made from mobile phones and call boxes, the last of the crew was finalized as the pieces in the jigsaw, a picture of a sinking ship, began to fit together.

At the end of the month Bobby went to meet Daniels to pick up a list of the radio frequencies we were to use on the job. That list went straight to Sam.

May

Sam's operations manual was drawn up and distributed among those who needed access to it this early in the operation. Immaculately typed and running to fifteen pages, essentially the document was a how-to guide. The whole smuggle was in there, every procedure we'd need to go through in order to load, transport and unload what had become the staggering total of sixty-five tons of Thai dope to America.

Five days into May, Bobby and Sammy went to meet Daniels and the Fisherman, Larry, and Henry, the Fisherman's friend. They once again talked through the details of the offload from the *Encounter Bay* into the small fleet of non-existent waiting fishing boats. On the same day the DEA threw their hat into the ring when undercover agent Brad Morgan handed over $650,000 to Daniels in Hong Kong to help pay for the weed. That money bought them a certain bust. That night, the Colfleshes and I once again met up with the Fisherman and his friend in Room 234 of the Peninsula Hotel, Hong Kong.

We went through the operations manual with them page by page. Sam told Brant his codename for the job would be *Guido*, Sam himself would as usual be known as *Haig*, his brother as *JT*, and me as *Fox*. As always, Sam focused on the detail.

'So we'll let you know when the Mothership is closing in on the rendezvous site. At that point we'll let you know which of the possible locations listed in the manual we'll be using. There are abort codes listed in case there's a problem as well as the codes for you to let me know that all's well. You'll have time then to make your final preparations and have everything in order at your end. The more prepared we are, the less risk we take.'

We arranged for them to meet Bobby in Washington in the run-up to the offload in order to collect the portable radios they would be using during the job. In order for us to be able to contact Brant in the meantime we were given the fax number by which to reach him at the dock. In reality the fax machine sat on a DEA desk.

A couple of days later, on 7 May, Brian Daniels was busy buying a boat to bring the dope from the beach in Vietnam to the *Encounter Bay*, which was by now referred to by all involved as the Mothership, as per the operations manual. With the help of Tai Farman, an associate of his who fronted the boat deal, Brian bought *Meridian*. Brian and Tai then went on to discuss arrangements for getting the cash to pay for the weed to their supplier. On 16 May I went to have a look at *Meridian*, to satisfy myself that the craft was able to handle the onload in Vietnam. Daniels had chosen well and the boat looked fine.

More money moved around, more men met in hotel bars and departure lounges as more suitcases got passed from hand to hand. Brian Daniels and Bobby received the

$650,000 the DEA were putting up. Bobby picked up almost half a million dollars from Daniels' confederate Jack Corman in Hong Kong and dropped it off with Brian in Thailand. When Brian had the necessary cash together he sent a part-payment on the load to his supplier in Laos. Once that was received and divided among the suppliers, the dope was shrink-wrapped, ready to be loaded on to trucks and driven by convoy to Da Nang, Vietnam.

At the end of the month Sam had a meeting or two to finalize onload plans. He and Bobby went once again to meet with Brian Daniels, to talk more about the onload, and nail down the details of how they would move the weed from the beach at Da Nang to *Meridian* and from there on to *Encounter Bay*.

Meanwhile, in America, Larry Brant had outlined the planned seizure of the *Encounter Bay*, briefing officers of the Thirteenth Coast Guard District on how exactly they would take down the smugglers.

June

Encounter Bay was moored in Singapore. On 2 June she left quietly, departing the harbour under cover of night and sailing to the waters around the small island of Batam in Indonesia where she dropped anchor and waited. Sam took command of the boat when he boarded her two days later, on 4 June, along with crew members Jeffrey Press, Terrance Nolan and Gary Robinson. As Sam was running the show from now on, all of the crew working on the journey to America were required at all times to be in uniform.

Once Sam was aboard and sure that all was in order he began his long journey by sailing *Encounter Bay* to Da Nang, a major port on the south central coast of Vietnam. Da Nang was becoming a popular spot as a departure point for drugs being smuggled out of the area, favoured by those looking for an alternative to Thailand where sentences for drug trafficking were famously severe. The night was velvet dark when he arrived but he soon met up with the *Meridian* and, it seemed, the whole Vietnamese army.

Of course it wasn't the whole army, but it was a sizeable chunk of it, under the command of a most helpful and efficient general. Altogether, with the army's help, the onload took two days. A convoy of camouflaged Russian army trucks, all loaded to the gills with fresh green dope, the thousands of bales of weed held in place by rope and netting sheets, emerged from the tree line, their headlights casting huge staccato shadows as they neared the edge of the dense jungle where the beach began.

The Vietnamese general delivering our weed that night rallied his troops and they took care of the task in hand, passing the endless bales hand to hand down the beach and then on to the *Meridian*. Meanwhile the general surveyed the scene from his position, standing in the back of his jeep. Up until arriving at the appointed onload spot, Sam had no idea of the Vietnamese army's involvement in the project and was, even considering the life he led, having a very strange night indeed.

Eventually the *Meridian* finished transporting the bales to *Encounter Bay* – at which point Sammy discovered that the sixty tons at most we'd expected had turned into around seventy-two tons, all packed into over eight thousand bales. Each bale was a foot and a half high and deep and three feet wide, and each sported Brian Daniels' trademark PASSED INSPECTION logo featuring his watchful American Eagle, a sure sign that the dope inside was his.

Once the loading was complete, *Encounter Bay*, with Sam at the helm and something like $300 million worth of dope at his command, set sail for Washington. This time he was going straight through, sailing around the world in one hit and not stopping even once en route to America. *Encounter Bay* was carrying more than five hundred tons of fuel, high-speed diesel, and she was more than ready to make the three-week trip in one steady burst. Aerial masts had been hidden in the boat's main mast to enable long-distance communication and receive any information from either Asia or America that she would need on the journey ahead.

Two weeks after *Encounter Bay*'s departure, on 25 June, Bobby flew to America to meet Larry, Henry and Jack Corman at the Red Lion Hotel in Washington. Sam had been in contact from the Mothership three days earlier and relayed a coded message that had meant that all was well and running to schedule. At the Red Lion meeting Bobby gave Brant a hard copy of Sam's operations manual as the time was fast approaching when he would need it to orchestrate his fleet to carry out the offload. Listed in the manual were the six possible offload rendezvous positions; all the DEA had to do now was wait to hear which one to meet us at.

During the final weeks of June we received three messages from Sam at the TradeMax offices. The telex messages were heavily coded but their meaning was clear. As far as the captain and crew of *Encounter Bay* were concerned their journey to America was proceeding exactly as planned and they saw no reason why the Mothership should not reach the seas off the coast of Washington at the time specified in the operations manual.

In anticipation of just that, on 28 June, the Coast Guard cutter *Boutwell* left its mooring in Seattle's Pier 36 and headed out into open sea, pushing thirty knots.

Two days later, the United States gained permission from the Panamanian government to board our vessel. The permission was believed to have been granted by the ousted Panamanian president Eric Arturo Delvalle, whose exiled government was then recognized by the US over the Noriega regime. Noriega's reign in Panama was drawing to a close; he had himself been indicted in Florida in February 1988 on drug trafficking charges.

Permission granted, *Boutwell* bore down on *Encounter Bay* with guns blazing, and it was all over.

Listening to the shells explode in the water around *Encounter Bay* from the Singapore Post Office, I spoke to Sam for what would be the last time,

'Just . . . Just come back, Sam.'

But of course, Sam never came back.

July

Panic stations.

On hanging up from my call with Sam, I wandered through the Post Office and back to the white Jaguar Sovereign. I drove home slowly, suddenly aware of every other car on the street as I prepared myself to break the news to May that our lives were about to change radically, that nothing would ever be the same again. She was devastated and deeply ashamed of what I'd done – she could barely bring herself to speak to me.

The children were too young to understand what was happening, unable to comprehend that unlike in the past, this was a business trip that Daddy would not be returning from anytime soon. Attempting to say my goodbyes to my family brought home for the first time the true horror of the situation I was in. I stared hard into the faces of Nicole, Nicholas and Nigel, committing to memory every detail of their beautiful faces, every eyelash, the smell of their skin, the feel of their hair and the turn of their mouths. I began to feel a profound and all-encompassing sense of loss as I packed clothes and belongings into two suitcases, unsure of what I would need, where I was going.

The good times were history, my family and the friends I'd grown so close to, lived side by side with for so many years and shared the great adventure with were gone. The life we'd lived would soon be little more than a collection of memories that would eventually all fade into a dream.

I needed to see Bobby. I drove to Singapore airport and

took the first available flight to Bangkok, paying cash at the last minute for the ticket. Once there I booked into a cheap hotel for a few days and waited and watched. When I was happy that Superstar wasn't about to be raided, I called Bobby and arranged to meet.

On 2 July Bobby had met with Brian Daniels in Bangkok to discuss the intercepted load.

A day later, at a small, quiet bar along the street from Superstar, Bobby and I met in a daze, both of us unable to fully comprehend the enormity of the shit we were in, staring at each other in silence before spilling out machine-gun fire monologues of possible ways out, all useless. Bobby told me that he was ready to quit, to hand himself in to the authorities and leave his fate to the gods and American justice.

'My mind's made up, Fox, I can't run.'

'This could get bad though, Bobby, this could get very bad. You're not going to walk away from this with a slap on the wrists, they'll want blood, they'll want to put us away for a long, long time.'

Bobby was based in Thailand, his family was there, happily living in the house that he had built for them and he was, it seemed to me, in a far more vulnerable position than I was. My only alternative option, my only way out, to disappear and live life on the run, held no attraction whatsoever for Robert Colflesh.

'I can't do it Bobby,' I said. 'I can't give up. I'm going underground.'

We shook hands. 'Good luck, Fox, it's been nice knowing you.'

Bobby tied up his affairs and handed himself in. It was

a brave move, and I still respect and admire him for it. But I believed I had too much to lose and held on to the staunch refusal to believe the ride was over. I was going on the lam, cashing in what I could and leaving my family behind, who I figured would be safe in Singapore and definitely better off without me. I saw no choice but it was a bad decision made in haste, a wrong move inspired by panic, the after effects of which would ripple across the surface of my life for years to come.

On 4 July, Brian Daniels decided that he too would get the hell out of Dodge and bought a ticket on a flight from Singapore to Zurich scheduled to leave three days later.

On 5 July my boat *Encounter Bay* was towed into Seattle. She was battered, bruised and pockmarked with the scars of fifty rounds fired by the Coast Guard into her body before they finally boarded her. They arrested Sam and everybody else they found on board, including the Indonesian crew members. Government agents in Seattle examined the boat and began the long process of unloading the bales of weed, which were packed tight in containers and all individually triple wrapped in heat-sealed plastic.

I was inextricably tied into the job when the government search of the boat turned up the call receipt from the telex that Sam had sent to me in Singapore.

The bales of weed were loaded on to military trucks and driven with helicopter escort to the Yakima Firing Center, a US Army base in east Washington, where they were scheduled to be incinerated. Catch a fire. Over the next five days and nights everything we'd planned and plotted, twelve years of work and all of our schemes and revisions, went up in a cloud of sweetly scented smoke.

Two years earlier President Reagan had earmarked 1.7 billion dollars to tackle the drugs problem and introduced mandatory minimum sentences for traffickers and dealers. With his wife Nancy spearheading the 'Just Say No' campaign, drugs became the big issue of the day and the American administration was taking them very seriously. This was not a good time to get busted. The *Encounter Bay* seizure was played as a decisive victory in the war on drugs, mushrooming budgets were justified and the DEA and customs had a front-page headline haul. The photographs of the seizure show enough bales of weed to build a small house.

72 Tons of Marijuana Seized

> The Coast Guard has seized a Panamanian-registered ship with more than 72 tons of marijuana, after firing on it 600 miles from shore. Officials said the converted oil-supply ship *Encounter Bay*, which was towed into port here today, refused orders to stop on Friday. The cutter *Boutwell*, with permission from the Panamanian Embassy to board her, fired 60 rounds from machine guns, then threatened cannon fire before the crew surrendered. The 18 crewmen, including three Americans, were held for a court appearance.
>
> *New York Times*, 7 July 1988

Immediately following his arrest, Sam was placed in the Kent Correctional Facility in Washington, where he met Mark Bartlett for the first time. Bartlett was an Assistant

US Attorney, thirty-two years old and part of the Organized Crime Drug Task Force assigned to our case. Bartlett was to prosecute the case against us and had an impressive CV which marked him as being more than equal to the task. He had worked in the law since 1982, when he had received his degree from George Washington University, and subsequently gained admittance to the New York bar where he had worked as an Assistant District Attorney for Manhattan District. He left New York in 1986 and made his way to Washington where he was employed by the United States Department of Justice as an assistant US Attorney. Many years later, I would meet Bartlett too.

Sam's initial statement, that the dope smuggling was a fund-raising exercise for anti-communist insurgents in Cambodia and Laos, was duly ignored. Bartlett let his prisoner know, in no uncertain terms, the position he was in.

'Sam, we've just caught you in command of a boat carrying over seventy tons of marijuana. Basically, you're looking at twenty to life. All you have to offer at this point, the only bargaining chip you have in your possession, is information. If I were you, Sam, I'd think about talking, because if you don't tell me what I want to hear, or if I think that you're holding out on me, I'll push for the longest sentence I can and you'll be spending the rest of your life behind bars.'

Sam had no choice but to tell them about how we worked. He gave them the address of the San Francisco warehouse we leased through another of our fronts, the Leading Sale Investment Company. The warehouse was duly checked out and found to be full of the equipment and vehicles we would need to unload and sell a shipment, though there were no fingerprints. People in the warehouse were encouraged to always be mindful of the sign on the wall which read, 'Gloves will be worn at all times.' What they did find though, in the glove compartment of one of the vehicles in the warehouse, were the keys to the beloved cigarette boats *Mariposa* and *Kim Ono*.

I knew that our Hong Kong office, TradeMax, was bound to be raided, and I certainly didn't want to be there when it was. Due to the light workload that passed through the office we employed only part-time staff and temps occasionally to help us keep up the facade of a busy company. As soon as I heard about the bust I called the TradeMax office and asked the girl on duty that day to grab all of the files from the office and lock up for the last time, to go home and wait for me to call. Only then did it fully dawn on me that even though she worked for me I knew next to nothing about her and that all of her particulars, such as her address and phone number, were in the files she promptly and diligently removed from the office, never to be seen again.

I was officially on the run.

CHAPTER 12

SINNERMAN, WHERE YOU GONNA RUN TO?

A crayfish farm and a beard.

I spent the first few weeks after the bust preparing myself for life on the run. I left Bangkok and spent some time back on Batam, the Indonesian island where many of the men who made up the crew of *Encounter Bay* hailed from. We were known on Batam, having spent a lot of time on the island over the years, and I felt reasonably safe there. Before leaving I'd collected together all of the incriminating paperwork and documentation I could that linked me and my precious collection of aliases to the foiled operation and hightailed to Batam to collect my thoughts and set fire to my past.

While the documents linking me to twelve years of dope smuggling went up in smoke, I felt the uncomprehending eyes of the families of our boat crew on me, all local, all loyal, and all grateful for the prosperity that working for the strange group of Westerners had brought them. There was nothing I could say to ease their worries, and even less I could do.

I'd spent the last decade and more in a gang, surrounded by the same faces: the Colflesh brothers, Robert Lietzman, the various staff we employed and hangers-on we accrued. I'd had a family, a wife. And now, suddenly, it was just me. There was no real contingency for this, no plans had been laid just in case and there was no fund set aside for starting again. Going on the run began with a scramble to survive.

I wasn't even sure at first exactly who I was running from. The DEA would have wanted to catch up with me no doubt, the US Coast Guard was probably none too pleased with me either but where else was I a wanted man? The pot had been exported from Thailand but I had no idea whether the authorities there had been informed and wanted me for it. The same went for Singapore. Not willing to risk either, I stayed where I was. I was feverishly buying up every foreign newspaper I could lay my hands on in Indonesia and scouring the pages for any mention of the case. Cut off from contact with everyone else involved I was becoming increasingly desperate to hear what was going on and to find some clue as to where I stood. No news was very bad news indeed. The first reports of the seizure claimed that the bust had happened by accident, that the Coast Guard had got lucky and happened upon *Encounter Bay* during a routine sweep of the area. Cecil Allison, captain of the Coast Guard cutter *Boutwell* that had chased down and captured *Encounter Bay*, was grilled on the issue at a news conference. He flatly denied that had had any intelligence information on the ship.

This version of events didn't ring true to me at all. The

Coast Guard had been too well prepared and had known far too much to have just stumbled upon us. It later came to light that the seizure had been reported as dumb luck in order to lure Brian Daniels into a false sense of security, in the hope he would still return to the US where he could be arrested. But Daniels hadn't fallen for the story and was instead arrested in Zurich.

At ten in the morning on 25 July Brian Daniels met two men, known to him as Bill Bartelucci and Jim Robinson. Bartelucci and Robinson were Americans with mob ties who'd been doing some piecemeal debt-collection work for Daniels, picking up money he was still owed from different dope deals, collecting the money in America and sending it out to him in Switzerland. As such they had almost unlimited insight into Daniels' operation, how he worked, and who he worked with. The two men were in fact undercover agents. Now, Jim Robinson showed Daniels his ID card containing his real name, Special Agent James Harper, and promptly arrested him on suspicion of drug trafficking offences and money laundering. He wasn't giving up without a struggle though and hired a lawyer to fight extradition.

I later discovered that two days later, on 27 July, almost three weeks after the bust, I was named in my absence on an indictment that charged me with violating Titles 46, 21, and 18 of the United States Code, for aiding and abetting a conspiracy to import and distribute in excess of one thousand kilos of marijuana in the United States. An arrest warrant bearing my name was issued by United States District Court Clerk Bruce Rifkin on the same day.

I was, quite rightly, regarded as a principal in the *Encounter Bay* case and according to the United States Code, 'Whoever commits an offense against the United States or aids, abets, counsels, commands, induces or procures its commission, is punishable as a principal.'

On 24 October the cases against the Colflesh brothers and assorted crew members of the *Encounter Bay* were heard in front of Judge John Coughenour. As far as Chief Judges go, Coughenour was considered something of a maverick. Born and raised in the Midwest, he was a motorcycle enthusiast who spent as much time as possible riding his Harley and lived part of each year on a boat. But quirky reputation notwithstanding, Coughenour was tough. He'd been hand-picked for the federal bench by none other than the staunchly anti-drug Ronald Reagan and was marked by a no-nonsense approach to the law.

Bobby and Sam had both been charged with possession with intent to distribute more than one thousand kilograms of marijuana. Sammy had retained the services of Howard Weitzman to act on his behalf in the case, perhaps reassured by the fact that Weitzman had defended *Back To The Future* aluminium carmaker John DeLorean in his high-profile cocaine and embezzlement case. As well as DeLorean, Weitzman's impressive celebrity client roster includes Michael Jackson, Marlon Brando, Magic Johnson and Courtney Love. During an initial federal court hearing Weitzman raised the question of whether the American authorities had been within their rights to 'go out and pirate a boat' flying a Panamanian flag while sailing international waters. I liked his style.

He questioned the Coast Guard's witness Lieut. Thomas Rogers as to where the intelligence leading them to the *Encounter Bay* had come from, receiving the answer, 'I believe that's classified information'. Weitzman's efforts to have the case thrown out failed and the brothers, courtesy of an eventual plea bargain whereby they agreed to testify against Brian Daniels, received sentences of ten years each. Ten years may have sounded like a lot but I knew that compared to what they could have got, Bobby and Sam had got off lightly. Before reaching the plea deal the Colflesh brothers had each faced a possible, indeed very probable, life sentence. According to Judge Coughenour, Bobby and Sam's military records had played in their favour and convinced him to make a deal.

Of the other seventeen co-conspirators charged, New Zealander and *Encounter Bay* chief engineer Anthony Sayers received one year and one day in prison, Jeffrey Press was given seven years, American deckhand Gary Robinson was given one year and one day, and Terrence Nolan, a US citizen and deckhand, was sentenced to five long years. The rest of the crew members, mainly from Batam and Singapore, were sentenced to six months each.

Press reports also began to filter through of the Vietnamese army's involvement in the smuggle. Throughout the run-up to the case, the Coast Guard had been reluctant to discuss the scope of the operation that had brought about the *Encounter Bay* seizure. But once the case was heard in open court, details of every aspect of the job began to come out. US Attorney Jerry Diskin was questioned after the case as to whether any members of the Vietnamese government or military were under investigation by the American authorities, but declined to comment. He also refused to comment on whether the Vietnamese government was involved in drug smuggling activities and had accepted pay-offs. It was a tricky issue. Since 1986, the American government had barred friendly relations with nations whose leaders engaged in drug smuggling 'as a matter of government policy'. Vietnam though, had never fallen foul of that year's Anti-Drug Abuse Act and had recently been attempting to mend its relationship with America in order to take part in much needed trade to stabilize its shaky economy. No one seemed to have mentioned this to our general or his troops.

Although they didn't officially consider the Vietnamese government as drug smugglers, the Reagan administration still refused to recognize Hanoi until it ceased occupation of Cambodia and resolved the issue of the Americans still listed as missing after the Vietnam War. The desire to find out the fates of soldiers still missing since the conflict had been a major factor in America not officially denouncing Laos as a nation that benefited from drug smuggling, despite much evidence to the contrary. Drugs and politics were making for messy bedfellows and uneasy alliances.

It dawned on me, while lying on the metal bed in my sparsely furnished Indonesian hotel room, surrounded by newspapers opened at the pages that covered the bust, that I had, by virtue of my life thus far, left myself almost completely unemployable. The experience I had gained in the world of international trade was not exactly of the type that I could boast about to legitimate potential employers. Neither had I any underworld connections despite having been a successful criminal for the last twelve years, nor did I have friends in the straight world. I was wanted in at least two countries, perhaps more, so strolling into a local job centre and applying for the positions on offer was completely out of the question. I was a forty-four-year-old ex-smuggler who hadn't had a proper job for twelve years. Luckily, that was a problem I would not have to face for a while as I had made it out of Asia with enough cash to start a little business somewhere, and hide out until the heat wore off. Of course, I had no idea how I was going to manage the task or how long it would take.

Most of the millions I had made over the years were gone. Everything the authorities could tie to me would be immediately seized. What was left was tied up in property and assets spread all across the world, a world I could no longer travel with impunity. Suddenly my years of reckless abandon with money, seemed wanton and foolish. The truth was that I had become almost disdainful of the money I was making. When it is so easily earned, it soon becomes something abstract, something always there yet somehow valueless. That was all about to change. There were a couple of Halliburton suitcases left over in Singapore from some smuggle or other, souvenirs of a time that was now past, so I filled them with what little cash and all the documents I could lay my hands on and took them with me as I headed back to where the whole thing had started, back to Australia.

I figured Australia to be safe. Save leaving the country without a passport I had never broken any laws there. Travelling, though, required some thought, and any move I made would have to be double-checked and scoped from all angles. Already paranoia was becoming a way of life, one eye permanently cocked for the nearest exit.

On previous trips home I'd bought myself a property in Cairns and three parcels of land, as well as a section of a beach in Wongaling which I had given to my mother and where she had built the house in which she now lived. The purchases had been a kind of insurance policy should anything go wrong, and things had by now gone about as wrong as they could.

But a life lived on the run soon becomes very expensive. Where before I had amassed a collection of credit cards in different names and thought nothing of using plastic to book first-class flights, traceable credit was no longer an option. I had no real idea of what the authorities knew or how many of my identities had been compromised since I had left Thailand behind, so everything now had to be bought with cash. If I needed a car, which I frequently did as Australia is a big place, then hiring a vehicle was out of the question. Rather I would have to buy the thing outright, something older than I was used to but reliable, something that would blend in with the other traffic on the roads and not bring unwarranted attention to the driver. I also had use in Australia of the car I had bought for my mother, a champagne-coloured Mercedes 380 SE, which, although it was a beautiful car, was a bit too conspicuous, so I used it sparingly.

I changed the way I dressed, losing the loose silks and brushed cottons and opting instead for inconspicuous casuals. I let my hair grow longer and I grew a beard. The only clue I left to the life I had lived was the watch on my wrist, the Rolex GMT that I couldn't bear to part with. Thus newly attired, I decided that I should look up an old friend, Ned.

Since we had met in the 1960s, Ned and I had stayed in touch. We hadn't seen an awful lot of each other but I had made a point of looking him up on my visits home to see Mum and he had been out to visit in Hong Kong and Singapore occasionally, helping out while he was there with the paperwork required to move money around the various companies I had set up. What mattered to me now was that I considered Ned a friend. Fortuitously, as well as being one of the few people I knew in Australia, he was a qualified lawyer – and one thing I needed right now was a lawyer. I also needed a buffer, an official body between me and the world. I was going to have to be very careful when it came to making investments or spending money. After making initial contact I began to spend the time I suddenly had so much of at Ned's office as I pondered the question of what the hell I was going to do next. We agreed that Ned would act on my behalf. If I needed information about the progress of the case being built against me then he would be able to get hold of it without giving away where I was. With Ned on my side, I thought, I might just make it.

I was the lucky one. On 14 Feburary 1989 Brian Daniels was flown from Zurich to Seattle-Tacoma International airport, having lost his seven-month battle against extradition. As soon as he landed he was taken to jail to await trial for the *Encounter Bay* job among the other charges levelled at him. Like the Colfleshes before him and me too, were I to be caught, Daniels faced the very real prospect of spending the rest of his life behind bars. Daniels' first scheduled appearance before a federal magistrate was set for 15 February, the day after he hit American soil. Later that year, on 1 June 1989, almost a year on exactly from the *Encounter Bay* seizure, the Grand Jury for the Western District returned a ten-count superseding indictment, basically a charge sheet, which named me, as well as Brian Daniels, Tai Farmwan, Thomas Sherrett and others related to the case. I was named in counts I, III and IV of the indictment, and charged in my absence with 'Conspiracy to Import into the United States from a place outside thereof, in excess of one thousand kilograms of a mixture or substance containing marijuana'.

It was while sitting in Ned's office one afternoon that the idea of setting up a crayfish farm was first mentioned. Crayfish are the fish Elvis sang about in *King Creole*, scaled-down versions of lobster. The Australian Red Claw crayfish we would be farming went by the name *Cherax quadricarinatus*, and are similar to crawdads, mudbugs and yabbies. They are ugly to look at but good to eat and, according to Ned, easy and profitable to farm. The other option we discussed for a while was prawns but in the end the crayfish won out.

Farming the crayfish would involve firstly buying a plot of land large enough to hold around ten pools in which to house the fish, and secondly working incredibly hard to ensure that they grew into something worth selling. By that point I was ready to try anything. Inactivity didn't come easily to me. I may have run around the world seemingly without a care for the last decade but I had worked hard too. The more we discussed the idea the more enticing it became. If we were to buy a crayfish farm it would have to be out of the way somewhere, far from prying eyes and awkward questions. The long hard work it would involve in order to get the project off the ground would be a welcome relief from the long days I was spending with little to do but drink myself numb, trying to cover the hurt I felt at being separated from May and the kids.

The booze dulled the pain a little at first but didn't really touch the sides. There is nothing like coming close to losing everything to show you what is most important. I was still in occasional touch with May and the children but contacting them was a complicated affair. I took it as read that the authorities would have May's phone tapped so we had an elaborate system in place to circumvent this. I would drive for one, two hours in my newly acquired car to the most remote call box I could find and phone May who would be waiting for the call at a pre-arranged place, at the home of one of her family perhaps, which was unlikely to be bugged. We would rotate the numbers I would call in case the authorities were tailing May.

Although a loyal, loving wife and fantastic mother, May made for a terrible criminal. My years as a smuggler had meant that security and secret-keeping were second nature to me, but the deceptions and intrigues needed just for us to stay in touch did not come naturally to May at all, as I found out the first time I called home and May picked up.

'It's me.'

'Oh Micha—'

I hung up before she'd finished saying my whole name.

Rather than make me feel better, the snatched phone conversations merely served to highlight the seemingly unbridgeable distances between myself and my wife and family. To say that May was not happy when the details of my crimes were brought to light is putting it mildly. She was shocked, furious and outraged at what I had done, she was embarrassed in front of her family and worried for our children. Any justification I tried to present highlighting the difference between hard and soft drugs held no sway with her. I had let May down badly and as we conducted our clandestine conversations I felt on more than one occasion that I was losing her.

I needed to do something to take control of my life and look towards the future. So I went ahead and bought a crayfish farm. Ned found the perfect location in Queensland. We were virtually buying a ready-made business and merely had to move in and get to work. The land was for sale for Aus$400,000, and Ned himself had no money to put into the venture, now turning into a partnership, so I sold a property I owned, the flat in Cairns, and put all of the money up. Ned was fronting the deal and so suggested that I should grant him power of attorney over my estate. Basically by signing the agreement with Ned I was authorizing him to act on my behalf in any and all legal and business matters. As far as what was left of my income from smuggling and the assets I had acquired, he now controlled it all. And why not? He was my friend after all.

The farm was situated slap bang in the middle of the desolate Australian landscapes so similar to those my father had flown over during his tenure as a bush pilot. They made a fitting backdrop, the lonely surroundings suiting my mood at the time perfectly.

Did you know crayfish take years to grow to a size large enough to sell them as food? In the meantime, they require some serious looking after. We built ten pools on the land I had purchased, each 2.5 metres deep and measuring about 30 metres square. Because our crayfish were normally found in rivers we had to keep the pools constantly aerated, which we achieved by installing a sprinkler system. Crayfish are migratory by nature and therefore were constantly trying to escape so we had to erect inward sloping walls at the top of the pools, which would prevent their claws from gaining enough purchase to escape.

Not only were the little bastards always trying to get away, but they would often eat one another too. Fortunately for us, they bred at such a prolific rate that we could accommodate the cannibals among their number. A more worrying problem was the fact that they were a popular snack with flocks of local cranes, beautiful birds we fired at with double-barreled shotguns to dissuade them from making free with our crop.

We employed a Fijian marine biologist to work onsite and ensure that as well as being well fed and watered, the lobster also remained in the best of health. The rest I did myself. On any working farm there is always a long list of jobs to do and duties to take care of, and ours was no different. Much of the work was back-breaking labour, mending, fixing and making new beneath the unforgiving Australian sun. At the end of the day I had little energy left for anything but drinking myself into oblivion and dreaming of better times. Living accommodation took the form of a large three-bedroomed house. I told Ned that he should occupy the house while I would go back to my old ways and buy a caravan to park onsite and call home.

One of the reasons I had initially been so taken with the fish farm idea was that I saw it as being something solid that could provide a place for my former partners in crime to come to once they had been released from jail. By the time the Colflesh brothers had served their sentences the fish farm should be in profit and in a position to provide a decent income for all of us. It wouldn't buy us yachts and clubs, but if it panned out as I hoped, we could all earn a reasonable income from the venture. I was under no illusion that I would ever smuggle again. My greatest asset as a smuggler had always been my anonymity but, thanks to the *Encounter Bay* bust and the surrounding publicity, that was now blown far out of the water. No, I was definitely no longer a smuggler and instead had become a hard-working farmer. But I was bored.

The crayfish farm was situated near an area of outstanding natural beauty regarded as one of the last truly wild environments on the face of the earth with virtually untouched tropical rainforests and savannahs with a climate to match. Home to a large number of Australia's surviving Aborigine population, the area also boasts a five-star camping facility where campers, rather than roughing it in the usual sense, are housed in luxury serviced tents with guides on hand to walk them through the area's wildlife: rare species of frogs and butterflies found nowhere else on earth, a unique treat for the nature buff with an unlimited holiday budget. Even the beauty of the landscape left me numb.

For a while the new computer I bought captured my attention. PCs at the time were still expensive and far bulkier and harder to operate than they would soon become. After many long nights spent trying to work out the seemingly unfathomable mysteries of programming code I gave the thing up as a bad lot, and returned to the solace of the bottle. Ned, though busy, was often on hand as a drinking partner, but I missed the familiar faces from my old life. I decided to buy a boat.

I chose a sailboat, a beauty large enough to live on, and had Ian do the necessary in order to free up some of what was left of the sale of the Cairns esplanade apartment in order to pay for it. I chose the boat on the strength of its name and for as long as I owned the vessel it retained the apt title of *Sanctuary*. The boat was close enough to the farm that I could easily commute to work in my old 4x4, yet far enough away that I felt I had some life outside the daily grind of feeding and watering a million hungry, ugly, cannibal lobsters.

Once I installed myself on the boat I began to wonder what my old friends from the *Delfino II* days, Jim and

Moira, were up to. Luckily, they were between maritime engagements and more than happy to come and visit. The sailboat was not really built for three and living conditions were a little cramped but we made the best of it and I have some fond memories of the time we spent there. Jim was growing older and the Australian climate suited him so he'd often visit, living aboard with Moira while I left them to it and spent my nights at the caravan.

And in this way the days slowly turned into weeks, the weeks into months and the months into years. Then, as we approached the second anniversary of setting up the farm, Ned came to me with the news I had been subconsciously dreading since I had first arrived.

CHAPTER THIRTEEN

UNLUCKY THIRTEEN

Another moonlight flit.
Two suitcases and a small boat.

'Bad news, Mike . . . They've found you.'

'What do you mean? Who has?'

'The Australian police. They know you're here and they're coming.'

'Shit.'

I didn't need telling twice. I'd made the mistake of feeling I'd got away with it and although circumstances hadn't been ideal over the past two years I'd started to feel settled on the farm. That had been a mistake, and they'd caught up with me. Of course they had, it was naive of me to ever think they wouldn't. Luckily, one of Ned's contacts had come through and tipped him off and given me a head-start, but I had no idea how long I had. I imagined the police on their way there and then, in convoy maybe, rubbing their hands and practising their stern looks for the front pages of the local rag. I pondered how they'd got me. The phone calls to May and the family? Or had someone recognized me? But in the final analysis it didn't matter. What mattered right now was that there was no time to waste. Within minutes of Ned's announcement I was preparing to leave the farm and Australia behind.

Flying was out. The authorities were bound to have the airlines covered. No, I was going to have to leave Australia surreptitiously, just as Lietzman and I had done all those years before. The nearby Cape York Peninsula offered the ideal spot for what I had in mind: it was quiet, as far off the beaten track as it's possible to be with a deserted coastline. My hastily concocted plan was to sail over to New Guinea. I'd worked there as a young man and knew the island reasonably well, well enough to be secure in the knowledge that boarding a plane there would be a damn sight easier and less dangerous than it would be in Australia. Since gaining independence from Australia in 1975 New Guinea had been self-governing; what law enforcement there was on the island would not, I hoped, have been informed of the warrant for my arrest in Australia.

I crammed all I needed into two chrome Halliburton suitcases: all the cash I had to hand, some fake passports and sundry items of clothing. As soon as I was packed I jumped in my car and headed to Brisbane. Once there I bought a small motor boat for cash and hitched it to a trailer on the back of my car. I packed it full of my fishing equipment, a disguise of sorts, so that to anyone I passed on the roads I would hopefully look like just another fisherman about to try his luck in the nearby waters.

What I had in mind, though, couldn't be achieved alone. I was about to drive my car, boat and trailer to the most remote beach I could find and set off from there, but setting sail would leave behind the car and trailer, both covered in fingerprints and tell-tale signs if anyone were looking. I enlisted some help to get out of the country, calling one of the few acquaintances I'd made outside of my small circle since arriving. Robbie agreed to come along with me and see me out to sea. Once I was on my way to New Guinea and a new life he would hitch up the trailer to the car and drive the clues far enough from my point of departure that they would not give away what I was up to.

We drove through the night from Brisbane without stopping. As soon as we got to the coast, the morning after I had received the news of my impending arrest, we discussed the finer details of my proposed journey. Even as we spoke, the weather on the peninsula began to take a turn for the worse. Robbie looked up at the gathering storm clouds, and then over at me.

'It doesn't look good, Mike. If I were you I'd think about a raincheck. I reckon if you leave now you'll be lucky to make it a couple of miles out before the storm hits. That boat of yours wouldn't stand a cat in hell's chance out in this.'

Robbie was right. As we stood looking out over the ocean the wind began to blow up around us and light rain began to fall. We watched as the sky darkened further and listened to the first rumble of thunder and crack of lightning.

'Shit. This is all I need. How long do you think the storm'll last?' I asked, feeling twitchy.

'Hard to say, mate, maybe a day if you're lucky, maybe

a week if you're not. Best idea is to stay here tonight, sleep in the car and wait it out.'

Besides the weather there was also the question of fuel to consider. The 150 kilometres from Australia to New Guinea, alone in a small boat, is quite a trip. The boat needed fuel, a lot of it, and this was not a part of the world inundated with gas stations. After spending an uncomfortable night sleeping in the car at the beach we awoke to a brighter day. With hot sun now shining we set about locating a local public service works, a supply station for government vehicles. We bribed the lone officer working there to supply us with what we needed and then lugged the heavy cans of fuel cross-country for three miles to my proposed departure point. The temperature hit 40 degrees as I attempted to carry the bladder, sloshing this way and that, across the miles of rugged terrain and back to my boat.

Finally, by the afternoon of the second day I was ready to leave. The boat I was taking had two fuel tanks and an onboard motor, as well as the spare motor that I would need later. I'd also stowed an inflatable dinghy on which I'd complete the last part of my journey.

After a little pushing and shoving we got the boat off the trailer and into the sea. I said my goodbyes to Robbie, thanked him for his help and prepared to sail to New Guinea. But early on in the journey it became obvious that things would not go quite as smoothly as I had planned. Because of the weight the small boat was carrying, a huge amount of fuel plus me and my two suitcases, it was refusing to sit properly on the water. Before I even had a chance to consult the charts I'd brought along to guide me on the voyage I noticed that the boat wouldn't plane, that is, it wouldn't get the lift it needed to lie flat on the water. Instead it was dragging its way through it and using up far more of its precious fuel than it needed to. I should have been able to easily manage fifteen knots but was only doing about four. No matter what I tried – laying flat across the front of the boat, moving the suitcases and fuel to the front too – the boat refused to lie as it should on the water.

I had to go back and start again. But it wasn't as easy as all that. If Robbie was gone I was fucked. Launching the boat in the first place had been a challenge for both of us – there was no way I could get the boat out of the water by myself, let alone launch it again. This was not the smooth getaway I had been anticipating.

A couple of hours after leaving I was back at the deserted beach and, luckily for me, Robbie had decided to hang out in the area for a while, taking the opportunity to do some fishing and drink a beer or two from the cooler in the car before heading back to civilization.

'Fuck's sake, Mike,' he said, astonished, 'you should be halfway to New Guinea by now. What happened?'

It was lucky I'd turned back when I had, another hour and I would most certainly have missed him. Robbie was a sight for sore eyes but more than a little perturbed when I explained to him that in order to start my journey again we first needed to drag the boat out of the water where it was now anchored, pull it up on the beach, and start the whole process from scratch.

'Jesus Christ, mate. You said on the phone you just needed a bit of help with a boat, this is turning into a bloody marathon,' he grumbled. 'I wish I'd taken off now.'

But Robbie soon relented and after much hard work we eventually dragged the motor boat back up the beach. I was exhausted and leaving again straight away was out of the question. Sailing to New Guinea would be challenging enough without attempting it while I was in such a state. We lit a fire on the beach and cooked the fish Robbie had caught, emptied the cooler and slept there. And so, refreshed and ready for action, I set sail again on the morning tide. We'd redistributed the weight on the motor boat and got rid of as much fuel as we safely could without jeopardizing the mission. This time I was determined the plan would work. It had to. For all I knew, every policeman in Australia was on the lookout for me and I had no intention of being caught while there was still the slightest chance I could make a break for it.

The weather at least was with me and I cast out into clear blue waters beneath a cloudless sky, crossing everything I had in the hope that this time the boat would plane. But it took a while. When I first got out into the sea the boat fell into the now familiar routine, nose in the air and fighting the sea as it dragged over the calm water. Eventually though, after screaming, yelling and calling it every name I could think of, the boat levelled off and began planing. I shouted my relief to the gulls overhead and turned back to head for the beach I'd just left. Robbie had stuck around, waiting to make sure that this time I could sail and walked out waist deep into the water, fish swimming around his hips as we shook hands and said goodbye.

'Well, so long, Mike, you're a good bloke and all that, but try not to come back this time.'

'Robbie, you're a saint.'

I was off.

It was the most beautiful day I could remember for a very long time. A cool breeze blew across the surface of the sea taking the edge off the power of the beating sun. I didn't even have a canopy on the boat to provide any shade, all there was as I headed out into open water was me, a collection of fishing equipment and two Halliburton suitcases packed with everything I'd need to start a new life.

Staring down through the crystal-clear water at the shimmering schools of fish and softly waving coral reefs I realized that for the first time in as many years as I could remember, I was completely and utterly alone. Throughout my childhood, working life and smuggling career there had always been people around. While I was smuggling I had surrounded myself with the same handful of people; we'd worked and lived together, bound by mutual respect and trust, our fates linked by crime and the secrecy it musters. But out in that boat, on the run from Australia and heading to New Guinea, there was no one left but me. The sun was shining, the weather was glorious, and I wasn't beaten yet. For a while on that tiny motorboat on the way from Australia to New Guinea, I felt free.

My happiness was short-lived. I thought at first I was imagining it but no, that definitely was a plane I could hear and it was definitely heading straight for me. A second or two later I saw it, a small Australian Coast

Guard plane moving closer and closer by the second. I struggled into action, desperately fumbling with my fishing rods and gear, trying for all I was worth to maintain the illusion that I was out for sport rather than escape. I acted the part as well as my heightened senses and newly sweating palms would allow, hurriedly casting a line over the side of the boat while affecting the most casual glance I could muster up at the plane. It took an eternity to pass but eventually it did just that, leaving me to my fishing and relief. I laughed out loud when I realized they weren't after me and sped up towards my destination.

Hours of blissful sailing later, just as the charts I'd brought with me began to tell that I should have land in sight, sure enough, there it was. I idled the engine and prepared to disembark. The first order of business was to inflate the rubber dinghy I had bought with me and fit the spare outboard motor to its stern. I put in the suitcases and some fishing gear, then took out the axe I had bought for this very purpose and began hacking away at the hull of the motor boat. Just as I couldn't risk my car and trailer being found abandoned on the beach at Cape York, nor could I leave a perfectly good boat covered in my fingerprints floating off the coast of New Guinea. The boat was remarkably robust and held up well to a concerted attack from the axe. I was sweating before I managed to create a hole in the hull large enough to start taking on water. I turned the boat's wheel full right and tied it off there with an old length of cord. Then I hopped into the dinghy, leaned over to the motor boat and put it in gear and watched as the boat began to turn in one giant thirty-foot circle. The idea was that it would take on water and sink but this boat didn't seem to want to die. I caught up with it, stopped the engine and put the boat into reverse, repeating the process and climbing back on board the dinghy to watch the boat turn the huge circle, but backwards now. At last it began to take on water, moving nearer and nearer to the water line with each circuit.

After a very long ten minutes the boat lost its battle with gravity; its engine was swamped and it had nowhere to go but down. I felt a small twinge of sadness watching it disappear below the surface and send up a short Morse code goodbye in bubbles before I fired up the engine on the dinghy, made sure my suitcases were secure and headed off for the nearest beach.

I had sunk the motor boat just two miles or so off New Guinea so it wasn't long before I was navigating the dinghy into a small gap between some rocks that met the sea. At that moment a native of the island happened by and assisted me on to dry land. I wanted to create the impression I'd just sailed in from a yacht moored somewhere just out of sight and took my helper's lack of quizzical expression as a good sign. Once I had clambered up on the rocks and pulled up my suitcases and fishing equipment behind me I asked him where I would find the nearest hotel. He showed me and I set off to check in, leaving the dinghy where it had landed, hoping that it wouldn't be too long before someone came along and stole it.

The hotel was small and clean and the staff there friendly and helpful. I spun my yarn of just having come off a yacht moored close by and again no one so much as raised an eyebrow. As I checked in I asked how I could make my way to Port Moresby, the only place in New Guinea where I could catch an international flight.

I was going to London.

CHAPTER FOURTEEN

WELCOME TO LONDON, PILGRIM

Camden market and the new gang.

It was 1990 and by now customs and passports checks, particularly in the world's larger cities, were no longer the simple queue-stamp-and-go affairs they had once been. I spent the whole flight to Heathrow ordering more and more miniatures from the smiling stewardesses, an odd race who somehow seemed to manage to look very young and very old at the same time, pickled by the mediated air in the jet-stream of international travel. But fear of what would befall me when I touched down ensured that the small plastic bottles of Johnny Walker Red and Gordon's Dry Gin I knocked back with abandon had little noticeable effect in allaying my anxiety. As the landing gear deployed beneath me and made first contact with British soil, I felt distressingly sober.

I trudged towards Nothing To Declare with sweat beginning to trickle from my collar and down my spine and a throat so dry that I couldn't swallow. The two Halliburtons, dented now and aged by their journey thus far, felt heavy in my clammy hands as though they could slip from my grasp at any moment. I still had no idea if British law enforcement were part of the search for me and half expected, as soon as I produced my Michael Young passport at passport control, to be surrounded by drawn guns and angry stares. But I didn't see a single uniform and made it through customs without incident, emerging gratefully into the grey air of a wet west London.

I hadn't actually thought much beyond landing. Now I was here, in a city where I knew absolutely no one, I had to plan my next move. First things first, I hailed a cab. The driver who picked me up was chatty and, riding the wave of adrenalin my recent event-free negotiation of customs had inspired, so was I. When he asked me where I was headed I took a moment to reflect on the question in a broad sense and had to stop myself from telling this stranger that I was headed towards freedom, perhaps even a new life. When I realized what he actually wanted were directions I remembered an area I had travelled through and liked the look of on my trips to our 'office' at 15a Norfolk Place.

'Do you know any decent hotels in St John's Wood?'

'Certainly do, my friend.'

'Okay then, take me there.'

An hour after touching down on English soil I was reclining on a hotel bed with a view overlooking the street, wondering what the hell I was going to do next.

Before I'd left Australia I'd arranged with Ned that he would start to slowly dissolve the assets I had left there, the few parcels of land and the boat, and forward the money to me in London. It also wouldn't be too long until the crayfish on the farm reached the age where we would be able to harvest our first load for sale and therefore start seeing some money back on the investment I had made. Until that money began to trickle through I would have to take care with my finances. Living in hotels was not going to be a long-term proposition and so I set about wandering the streets of St John's Wood in search of a flat to rent.

I found a small two-bedroom apartment that suited my modest needs perfectly. It would serve as an ideal base and provide enough room for the family when they visited, which I hoped would happen sooner rather than later. May and the children had remained in Singapore since my rather hasty departure and it had been a full two years since I had seen them. Aside from brief phone calls and the occasional letter we had had virtually no contact at all. Top of my list of priorities once the flat was secured was finding a way I could see my wife and family away from the eyes of the authorities who, for all I knew, were still watching them.

I began to take in the town, wandering through London's ever-changing postcodes from Clapham to Kensington searching for a way to make a living. I was a dazed *flâneur*, alienated and intrigued by the city in which I now found myself. Like waking from a dream, there would be a moment every morning, a glimpse of peace, before the full realization of where I was and what I had lost hit home. They were tough days, the easiest passed on a kind of autopilot while the hardest seemed made up of a never-ending series of regrets and what-ifs. I was lucky to be free and I knew it, but it wasn't enough. If I was to get through this, as I knew I had to, then I had to make my situation work to my advantage and claim back those parts of myself I was beginning to think I had lost.

On the plus side, London offered the promise of anonymity every bit as complete as the Patpong Road ever had. The city's underground culture had undergone something of a quiet revolution in the last five years, ever since a group of enterprising souls had begun to import and sell a new drug, known as ecstasy, into the capital. Along with the culture that went hand in hand with the drug – house music from Italy and Detroit, rave parties in abandoned warehouses and a frightening affection for baggy clothing in bright day-glo – there had been a resurgence in a lifestyle not reliant on the homogenized high street. One of the areas benefiting from this cultural sea-change was Camden market.

Camden market in the north of the city spread from Camden Town underground station all the way up to Chalk Farm, its length covered by hundreds of stalls and shops selling everything from bootleg Ramones and Smiley-face T-shirts to one-off dresses fashioned from lurid 1950s curtains, and all soundtracked by the high-points and avant-garde extremities of musical history emanating from the ghetto blasters and stereo systems rigged up to the colourful stalls and turned up to eleven. Would-be fashion designers and artists used the space to exhibit and sell their wares, their own designs mixed in with second-hand Gucci loafers, vintage sportswear and twelve-hole Dr Marten boots.

Although relatively busy with a steady stream of trade

throughout the week, Camden really came alive at the weekend. On a good day up to 200,000 sightseers and shoppers would stream out of Camden Town and Chalk Farm tube stations, which book-ended the market.

As with any small community, the market bred its own brand of folklore, tales which were swapped by traders and punters alike over long afternoons as tourists, students, and fashion designers swarmed over the place searching out vintage Levis with selvedge inner seams and cinch-back buckles, or the rare Northern Soul and Psych singles, so collectable that they could fetch hundreds. The market stories became Chinese whispers, made real by the very retelling and gaining in veracity the further they became untethered from truth. There was the guy near the stables, his entire inventory laid out before him on a ratty blanket in front of his beaten-up old suitcase, his stock, were he to sell it all, worth less than the price of a decent bottle of wine. He'd managed The Beatles, so the story went, back in the early days of the Chuck Berry covers in Hamburg in the leather suits and pointed black boots. He'd then fallen out with the Fab Four and declared that they would never work again, just before they became the biggest band in the world. There was the lady from north London selling art deco, the prize piece on her stall a fine example of an original pewter ashtray designed in the thirties and known to those in the trade simply as *The Echo*. Antique dealers and collectors would greedily snap up the ashtray and head off happily, complete unaware that their lucky find, their original piece of design history, had been cast and fired only the week before and left to cool along with a shelf of others all exactly the same, in the basement of the woman's north London home.

I liked Camden from the first time I visited. Its vitality and vigour put me in mind of Thailand and I became convinced that it was the perfect place for someone like me, essentially a non-person, to find a comfortable niche in which to hide. I began returning to the market again and again, strolling through its maze of stalls and shops, dodging its buskers and lowering my eyes when passing its policemen. On one of my walks through the market I noticed a stall selling renovated second-hand furniture, old chairs, tables and wardrobes that had once been discarded but since given new life, like the one I needed, by being stripped down to the wood, smartened up and varnished. The stallholder was called Gareth, a friendly soul with an open face. I began to strike up conversations with him on my increasingly frequent visits to the market. His business was obviously ticking over but it was apparent that the enterprise was not running at its full potential. After a few weeks, Gareth and I struck up a relationship, casual at first but gaining in momentum until I finally put the idea to him I had been mulling over since we'd met.

'How would you feel, Gareth, about taking me on as a partner?'

I offered to make a cash investment in the business, initially of a thousand pounds, money that would allow Gareth to increase the stock he held and eventually, therefore, the profit he made. For investment, not only of my money but my time as well, I wanted half of the business. Gareth agreed and the business, with both of us at the helm, was from then on known as Dream Street Designs.

Gareth sourced his stock at auction houses dotted throughout London. I began to attend the auctions with him and was soon caught up in the thrill and rush of bidding for pieces I thought could turn a profit. From house clearances to dead stock, the halls and auction rooms we visited were filled to the rafters with everything from the plain dull to the plain strange and all points in between. Mounted big game heads rubbed wooden shoulders with rusted suits of armour and dusty collections of old football programmes. Fruit machines and fruit bowls, ribbonless typewriters and rusting Edwardian bedframes all jostled for space in their attempt to catch a buyer's eye. It was a world easy to get lost in, everything on show there seemed to tell a story and I had to remind myself that what we were after was used furniture.

We set about picking up a collection of shabby tables and benches, tired wardrobes and unwanted desks. Once the furniture was back at the Camden workshop we set about the alchemy of renovation, stripping and sanding the pieces back to their original wood and turning the discarded into the desirable. It was a good business. With a good eye for a nice piece and some hard work and elbow grease, a table that we picked up on the Monday night at Southgate auction rooms for £20 would be snapped up on Sunday for £250.

Gradually, I began to make friends among the stallholders at the market, the faces who would gather early on Saturday and Sunday mornings beneath tousles of hair untroubled by brush or comb since the revelries of the previous night. The first subject under discussion as the market came to life was the size of their hangovers.

Ed and Steph ran a huge stall in the converted Midland railway arches, just opposite Dream Street. They sold second-hand and vintage clothes imported from Europe, rails of wool suits and leather jackets, tweed overcoats, trilby hats and summer dresses that seemed to run back for ever until disappearing into the vanishing point at the rear of their long thin shop. They called the business Archie's and it was often tough to make out there where the party ended and work began.

Apart from Ed and Steph, the staff at Archie's was often supplemented by a loose crew of friends and relations who converged on the business to pick up a new outfit or pass some time. Toby and Dan worked there on occasion. Toby was Steph's brother, a Rolling Stones obsessive whose laugh, on a clear day, would carry all the way to Brighton. His best friend Daniel called everybody he met Darling, even policemen. The pair would think nothing of half filling the petrol tank of their noisy white van, stuffed with antique dinner suits and adoring young ladies, and setting off for a drive through Europe, calling in the roadside recovery services every time they ran out of gas and arriving back at the market three weeks later to share the tales of their latest adventure. When out and about closer to home the pair perfected a pulling technique that involved them pronouncing proudly that they lived in Piccadilly, which wasn't a complete falsehood, as it happened to be where they had parked the van that night.

Besides Camden's answer to the Glimmer twins,

Archie's also provided a weekend home to Adrian and Chris. Adrian had the air of a downbeat aristocrat complete with pipe, frayed tweed and stout English walking shoes, and would later hit upon the genius idea of advertising his services as a house-sitter in *Country Life* and *The Lady*. So, despite the fact he was skint, he often found himself potless in a six-bedroom townhouse at the plush end of Mayfair. Chris would arrive for work straight from the clubs, gravel voiced and shiny eyed with last night's immaculately chosen outfit showing the signs of twelve straight hours of falling in and out of a succession of bars and parties along with his best friend and co-conspirator Kenny.

Opposite Archie's was the stall run by the Kyriacou brothers, a pair of characters straight out of a Cathi Unsworth novel. Half Cypriot and half Scottish with messy quiffs and loose-buckled engineer boots, the pair spent their weekends selling vintage Rock 'n' Roll Americana through a fug of cigarette smoke and matching hangovers before heading over the road to the Lock Tavern at the end of the day's trading to bet their pocket full of takings on a pool game with Ed. Along with their brother George, the Kyriacous had grown up in hotels managed by their father and recalled well the night in the late seventies when their dad had had more than enough of The Clash's on-the-road room-trashing antics and turfed the band and their touring party out of his establishment and into the mean streets of Crawley.

Just being around them all made the world feel a better place.

The only phone on the market belonged to the Russian

guy just along from Dream Street who sold jukeboxes. He had a huge stock of the things, vintage Wurlitzers and Rock-Ola's playing Del Shannon and Hank Williams 45s, and had an encyclopaedic knowledge of their history and inner workings. There wasn't one made that he couldn't fix. The combination of the great music he was always playing and the fact that you could phone from there made his store a very popular spot indeed. Just across from him was the luggage guy, who specialized in antique Louis Vuitton travel ware. People paid good money for the vintage luggage, often as much as they would if they were buying it brand new, and on the occasions when he would display a travel trunk similar to the ones we had used to transport cash back to Asia at the end of my smuggling career, I found it difficult to walk past his shop without smiling.

Three months after arriving in London I felt that enough time had passed since I left Australia for Ned to have sold my boat for me, and I was beginning to wonder where the money was. Most of the time I couldn't get Ned on the end of the phone; on the few occasions I could I would hang up with a very bad feeling.

'Ned, it's Mike. I need you to start sending me some of my money, the boat sold a while ago and I could really do with it here.'

'Yes, Mike, the thing is, there's been a few unexpected expenses on the farm, I won't be able to send all of the money straight away . . .'

The more elusive Ned became the more a question mark began to form in my mind over his claim that the Australian authorities had been looking for me and closing in. When he'd first told me that was the case I'd taken him at his word and left immediately but now, safe in London, something about the whole affair didn't quite ring true. I had never committed any crime in Australia. I had never smuggled dope into or out of the country and the more I thought about it the less likely his claim that I was about to be arrested became. The dark suspicions I was harbouring were soon confirmed.

I had given one of the pieces of land I had bought in Australia to my mother, a small piece of beach-front property where she built herself a house. It was a beautiful spot, dotted with ancient mango trees yielding sweet, stringless fruit just waiting to be picked. At night as the sun went down where the ocean met the sky the fruitbats would converge above the gardens of the house, flocks of them throwing dark ever-changing shapes in the twilight. Although I had made my mother a gift of the land it was still officially in my name, and therefore now under Ned's control. I phoned my mother one night from a call box at Charing Cross station and as soon as she realized who was on the phone, she broke down in tears.

'Oh, Michael, it's terrible. Some men came around, they said I have to leave, they said the house isn't mine any more and I have to leave. I don't have to leave do I, Michael?'

Using his power of attorney he had sold it right from underneath her. There was nothing I could do and she was forced to leave her home. Ned eventually embezzled everything I'd placed in his care. I never saw a penny from the sale of the fully grown crayfish after all the back-breaking work I had put in. He sold all the property

I had in Australia and pocketed the profits. Predictably, Ned became impossible to track down. He was no longer reachable at his office or at any of the numbers I had for him.

Some research and a few questions asked on my behalf in Australia pointed to the fact that I wasn't the first person he'd screwed over and it was very unlikely that I would be the last. At first I felt bitter and angry. What he'd done to my mother infuriated me and still does, but in order to carry on and not become consumed by the resentment I felt towards the man I had to let go somewhat. Perhaps the distance between him and me helped. If we were in the same room I doubt I'd be able to remain quite so Zen about the whole squalid affair. It is a shame though. If Ned put half the time, effort, thought and resources that he put into swindling his friends to more constructive use he could probably do very well for himself.

How are you, Ned? Sleeping well?

Dream Street was not turning over enough to make me a millionaire again in a hurry, but it certainly provided me with enough ready cash to live on and get by. I lived alone in London and spent the majority of my time working, I had curtailed my extravagant tastes and was, on the whole, managing quite reasonably. The people who needed the money and would benefit from it far more than me were the very people I had most harmed with my criminal career, the people I had left behind in Singapore, May and the children.

The separation from my family was becoming unbearable. It had been three years since I went on the run and I was sure that I could risk seeing them once more. Visiting them in Singapore was out, too dangerous, and I felt that asking them to come to London was fraught with risk too, so I arranged to see May and the children in Germany. I arranged the German trip via call boxes dotted throughout London – Charing Cross station was a favourite but there were lots of others. I would travel to phone boxes in Little Venice, Maida Vale, Bayswater and Soho, anywhere far enough away from my home in St John's Wood and my work in Camden that I felt sure I wouldn't be leading anyone tracing the call straight to me. I also wondered whether anyone would still seriously be looking for me; it had been three years since the *Encounter Bay* bust and I hoped that by now they might have given up on me. But it wasn't something I was prepared to bank on.

The flight to Germany went without a hitch. My fake passport was barely given a second glance as I passed through customs and headed off to see May, Nicole, Nicholas and Nigel. I had grown more and more excited as the trip approached, sure that it would be a roaring success and the scars of the last three years would heal as soon as the five of us were all together again. But that was not to be. My children were still young, too young to be capable of understanding the situation we were in and were freaked out by my appearance out of the blue. The beard I had grown meant that Nicole didn't recognize me at first and burst into tears as I approached her. I was heartbroken and as soon as I was at a sink I shaved the thing straight off. May was still angry with me – it was obvious from the moment that we met up that if it weren't for the kids seeing their dad she wouldn't have made the trip, and I didn't blame her. From Germany we made our way to Disneyland in Paris where I wore Mickey Mouse ears and basked in the light of my children's smiling faces.

Despite all of the difficulties of the trip, saying goodbye to them all at the end of the three weeks was heartbreaking and on the plane back to London I swore to myself that the situation would not continue as it had, that we would be a family again, no matter what.

I felt that the Michael Young identity I was using had enough back story and documentation by now to appear more than credible. I had even obtained a National Insurance number in the name. Obtaining the number wasn't easy and involved me being called in for an interview to explain why I had waited until I was in my mid-forties to get it, and where exactly I had been up to that point. The official interviewing me made no effort to hide his exasperation as I spun him my yarn.

'So what I don't understand, Mr Young, is where you've been until now.'

'South East Asia, Australia and America. I left Britain as a teenager and haven't really been back since, but I'm ready to settle here now.'

'Lucky us,' he said, his voice dripping sarcasm.'So let's start from the beginning again. What date did you leave Britain?'

As I retold the story I had practised I could feel the man's patience wearing thinner by the moment. After an hour in my company he threw up his hands, collected his papers and left the interview room, telling me I was free to go. Within a month I had my National Insurance number in the name of Michael Charles Young. I was getting more real by the day.

I was working hard, running a business, paying rent and living something quite close to a normal life. The fact that no one seemed to have followed May and the kids when they came to meet me in Germany convinced me that they were no longer being scrutinized so closely at that end, so I asked them all to come and live with me in London. After much persuasion May agreed to the idea and soon, rather than living alone in the St John's Wood flat, I was sharing it with my wife and my three young kids.

Having the family back around me was heaven. The kids were as noisy and playful as children their age the world over and the loneliness I had felt for the years leading up to them all re-entering my life soon drifted away. The flat was too small to house us all comfortably for long but I had an idea as to how we would solve that little problem, and hopefully provide a little security for May and the children too.

My grandfather had died in 1989 and left me a not insubstantial amount. I was in touch with the lawyers handling the will by post and signed over all of the legacy I received from my grandfather's estate to May. Once the inheritance tax was paid there was enough left over to buy a house. Finally we would all have somewhere safe we could call our own, a base from which to rebuild our life together. When I signed the money from my grandfather over to May I suggested she be sure to put it into a dedicated bank account, to open one if necessary. The reason for the single dedicated account was quite straightforward. The money from my grandfather was clean, completely legal and above board and should the worst ever happen, it should therefore be untouchable.

We eventually found a property to buy with the money I had signed over to May at 351 West End Lane in Hampstead. The house was expensive, at £210,000 it swallowed up pretty much all of the inheritance, but it was beautiful. It was handy for work at Camden and close to Hampstead Heath, the park in north London that offers the most stunning views of the city. Hampstead is renowned for once having been the neighbourhood favoured by artists and writers: William Blake lived there, as did Kingsley Amis, Peter Cook and the mighty T. S. Eliot. Richard Burton and Elizabeth Taylor had a home there too. It's a swanky part of town.

The ground floor of the property had been built as a shop front, which had great potential as far as the Dream Street business was concerned. As soon as we moved in I turned the shop into a combined showroom and storage space for the furniture business and had a sign painted and hung to announce that we were open and ready to trade.

Of course I couldn't leave the building quite as I found it and just as I had on pretty much every property I had ever owned I set about planning and designing the changes I wanted made to the place before I called in the builders.

CHAPTER FIFTEEN

BUSTED. 1993

Those are policemen, not tourists.

At the start of 1993, while considerably more than three sheets to the wind, I took a tumble down some steps at Camden market. I managed to deal with the injury though, and found that a jam jar, secured around the neck by a length of cord and filled with a generous measure of gin and tonic, meant that the crutches I was forced to wander around on for a while didn't interfere with cocktail hour, which usually began at around eleven in the morning and lasted for the rest of the day. Cheers.

As happened periodically, the shoppers and stall-holders who filled Camden had undergone, seemingly overnight, yet another marked change in appearance and demeanour. Grunge, flown in from Seattle, had replaced Acid House as the pop cultural force to be reckoned with. I now found myself negotiating my way past the dark eyes and troubled stare of Nirvana's Kurt Cobain on a thousand T-shirts making their way along the Chalk Farm Road as his band's tune, 'Smells Like Teen Spirit', refused to go away.

We were doing well enough to employ Dan and Toby

on an ad-hoc basis, to deliver furniture or pick up stock in their clapped-out old van, stuffed to the gills with Victorian frock coats, John Le Carré paperbacks, and empty Marlboro Light packets. We also hired more staff to help in the business of renovation and were gradually taking over more and more buildings at the Stables in Camden. The kids were settling well into their new schools. Things were good.

In America though, that country now adjusting to Bill Clinton as its newly elected head of state, a chain of events was being set in motion, completely without my knowledge, that was to radically affect my life from that point on.

Mark Bartlett, the US Assistant Attorney responsible for putting my co-conspirators behind bars, had not forgotten about me. Bartlett's record of bringing dope smugglers to justice was second to none; the Colflesh Brothers, Brian Daniels and Brian O'Dea to name but a few all languished in jail thanks to his tireless work. As last man standing from the *Encounter Bay* bust I was definitely unfinished business as far as he was concerned.

Up to that point, America's War On Drugs had cost an estimated $100 billion. Prior to his election Bill Clinton had stated that 'you can't get serious about crime without getting serious about drugs' and for a while looked as though he took the problem seriously enough to radically rethink the policy he had inherited from the right-wing hardliners Reagan and Bush Snr, instead focusing on the root causes of drug problems. But once in office Clinton's stance on the subject soon became virtually indistinguishable from that of his predecessors. The War On

Drugs continued apace, and as far as it was concerned, I was still an enemy. Bartlett weighed up his options and decided that his best chance of catching up with me would involve finding the best man for the job. That man was Fran Dyer.

Dyer was an accomplished American Treasury agent, at that point working at the Criminal Investigation Division of the IRS. His career had begun back during the Vietnam War when he was an Air Force officer assigned to their Office of Special Investigations. While working as a Detachment Commander at the OSI he had supervised a team specializing in counterintelligence operations of the 'utmost sensitivity', leading one counterespionage operation that resulted in the eventual capture and arrest of a real honest-to-goodness Russian spy. Since 1981 Dyer had specialized in the investigation of narcotics trafficking and money-laundering operations and was considered something of an expert in the field. His investigations over the years had led him to work in smuggling and spending hotspots in the US, Europe and Hong Kong. Dyer had a high arrest and conviction record, which didn't bode well for me, and routinely worked alongside the DEA, the FBI, US Customs, and numerous foreign police agencies. All in all, this is not a man you want on your tail.

Fran Dyer had been investigating the Shaffer brothers, the notorious millionaire playboys who had operated out of Thailand and had, along with Brian Daniels, been behind the huge 42-ton load of weed that had landed in California in 1987 and saturated the market, causing the dope we smuggled in that year to be worth half what we had expected. Dyer's pursuit of the Shaffer brothers had led him to look closely at Brian Daniels, and that investigation led him in turn to focus his attention on me.

The manhunt to track me down that followed Bartlett's appointment of Dyer would involve information sharing and cooperation between members of the US Attorney's Office, the American Treasury Department, the Australian Federal Police Department, the DEA and Scotland Yard. It must have cost a fortune. Early on in the investigation, Dyer received what seemed like a break when he got word via a confidential informant that I was in England. Dyer decided to act on the information and contacted the International and Organized Crime Branch at Scotland Yard. Dyer knew I was fond of changing identities so a couple of Scotland Yard detectives made their way to the British Passport Office in Hayes in Middlesex to see if they could find a clue as to where I was through the aliases I used. They didn't know all of the names I'd collected over the years but they had my real name, Forwell, and my busiest alias, Michael Charles Young, to go on. Prior to 1988, the records at the British Passport Office were not computerized so they began hunting me out among the boxes of information corresponding to the 3.5 million passport applications made annually in the UK. Eventually this donkey work hit pay-dirt. Officers found my application for a passport under the name of Michael Charles Young and compared the photograph pinned to the form to the image of me that Dyer had sent them. It was the same guy.

Scotland Yard now had all the details of the Michael Charles Young alias to go on rather than just a name.

The rest of the passport application was useless to them – I had completed the form and obtained the passport pretending to be a civil servant from Preston. But once armed with the details of the Young alias they ran a credit check on me, or rather, him, and came up trumps. Over the years I had obtained credit cards in the names of many of the aliases I had used and I was still using the Visa card in the name of Young. Luckily I had neglected to let the credit card company know that I had moved and it had remained registered at the St John's Wood apartment I had rented two years previously, before the family and I had left for Hampstead. They checked out the flat and missed me, but they were inching ever closer.

Checks on transactions carried out on the Visa card revealed that it had recently been used to buy petrol at a garage in Chalk Farm, over the road from Dream Street in Camden. Piece by piece the jigsaw was beginning to fit together. Another snatch of information Dyer had received from his informant and passed on to Scotland Yard was the fact that I was now working at a London market, and here were credit card receipts for petrol bought in the middle of one of London's busiest. Forecourt CCTV footage was requisitioned from the garage corresponding to the time shown on the receipts and sure enough, there in grainy black and white was the white Volvo I was using for the shop, driven by a Chinese woman who matched perfectly the description of May that Dyer had forwarded. The registration number of the Volvo was sent through to the DVLA in Swansea who came up with an address, 351 West End Lane in

Hampstead. Now all the English cops had to do was watch, and wait.

The surveillance operation lasted just shy of a month. When the three officers originally on surveillance duty caught sight of May and followed her as she took the kids to school they knew they had found my family and that I wouldn't be far behind. Four more officers swelled the number of policemen looking for me to seven who between them mounted twenty-four-hour surveillance on the Hampstead address. On the twentieth day of watching the house through binoculars from their nearby vantage point they positively identified me as I climbed out of a Transit van and let myself in to the Dream Street showroom on the ground floor.

They came for me at work, at Camden market, on Sunday 28 February 1993, the same day that American forces laid siege to David Koresh's Branch Davidians commune in Waco, Texas. By April, Koresh's messiah trip had turned out bad; his weapons cache and refusal to submit had left the would-be Jesus as a marked man, surrounded by the authorities on all sides and buzzed by helicopters and itchy trigger fingers.

My capture and arrest was far less sensational than the bloodbath in Texas. The result of all the time and money it must have cost to catch me ended when four nondescript men entered the shop and headed straight for me. The second I laid eyes on them I knew exactly who they were and precisely why they were there. The open-minded look and trace of a bohemian attitude that marked our customers in the store was notable by its absence in the appearance and demeanour of these most unwelcome visitors. I also knew that I was tired of running and that even if I weren't, I had nowhere left to go.

'Michael Young?' one of them demanded.

'Um, yes . . .'

'I am placing you under arrest for possession of a falsified passport. You do not have to say anything but it may harm your defence if you do not mention anything that you later rely on in court. Anything you do say may be given in evidence against you.'

I tried to think practically as the words the policeman was saying sank in. As it was a Sunday the kids were not at school and had come into work with me and were happily playing in the shop, oblivious to the fact that their father was being arrested. My first priority was the children, so whilst the cops were busily arresting me I was frantically trying to make surreptitious arrangements to have them looked after until I could contact May and have her pick them up. It wasn't the best day I'd ever had at work.

As Camden began to fill with stalls and food stands, as the vintage clothes were hung on rails and the out-all-nighters turned up for a Bloody Mary breakfast after dance-floor adventures in the West End or raves out in the country, still saucer-eyed from the ecstasy and the coke, I left Camden market for the last time, watching it all disappear from the back of an unmarked police car.

It was over.

After formally charging me they drove me to the house. I had set up a small office of sorts in the basement and kept a small desk and filing cabinet there where I stored pretty much everything.

I tried to answer all of the questions they asked of me with a blank stare and a demand for a lawyer, which I was told would be addressed in good time. The four policemen made the most of their search warrant and went through every scrap of paper in the place. Most of the paperwork relating me to the smuggles I had carried out with Lietzman and the Colflesh brothers had long since disappeared; what hadn't been irretrievably lost when I instructed the secretary at TradeMax to grab everything and leave had been subsequently burned in my bonfire on an Indonesian island. But I hadn't been quite as clever, or quite as thorough, as I thought I had. Before long, the policeman who seemed to be in charge of the operation was grinning at me with his most supercilious Cheshire cat look and proudly holding up for my inspection a collection of my pieces of handiwork from a previous life: forged passports in the names of Rodney Wayne Boggs, Michael Charles Young, Michael Leslie Stocks and Michael Escreet. As well as the passports they found a number of printed balance sheets relating to the last scams we had carried out on *Encounter Bay*. Fuck.

Once they had the passports I was bang to rights and tied in to almost every smuggle I'd been involved in out of Thailand. The operation to find and arrest me had been coordinated by Fran Dyer and the British police at New Scotland Yard on the understanding that once I was safely in custody I would be extradited to the States to face the music. In the meantime I was to be held on remand in Brixton prison, a foul building in south London dating from 1820, which during its unhappy history had provided cell space to the notorious East End gangsters Reginald and Ronald Kray among a legion of other poor creatures whom history has forgotten.

The shock to the system brought about by incarceration in Brixton was profound. It is a truly abysmal place that blocks out light and hope and victimizes the soul. I was allocated a cell on D Wing, the top tier usually reserved for hardened criminals, and expected to immediately fall into line with the jail's harsh regime. One particularly humiliating aspect of life there was the ritual of slopping out. As inmates, most of whom were on remand and awaiting trial, we spent most of our time locked in our cells. The cells were basic stone squares often with condensation running down the walls and no plumbing whatsoever. Toilet facilities in the cells were provided by a plastic bucket that sat in the corner of the room and was emptied every morning of whatever waste it had received during the previous night. The practice of slopping out was eventually outlawed not long after I was moved from Brixton, having rightly been judged as inhumane.

The charge sheet listing my crimes ran to five pages and contained almost every weed smuggle and dope scam I'd ever had a hand in. They had the complete low-down on almost all of my criminal endeavours, virtually every ton of weed I'd ever smuggled was down there in black and white. They had dates, departure and arrival points, the names of the ships we'd used and how much dope we'd loaded into them. Under the heading

'The Government Of The United States Of America V Michael Gleave Forwell' there were eighteen charges listed in total, each a paragraph long and detailing how and when I had infringed the Misuse of Drugs Act 1971, in order to get my dope into America. The only jobs they'd missed were the picture frames, the fish tanks, the *Diana* and the Four X, all of which had taken place before I hooked up with the Colfleshes. Perusing the pages to the accompanying soundtrack of cell doors slamming and fellow prisoners shouting messages and insults along the cold halls of Brixton prison made for a most alarming read.

My situation didn't look good at all. Many of the crimes they were charging me with carried a mandatory sentence of twenty to life and the chances of me being able to make a deal were slim to zero. I had nothing that they wanted, nothing to offer them but the rest of my life.

I knew I would have to fight extradition to America. Staying in Britain and being charged for the same offences would still have resulted in prison time if convicted, but nothing like the amount I was looking at if found guilty in the States. The maximum sentence I could have been awarded by a British court was fourteen years. In America they could lock me up and throw away the key. What I didn't know at the time was that if the authorities hadn't caught up with me and arrested me when they did, there was a very good chance I would have got away with it for ever. From the moment I was charged in absence with my crimes back in 1989, the clock had begun ticking and they had five years to get me. If I'd managed to stay beyond their grasp for another year the statute of limitations would have run its course and I would have been home free. It dawned on me that this must have been a big factor in why the American authorities ploughed so many resources into going after me when they did.

A few weeks into my stay at Brixton I was told that I was being moved to another prison. I didn't think too much of the news at first – after all, what did it really matter which prison I was in – until they told me I would be taken to Belmarsh. Unlike the Victorian nightmare of Brixton, Belmarsh is a modern, purpose-built jail. It is situated near Greenwich in London and infamously its population was and is made up largely of terrorists. When I arrived the Provisional IRA member Paul Magee was locked up there along with other members of his organization. I got on reasonably well with the IRA members I met at Belmarsh. Many were there for what some may consider unforgivable crimes and I would never condone their actions, but at the time they considered themselves to be at war with a hostile force who had illegally occupied their homeland, and war usually soon becomes a litany of unspeakable acts perpetrated by both sides. The Kurdish revolutionary Marxist group PKK, which sought by violent means, such as suicide bombings, to establish an independent Kurdistan, also had members held at the jail. The organization had been suspected of trafficking in drugs, namely heroin, in order to finance their terrorist campaign. Since the Turkish military coup in 1980 many of its members had fled to Europe. Once PKK members began to settle throughout mainland Europe they had set about establishing a narcotic supply and distribution chain and trafficking in the heroin which originated in Afghanistan, Iran and Pakistan.

It seemed odd that I had been moved to Belmarsh; throughout the prison system the jail had the reputation of housing far more dangerous men than me. Security there is tight, it has a relatively small population but those who are there are watched like hawks. One afternoon in my cell, once again turning over in my mind the myriad details of the extradition problem, trying to think of anything, no matter how remote or unlikely that could aid my case, I heard a raised American voice out on the landing, a voice calling me if not by name, then at least by my nickname.

'Where's The Fox? Fox, are you in here?'

One of the secrets to making jail time pass is to keep your head down as much as possible, to try and remain invisible for as long as the sentence lasts. By shouting my name out all over the landing this new American prisoner wasn't helping my cause at all.

On the next association break I kept an eye out for the man who'd been calling my name and, sure enough, before long he appeared.

'You're The Fox right? I've heard all about you.'

The man before me had close-cut blond hair and stood at maybe five foot tall, and as he spoke I noticed that he had one green eye and one blue.

'Oh, really. And what have you heard?'

'You got busted for smuggling all that pot, you, Daniels and the Colflesh brothers. I heard all about you.'

As the man continued to talk in his quick-fire

American accent it seemed that he wasn't exaggerating, he did know all about me and my case. Not just me, but he also seemed very familiar with the cases of the guys I'd been busted with. It was all a little unnerving.

But on and on he talked, and after a while something he told me snagged my attention and caused me to take this strange stranger a little more seriously. He began to tell me that he had an uncle in the American Secret Service and that there had recently been a case in the US that could, certain circumstances permitting, have a bearing on my own. He said the case had recently been thrown out of an American court after it was discovered that one of the officers involved had been accepting bribes. Because of the greed of one man, the whole case had crumbled.

'You need to check out all the agents working your case, make sure they're all kosher. If one of those guys has been dipping his hand in the cookie jar, you could walk.'

I told him I would have no idea where to even start; most of the important agents involved in my case were American, I was currently stuck in a British jail with no way on earth of getting hold of that kind of information.

He told me he could help. 'Just get me a list of all the agents involved in your case. I can take it from there.'

'And why would you do that? Why would you want to help me?

'No reason, man, just to help, and you never know.'

It sounded fanciful but at this point even the most random of long-shots seemed worth following up. After all, I had a lot of time on my hands.

Back in my cell I read through the papers relating to

my case and picked out the names of the agents involved: Fran Dyer, Larry Brant, Mark Bartlett, et al. Eventually, after going through the papers, I had a list of about ten names.

The American who'd asked for the list was a fraudster, on remand and waiting for his own case to come to trial. During the next association we met again and I handed him the list of agents.

'I'll check these out for you, Fox, let you know if I come up with anything.'

But nothing came of it. As the weeks passed dark rumours began to spread through the prison concerning the fraudster. He was branded a snake, not to be trusted and was eyed warily by his fellow prisoners as he sat in front of the shared television set declaring that 'Knowledge is power, gentlemen. Knowledge is power.'

There were more worrying developments to cope with too. The authorities had elected to go after May as well as me and were gearing up to charging her with living off the proceeds of my crimes. It seemed ridiculous, I'd never involved May in the true nature of my business – she had been too busy throughout our marriage raising our children and looking after our homes to engage in any smuggling, even if she had been so inclined. But they were deadly serious, and were soon mounting a case against May every bit as comprehensively as they had against me.

In the case against May, the money I had inherited from my grandfather became a key issue. Although I had warned her to keep the money separate, to put it in a dedicated account and not to mix it with any other money, the inheritance had ended up travelling through accounts which dated back to my smuggling days and looked to the authorities like cash I'd made from dope. May was not a criminal and patently unable to act like one. I'd signed the inheritance over to my wife and she had bought the Hampstead home with it so, *ipso facto*, according to the case against her, May had knowingly used the proceeds of illegal activity to buy property.

It seemed as though it was coming at me from all angles. Not only was I fighting extradition to America from a prison cell in Belmarsh but I was also trying to keep up with the case against May, which eventually came to court in the spring of 1994. She was scared, confused and disoriented by the situation she found herself in – and of course angry with me. On the few occasions when we were in touch, relations between us were decidedly frosty. By now we were communicating by letter, but we were not talking.

When May's trial started perhaps the most surprising and damaging aspect of her time in court was the witness at whom she found herself staring in disbelief across the courtroom as he testified against her. My old friend and partner Samuel Colflesh had flown to Britain in order to appear at the trial and the evidence he offered against my wife was damning, particularly that which revolved around events that had occurred in our Draycott Towers apartment in Hong Kong many years previously. The prosecution insisted that the exchange Sam had witnessed between May and me, when I had asked her advice on the numbers I should paint on the side of my *Kim Ono* cigarette boat, demonstrated that

May took an active role in the running of the smuggling business. Even without Samuel Colflesh's help though, letters I had written to May outlining how much money we had and where it was looked terrible; they alone probably would have been enough to convict her.

I found out about Sam's surprise appearance at May's trial in my cell in Belmarsh and felt many things at once: frustration, anger, stunned disbelief and profound disappointment.

The outcome of the case against May was covered in *The Times,* the day after the judgment was delivered, on 30 July 1994.

Wife jailed for launder of massive drug profit

> The wife of an international drugs smuggler who helped to launder millions of pounds of profits from a billion dollar drugs empire was jailed for three years yesterday and had assets worth £900,000 seized.

Sentencing May, judge Mota Singh told her: 'It is not disputed that your husband was involved in trafficking drugs on a massive scale. Your defence was that you had no knowledge of his activities. The jury verdict shows you knew and you helped him to launder the profits.'

Which was bullshit, but by now it didn't matter.

May was devastated. Having been sentenced to three years it was likely that she would have to serve at least eighteen months behind bars, and it was all my fault.

Nicole, Nicholas and Nigel were sent back to Singapore to be looked after by May's sister and she began her sentence, first in Holloway and then in an open prison. The house in Hampstead was seized and sold as was all of the jewellery I had given her over the years of our courtship and marriage, worth about £300,000 in all. In total they seized almost a million pounds' worth of assets.

At around the same time that May was sentenced I finally lost my extradition battle. Over the last two and a half years I had become a reasonably competent jailhouse lawyer and tried every legal manoeuvre I could come up with to stay out of America. I found myself consistently blocked at every turn. At one point I had enrolled the services of an American lawyer famous for his record of successfully representing drug smugglers. I paid the lawyer $10,000 to secure his services but soon found out that men like him didn't come that cheap. He was used to unlimited budgets and million-dollar fees and the money I sent ran out in a heartbeat. I think I received two letters from him in total before the fee I had paid him was all used up and more was required if he was to carry on representing me. Another way to get rich from smuggling is to defend the men who do it.

As it became apparent that I was losing the fight against extradition and would need legal help once I got to America, I sent a letter to the Public Defender's Office in Washington explaining the details of my case and outlining my needs. The office handled the allocation of legal representation to those who couldn't afford it, and that now included me. Something in the letter must have struck a chord with the lady who received it. She got in touch with me to say that because of the way the process was structured in America, now that we had had contact with one another before my arrival in the country it had prejudiced my case and I had forfeited my right to free legal representation from their office. This was not as bad as it sounded. Because I was no longer eligible for free legal counsel I would be provided with a private lawyer and all my costs would be paid for by the state.

It was a small victory but turned out to be an important one. I would soon be heading to America to face a sentence of twenty years to life and I had nothing to give, I held no information with which to bargain my sentence down and the fact I'd gone on the run rather than hand myself in when the last operation went pear shaped was just another item on a very long list of factors which could, and probably would, work against me.

By the time I left Belmarsh I had been there longer than any other prisoner and it had begun to feel something like home. I said my goodbyes to the friends I had made at the prison and attempted to prepare myself mentally for what lay ahead on the other side of the Atlantic.

CHAPTER SIXTEEN

AMERICA, SLIGHT RETURN

Just because I don't like them doesn't mean I want them dead. Unwilling Days and honking seals.

The second I touched down in Washington on 31 July 1995 I was met by armed men and shackled. Apparently, I was a Category A prisoner, lumped in with terrorists and murderers, prisoners considered volatile, a danger to themselves and others. This meant that as well as the chains around my waist, legs and arms, my wrists were secured by handcuffs, which, rather than linking each cuff with a short chain, did so with a solid four inches of metal called a Black Box. The solid metal linking each wrist meant that officers escorting me anywhere simply had to grab the bar linking my hands and pull, and I would have no choice but to follow. If prisoners in these handcuffs become hard to handle then calming them down becomes simply a process of sharply jerking the metal bar, and breaking both of their wrists. The reason for my being awarded Category A status on arrival became clear when I met Mark Bartlett for the first time while I was being held in Tacoma, and broached the subject with him.

'We received word, Michael, that you intended to take out hits on the agents assigned to your case. We were given information that you had made enquiries into having the agents killed. There was a list, and we have a copy.'

At first I had no idea what the attorney was talking about. Then it dawned on me. The American fraudster I had met in Belmarsh prison, who insisted that if I gave him the names of the agents assigned to my case he would personally have them checked out, had taken the list I gave him and used it for another purpose entirely. He had tried to use it as leverage in his own case, claiming that I had written the names down and given them to him like he was some Murder Incorporated assassin and I wished to hire out his services. It was nonsense, of course. Just because I didn't particularly like the men in question didn't mean that I wanted them dead. Suddenly all of the over-the-top security precautions I had experienced since my arrival in America made sense.

Mark Bartlett is a sensible man and when I told him I had no intention of causing harm to anybody he took me at my word, and from that point on I went from Category A to C, far more befitting a prisoner of my peaceful intentions.

As Bartlett was the prosecutor assigned to my case there were a few questions he needed to ask me.

'Okay, Michael. The situation is you can plead guilty, which I strongly recommend, or you can fight me. There's nothing I need to know from you. Sam and

Bobby have given me everything already, unless there's something you feel you can contribute, some new information you can give us.'

The jail I was being held in was opposite the Boeing factory. Outside the barred and locked windows of the room we were using I could see the great long fuselages and painted tailfins of the planes there. I looked out at them for a second or two and then back at Mark Bartlett across the scarred chipboard interview table.

'There's nothing I can tell you that you don't already know, and nothing I can give you that you haven't already got.'

Bartlett just nodded. 'So be it, Michael. The only thing that I can offer you is that I won't go too hard on you if you plead guilty. Otherwise you take your own chances.'

Basically, I had no choice.

May was released from prison having served eighteen months of a three-year sentence in August 1995. Most of the fine she had been ordered to pay at her trial, however, £750,000 pounds in all, was still outstanding minus the money deducted after the confiscation of the jewellery and the house, and likely to remain so.

Knowing that May was out of prison felt like a weight off my shoulders. At last the children would be back with their mother, edging closer to normality after everything I had put them through. More good news came in the shape of the defence counsel I had been allocated. His name was Russell Aoki, a young Japanese-American lawyer with a serious face and a good smile. He was diligent, hard-working and genuine, and we hit it off right away. To a man in the position I found myself, little things suddenly meant a lot, and Russell Aoki's displays of generosity over and above his official duties, like tracking down and buying me underwear from Marks & Spencer, touched me deeply.

I had decided to take Bartlett's advice and plead guilty, which I did on 21 December 1995. My sentence was to be handed down the following March. The pre-sentence report and United States Recommendations presented to the judge in anticipation of my appearance before him were short on light relief:

> Mr Forwell's positive points cannot overshadow the magnitude of the criminal organization or his role in the organization. Mr Forwell, along with Mr Lietzman established himself as a major player in southeast Asian marijuana trafficking. Mr Forwell eventually brought the Colflesh brothers into his organization and they gradually assumed much of the day to day management of the organization. However, Mr Forwell was always a primary partner within that organization. There is no question that, in 1988, Mr Forwell was fully anticipating to share on an equal basis with the Colflesh brothers the tens of millions of dollars in profits gained from the 72 ton importation.

And there was more:

> Mr Forwell stands before the Court as a defendant in the largest marijuana seizure case in this district. He is one of the last defendants to be sentenced because he

> became a fugitive shortly after the vessel carrying the 72 tons of marijuana was seized off the Washington Coast. The defendant remained a fugitive for five years before being arrested in England in 1993. He lived under an alias and turned all his property over to his wife. Mr Forwell's guideline range is for a minimum of almost 22 years. However, the Plea Agreement entered into by the defendant and Government stipulates a maximum sentence of twenty years. If the Court accepts the Plea Agreement, we would recommend the maximum of twenty years.
>
> Mr Forwell denies that he was the mastermind behind this importation business. Whether or not he was, he certainly invested a lot of time and money into its success. The defendant points out that while involved in this importation business, he also ran a successful nightclub/discotheque. Therefore, one can only wonder what his motivation was for becoming so involved in the drug trafficking business.

I was appearing, as had the Colflesh brothers and Brian Daniels before me, in front of that motorcycling and sailing enthusiast, Judge John Coughenour. The venue for the trial was an unspectacular example of Washington civic architecture a short drive from the police station where they were holding me. The courtroom itself, when I entered it to face the judge, seemed huge. The generous dimensions of the room in which my future was to be decided were emphasized by the fact that there was hardly anyone there. Those few people already in their places seemed to radiate nonchalance, as if this day, one of the most important in my life, were just another day at work for them, which of course it was. A few court officials sat between me and the judge; Bartlett was there of course, as was Russell Aoki. On the wall above the judge's seat was the Washington State seal surrounded by a state flag and the Stars and Stripes. The walls and floor of the room were of varnished wood. The acoustics amplified every cough and shuffle, the ticking of the clock on the wall echoed throughout the room. At nine o'clock Judge Coughenour entered, and we began.

The prosecution had a solid case and with one or two exceptions pretty much everything they said was accurate, relevant, or both. Of the irrelevancies, I could only presume that they had been included to provide an atmosphere of guilt. An example was the discovery made in 1991 that Lietzman had an account at a branch of Credit Suisse in Zurich through which nearly five million dollars had flowed, and to which I had been a signatory though not the main account holder. If it was Lietzman's account then what did it have to do with me? It was also discovered and announced during the sentencing hearing that an account still existed in Lietzman's name at Bank of America in Singapore, which contained almost three million dollars.

I was pleading guilty to the two charges that faced me, those that still came under the wire of the statute of limitations, but I was still looking at a possible twenty to life. Aoki began at my sentencing by asking the court to impose a ten-year sentence, and set out his reasoning for the request in his statement to the court.

'We are asking the court to impose a sentence of ten

years and not the nearly twenty years recommended. We believe that this is fair because it's consistent with the original sentences of the defendants Robert and Samuel Colflesh, whose sentences were eventually reduced to fifty-two months. It reflects a statutory minimum.'

Well said, Mr Aoki.

The prosecution, led by Bartlett, were recommending that I serve 235 months in prison, a term just shy of twenty years. Twenty was what I had expected, and as far as it is possible to do so, it was what I was trying to prepare myself to receive. I had already been behind bars for almost three years back in England at this point and prison was becoming normal. To counter the prosecution's recommendation, Russell Aoki asked the judge to take into account that I had never used violence throughout my career and that although I very easily could have, I never indulged in the more profitable option of smuggling hard drugs. He also asked the judge to take into consideration that I had attempted to go straight after the bust, that I had started the lobster farm in Australia and worked hard at it and stayed out of trouble. He didn't mention that there isn't an awful lot of trouble that you *can* get into on a fish farm.

But Judge Coughenour was not convinced by all Russell Aoki's arguments, as he made clear while offering the reasons for the sentence he was about to hand down.

'I don't see any comparison between the Colflesh brothers and this defendant. The major distinction between them is that the Colflesh brothers cooperated in a very meaningful way.'

This didn't sound good.

'And with all due respect to Mr Forwell, and I have listened very carefully to what he has said here today and I am very moved by it, but the fact of the matter is that decisions were made and risks were taken. And unfortunately this is a very high-stakes game.'

With every word the judge spoke my chances of receiving the ten years Aoki was asking for receded. Mark Bartlett then helpfully pointed out that rather than hand myself in, as Bobby had done, I had chosen to make a break for it, and go underground.

Once Bartlett had spoken, the judge continued his line of reasoning.

'The case that I'm most concerned about in comparison to Mr Forwell is Brian Peter Daniels. I gave Daniels twenty-five years as I recall.'

Oh shit.

'And I made it clear to him at the time the major reason he was getting that much time, there were two reasons. One was that he didn't cooperate, and secondly I was convinced that there was a lot of money over in Europe that he now claimed he couldn't get his hands on.'

Judge Coughenour then asked Bartlett whether he believed that I too had millions out there that I had neglected to hand over to the authorities. Bartlett told the judge that as far as he knew, no, there weren't millions out there, pointing out that at the time of my arrest I certainly wasn't living like a man who had a huge cash reserve behind him. But Bartlett was also keen to point out that just because I was broke now, it wasn't through want of trying.

'This conspiracy had been established by, first of all, Mr Forwell and Mr Lietzman who then brought in Mr Colflesh. This had been going on for a decade. He talks about his sorrow over a mistake. This was not a mistake. This was a chosen lifestyle that had been going on for a decade.'

The clock on the courtroom wall edged past nine thirty in the morning as Coughenour weighed the arguments and gave his decision.

'Let's set the guidelines aside just as a kind of intellectual exercise and talk here about how much time is needed for this man to pay the price for what he did and the decisions he made after he knew he was found out. What is needed to get the message across to society that if you deal in marijuana in this magnitude and you get caught, you're going to pay a price.'

He sentenced me to fifteen years.

Immediately after being sentenced I was taken to the nearby Buckley jailhouse to await transfer to prison proper. The jail had recently played host to the Shaffer brothers following their day in court, which had ended as badly as mine. One small plus point of the stop-over was that the staff at the jailhouse were prepared, so long as I had the money, to pick up supplies from a local supermarket and hand them to me in my cell.

On leaving the jailhouse I embarked on a dizzying tour of the America they don't put in the tourist guides. On 4 April I was woken at 5 a.m. by the marshals, who have the job of transporting prisoners. I was already in my faded orange convict boiler suit, cuffed at the hands and feet, though thankfully no longer black-boxed, and taken aboard a minivan along with five male prisoners and two female to an airfield in Portland, Oregon. The shackles and cuffs are worn by every prisoner travelling through America and restrict arm and leg movements to the extent that walking becomes an undignified shuffle, and scratching an itch anywhere but on the wrist or chest is impossible.

Once at the airfield in Portland we sat in silence, shackled to one another in the back of the van as the midday sun beat down and turned the air inside hot and stale. We were awaiting the arrival of 'Con-Air', airline of choice for the discerning convicted wrongdoer. Our wait over, we were next ushered into the company of 120 others just like us, all shackled and cuffed aboard the old Boeing passenger jet, no doubt confiscated from ambitious smugglers working out of South America, and now used to airlift prisoners around the country.

The Stetson-wearing, tobacco-chewing deputies who manned the flights glistened with a film of sweat and regarded us all with undisguised contempt, exacerbated whenever a prisoner required chaperoning to the stinking, filthy onboard toilet. Lunch aboard the flight was a dry sandwich containing a minuscule slice of meat of uncertain origin served in a cardboard box that would probably have been far more nutritious than its contents. Eating while shackled required bending the head to the hands, which had travelled as close to the mouth as the ever-rattling chains would allow, bowing low in some sick parody of communion. I was a hell of a long way from first class.

The one privilege the deputies could not deny us in transit, though no doubt if they could have they would, was glimpsing the panoramic views through the window, the whole of America below us seemingly displaying itself in all its beauty to mock our lack of anything like freedom.

We landed at Sacramento, and I waited for my name to be called to signify that I would be getting off, but I waited in vain. While there we picked up some passengers and discharged others; the faces may have changed but the expressions never altered. I knew it was useless to ask where I was being taken; it would merely provide the deputies who had been charged with our care the opportunity to sneer, spit and hold secrets.

We landed next in Phoenix, Arizona, where the entire plane was emptied and a line of exhausted, manacled prisoners were herded aboard minivans in the hot sun and driven out to a detention centre seemingly located in the middle of the desert. After processing, filling in the necessary paperwork to administer our arrival, at around 7 p.m. the shackles were removed and I revelled for a time in the luxury of being able to take steps measuring more than twelve inches and to scratch my nose should I feel the urge. A fitful sleep at the detention centre was cut short at 3 a.m. the next morning when we were woken and shackled, and prepared for another long day in the air. Breakfast was a sweet doughnut and a crucible of apple juice, made all the more precious by the knowledge that it was the only food I would see until dinner, and dinner could be a very long way away. We were herded aboard 'Con-Air' and left once again in the care of those hateful deputies, and made our way skywards to Las Vegas.

On the flight to Vegas I found myself in a window seat and pressed my face hard up against the rectangle of clear plastic, blocking out everything around me but the landscape of undulating clouds.

Once back on the ground we were placed aboard a bus taking us to God knows where, which turned out to be the North Las Vegas holding facility. I was no longer sure whether it was day or night and disoriented to the point of ridiculousness as I stared out of the bus window at the flashing neon of the Vegas strip and looked into the faces of its lovers and losers. At the holding facility we were placed in a tiny cell where we would spend the next seven hours while we once again went through the interminable ritual of processing. Then we were each assigned a bunk in a dormitory sleeping fifty and handed a thin worn blanket and a woefully inadequate 'hygiene kit'. Thus passed the next three long days and cold nights.

Throughout my tour of America courtesy of the Department of Prisons I wore the blue plastic bracelet the guard had allocated me when I left Buckley. The colour-coded bracelets denoted your prisoner classification: blue signified that I was Federal, minimum risk, white signified a trustee, yellow signalled State misdemeanour and black marked the high-risk individuals. The bad guys wore black. The more dangerous the prisoner was judged, the better it seemed was his accommodation. Those wearing black bracelets never ate or slept with the general population but were instead provided single cells where they had their food delivered to them on a tray by the guards.

On Wednesday the 10th I was woken by a Las Vegas marshal at 5 a.m., and once again cuffed and shackled. We left without breakfast and were bussed back to the airport where we sat and felt the sun come up over the vehicle as we waited for another vintage Boeing to carry us skywards. We flew this time to San Diego and during the flight I caught sight of the Pacific Ocean. The last time I had seen the Pacific I had been crossing on a boat full of weed. It seemed like an awful long time ago.

From San Diego we flew on to Bakersfield where I, along with eight other prisoners, was loaded into a minivan for the final leg of my journey.

One pair regulation prison pants.
One short-sleeve regulation prison shirt.
Two sets regulation prison underwear.
One pair regulation prison shoes.

I was now prisoner number 252299-086 of Terminal Island prison, San Pedro, California, and likely to remain so for a very long time.

I had arrived at the prison hot, crushed and apprehensive. The step down from the marshal's minivan was too high for me to reach with my legs shackled so I fell out of the vehicle as the reinforced mesh door opened and got my first look at my new home as my face hit concrete warmed by the California sun. I was then led hobbling through the reception area, conscious that the dragging chains that bound my legs would mar the mirror polish of the floor some poor inmate had no doubt spent the entire morning buffing.

Once processed and given my prison uniform and handbook I was assigned to solitary confinement. Solitary is every bit as horrific and soul-destroying as it sounds. They put you in a room and leave you there. What made it worse was that I had no idea why I was there, since time in solitary is usually doled as a punishment. All soon became clear. In the American prison system, co-defendants in the same case are, as a rule, sent to different prisons. The reason for this is obvious and sensible: it drastically reduces the chance of them murdering one another in their sleep. By some oversight I had been sent to the prison in which one of the co-defendants in the *Encounter Bay* case, Brian Daniels, was serving his time. It took around a week for the governor of Terminal Island to have warders speak to both of us and assure himself that neither of us held any kind of grudge or hard feelings towards the other. Once he was satisfied of this I was released from solitary and assigned, as were all new prisoners, to Unit C, a steel and concrete rectangle containing bunks for around seventy men.

My first walk on to the main compound felt something like running a gauntlet. I was painfully aware that it offered my fellow inmates the chance to size up the new arrival. One of the first things that struck me about the prisoners as I tried to get my bearings was the fact that although we were all issued with the same items of uniform there seemed to be a million ways in which it could be customized in order to signify status and allegiance. The Mexican and Hispanic gangs wore their shirts buttoned at the neck and their pants low and baggy. The bikers had ripped the sleeves from their shirts in order to best exhibit their collection of winged Americana tattoos, Harley logos, naked girls, marijuana leaves and Old Glory. The black guys augmented their uniforms with bandannas in red and blue denoting their loyalty to Bloods or Crips, and as I walked into that yard it felt like every single last one of them was staring straight at me, the new scared-to-death English guy who didn't feel like he had a friend in the world.

Terminal Island prison is situated at the entrance to the Los Angeles harbour on Reservation Point. This rectangular stretch of artificial land mass, of which the prison occupies half, is surrounded on three sides by the ocean. Its waterside locale provides the reason for its having been renamed by inmates and guards alike 'Club Fed'. Charles Manson had been imprisoned there not once but twice. The first time he arrived as a young man in 1956 and spent a couple of years on the island after taking and driving away a 1951 Mercury coupe. Then he returned ten years later, in 1966, after having been caught attempting to cash a bad government cheque. Following his release from his second term at the prison Manson headed straight to the heart of the hippie dream and began gathering the lost souls about him who would later do his horrendous Helter Skelter bidding in the Hollywood Hills. Al Capone also served time there, as did acid guru Timothy Leary, convicted for dope offences in the sixties. Another infamous former inmate of Terminal Island was the New York Mafia foot soldier Henry Hill whose life formed the basis for Nicholas Pileggi's *Wise-*

guy, the Cosa Nostra kill-and-tell which Martin Scorsese used as the inspiration for his own tour de force, *Goodfellas*. Terminal Island was also home to one of the greatest crime fiction writers of all time, Edward Bunker, who began his writing career while in prison.

Since finding out that he was also an inmate I had been fascinated to finally have the chance to sit down with Brian Daniels. I reintroduced myself to Brian in the Terminal Island prison yard one afternoon during association and I liked him immediately. He seemed quiet and guarded by nature, but I suppose considering the circumstances he found himself in he had every right to be. I arrived in jail six years after Daniels and yet if I were to serve every last day of my sentence I would still be leaving before him. That must have been hard to take. We became friends in prison, or as close as two inmates can, and although declarations of that type are not really Brian's style, we got on well. I saw a lot of him during my time at Terminal Island. I took a job as a clerk in the hobby shop and Brian had discovered an interest in sculpture and got himself a prison job in the education department, so he was around a lot. But apart from establishing ourselves upon first meeting, I don't think we ever spoke once about the dope trade in the whole time we knew one another.

Terminal Island prison itself is a low-security facility and the more relaxed regime I encountered there was a welcome change from the shackles and black-box treatment I had received on arrival in America. Around 1,200 inmates are housed in the jail, more than double the 500 it was originally intended to accommodate when it was built back in the thirties. Ironically, given my last job before incarceration, one of the outlets for inmates at the prison is a furniture restoration business that sells its wares through a nearby shop.

If I look hard, really hard, there were moments that brought me pleasure during my stay at the facility. My living quarters were situated in the south yard of the prison and the education facility where I worked was in the north. The walk between the two passed along 'the breezeway', a 200-yard path with the prison factory wall on one side and the sea on the other. The path was separated from the water by three chainlink fences, razor wire and two or three feet of gravel. On the walk from home to work, which I made three or four times every day, the ocean was only about eight feet away, close enough that I could smell it. The smell of the ocean, mixed with the aroma of the diesel fuel from the Coast Guard cutter that was moored nearby could, if I closed my eyes and let my mind wander, take me back to happier times and boats full of dope.

Aside from Brian Daniels, I made some other friends at Terminal Island who helped make life easier. I got close to Steve, an exceptionally talented artist who hung around the education block, and I would often pass the time of day with the man they called the Reader. The Reader was always reading, he'd read every book in the library and devoured every single magazine and paper he could get his hands on. I suppose that reading provided the man with his escape, and no subject seemed to fail to capture his interest.

'Morning, Reader, what is it today?' I'd ask.

'Fascinating article here on the Pale Headed Brush Finch,' he'd say enthusiastically. 'Beautiful bird on the verge of extinction.'

Then the next time we met, 'Morning, Reader, what is it today?'

'Amazing . . . it says here that there are 365 different languages spoken in Indonesia.'

The Reader was inside for fraud, the details of which were so long-winded and complicated that even when he explained the crime to me I was still at a complete loss as to what he'd done, and how he'd done it.

Light relief also came on occasion courtesy of Revis, a huge guard who worked at the prison, usually assigned to the education department, who had had his promising American football career cut short by injury. Revis was a fair man, as nice as his post would allow.

'So tell me again, Mike. In England you can't pick the ball up, you just kick it, right? Don't sound right to me.'

At its worst for me though, prison life was utterly barren, tears shed in a desert. There were days when it felt like there was no art and no architecture left, no nature and no love. It was life in negative, lived out in a desperate house where the carpets, couch and anything flammable have been removed. Everything that remained had been bolted down and painted not quite white and not quite grey. In the garden the grass and flowerbeds had been concreted over. Even the air seemed third rate, used, stale and full of hatred. Everybody hated everybody else. Prisoners hated prisoners, prisoners hated guards, guards hated guards and guards hated prisoners. And round and round and round it went until eventually it felt like it was choking us all.

Racial tension abounded within the walls of the prison and the three main ethnic groups, white, black and Hispanic, stayed as separate and autonomous as the regime would allow. They even watched TV in separate rooms. I shared a cell for a while with Carlos, a Hispanic gang member, and returned one day to find Carlos in possession of a crude and deadly-looking knife.

'Carlos, you ought to be careful with that thing. What on earth do you want it for?'

Carlos replied without a moment's thought, 'To kill blacks.'

My days began at 6 a.m. when I would wake on the top tier of a steel-framed bunk bed and head hazily for the showers, hopefully in time to beat the first rush of inmates, many of whom were not morning people. Showered, shaved and abluted, I would head to the mess hall and partake of breakfast: miserable coffee, porridge and eggs. Once I had forced as much down as I could manage I would return to my bunk and make my bed, ensuring that my few meagre possessions were stashed in the two-foot-by-three steel locker attached to my bunk. Work call for regular and service workers in the prison was 7.30 a.m. But my job in the education department did not begin until 1.30 in the afternoon so my morning was spent reading or writing letters on my bunk, walking in the south yard or, if I could secure a pass, in the library. Most of the books stored in the prison library were law volumes, pored over by inmates hoping to unearth a previously overlooked legal loophole that they could crawl through. Most didn't.

At 11 a.m., having returned from work, the entire prison population was required to stand next to their bunks for the ritual of the stand-up count, where the warders would make their way among us, counting heads and ensuring that none of us had made a break for freedom. At midday the doors to the dormitory were unlocked and we would head back to the mess hall for a decent lunch of soup, salad and something, perhaps fried chicken on a good day. After lunch I would head off to the hobby shop at the education department, passing by the sea, and get ready to hand out the few tools and materials inmates were permitted to use in the workshop. The day's second stand-up count took place at 4 p.m. and required returning once more to my dorm to stand by my bunk to make sure I was still there. The hobby shop closed at 8.30, final lock-down for the night came an hour later followed by the sure sign that yet another useless day had passed: the final 10 p.m. stand-up count.

In order to combat the desolation of enforced confinement, I kept myself as busy as I could. As well as the job in the hobby shop I worked on the only computer in the facility that the inmates had access to. In a tiny glass-walled office I busied myself typing and printing out the weekend football schedules or the menus for holiday meals at Thanksgiving and Christmas. I made posters to advertise whichever film was being shown at that week's movie screening and tried my best to lose myself in the task at hand and ignore clocks and calendars.

Because Terminal Island is surrounded by water it is a

popular spot for mating seals. Seal love is neither a quiet nor a melodious affair, and they like to go at it at night. For some reason a lot of them chose the area just outside my dormitory window as the place to get it on. At first the concerto of horny honking was funny. After a while it became merely charming. The journey from mildly irritating to insanity-inducing was a short one and three years into my stay at Terminal Island I would have given anything for a decent night's sleep, uninterrupted by the gruff vocal gymnastics of sealus coitus.

There was a chance, which I had clung to from day one, that at some point I could be repatriated and serve out the rest of my sentence back in England. It was a slow process. In order to even apply I had to have spent two years in the American jail and once the application process was under way it was likely to take at least another two. Everybody involved had to agree to let me return. The British authorities had to declare no objection to taking me back, the American authorities had to declare no objection to me leaving, the governor of Terminal Island prison had to rubber-stamp the deal and I had to display my willingness by serving good time and staying as close as I could to being a model prisoner. The maximum sentence in Britain for the crimes I had been charged with in America was fourteen years, one year less than I had received in Washington. If I were to be returned to Britain it would be on the understanding that I would not be retried for my crimes there but instead be imprisoned for the fourteen-year maximum.

I had not seen my wife or children for years. The letters they sent told of three children who were growing up without me on the other side of an ocean. I kept my nose clean, dotted my i's and crossed my t's, and at night I listened to the seals honking outside my window and dreamed of the day I would see Nicole, Nicholas and Nigel again.

CHAPTER SEVENTEEN

FREE AT LAST

Andreas Kyriacou rolls himself a cigarette and asks the multi-million dollar question.

I remember walking along the Bayswater Road in London, away from Marble Arch and towards Notting Hill with tree-lined Hyde Park to my left and a line of statuesque Victorian hotels with their eyelash awnings in creams and whites standing proud and imperious to my right. Painters, wishing to show and sell their wares had hung pictures from the railings that separated Hyde Park from the pavement and as I passed I saw landscapes and oceans, abstract shapes in jewel colours and formal portraits in muted oils.

At Queensway underground station the shops had been too busy. The people coming and going in and out of them with such apparent ease scared and confused me. I had no idea if I were allowed into these shops, I didn't know how I would cope even if I were. I had no idea what things cost, or what they were worth. I pressed my face to the window and gazed in. The street was alive with a symphony of chirrups and bleeps. Mobile phones no bigger than a packet of cigarettes rang all around me, just walking along in Bayswater I was privy to conversations from a world I no longer knew anything about. The light had faded over central London and my family were less than a mile away.

It was the early spring of 2001, and I was out.

My petition to leave Terminal Island had been successful and after four years I was on my way back to Britain, to Wandsworth prison. My journey from the Island was every bit as interminable as the journey to it. Once again I was shackled and chained, herded on and off minivans and buses and eyed with something like hatred by the sweat-soaked redneck deputies aboard Con-Air. I had spent the next three weeks on the road and in the sky, never sure of where I was until I could find a fellow prisoner who knew, and even when he told me the place names just sounded like words, meaningless and empty, pointing to nothing and nowhere.

I passed through the Atlanta State Penitentiary for a while, as close a place as I have ever been to hell on earth. Fear seeped through the cracks in the brickwork there, malevolence lurked around every corner. Every pair of eyes seemed to be weighing me up, waiting for the moment when the guards left and I was unprotected, vulnerable. Seeing Atlanta brought home to me how lucky I'd been to have served my time at Terminal Island. If I had ended up in a place like Atlanta State Pen for four years, I'm not sure whether I would have made it.

Eventually, after losing all track of time and place I found myself in a holding cell in New York awaiting my one final flight, back to London. In that New York cell I was still dressed in the clothes I had arrived in; the orange convict boiler suit and mismatched flip-flops – the colour of dejection. I was due to receive my own clothes to travel home in, clothes I had last worn four years ago and it felt important that I receive them, and the dignity they somehow embodied. I asked the guards about the clothes when I saw them. Nothing. As the time of my leaving approached ever nearer I asked again and again. Still nothing. I got brushed off, knocked back and ignored. My resistance was low and my priorities were all out of whack. This was my world now. I needed those clothes, but they weren't coming.

Since he had represented me four years previously I had stayed in touch with Russell Aoki. I managed to get a letter out to him explaining the clothing situation and I hoped and I waited. Two days later the biggest guard, the ugliest with the deadest eyes and the cruellest mouth, stopped at the door to my cell and looked in on me, lip curled in disgust, voice filled with barely suppressed rage. 'You makin' trouble for me, you Limey fuck? You make trouble for me, boy, and so help me I'll leave you where I fuckin' find you.'

At 4 a.m. the next day I was woken and handed my clothes and told to get ready quickly. They didn't offer breakfast and I didn't care. I was heading to England, the nearest thing I had to home.

On arriving back in the country I was sent to Wandsworth prison where I remained for six months. Wandsworth was as different to Terminal Island as it was possible to be. Like Brixton, Wandsworth was a Victorian jail and the site of some 135 executions in the years between 1878 and 1961. The gallows had finally been dismantled in 1993 and the site where they had once stood had since been turned into a cafeteria for the prison officers who work there.

While at Wandsworth I had achieved a dubious kind of notoriety among my fellow inmates when *Reader's Digest* magazine printed an eight-page article about my career and capture under the title 'Tracking The Fox'. The magazine had been published two years before I arrived in Wandsworth but had remained in the library. Prisoners enjoy reading about crime and it was dog-eared and tired by the time I got to look at it. There were pictures too, a collection of fake passports and stamps, a cigarette boat speeding into San Francisco harbour, a ship where they found over seventy tons of dope, neatly packed and ready for sale.

The man in the piece, an Englishman named Michael Forwell who worked with a partner called Robert Lietzman and two brothers named Samuel and Robert Colflesh, seemed vaguely familiar to me. But if I had ever been that man, I certainly was not any more. I knew who I wasn't, and that was a start.

After six months I was transferred to Coldingley, a Category C prison that focuses on preparing prisoners to return to the outside world. I had learned the lesson in Terminal Island that doing some work in prison alleviates somewhat the awful drag of days spent behind bars, so I took a job in the sign shop. I passed the time working on the computers, designing the blue-and-white wall signs that were then made up and sent out to other prisons. I made signs letting the inmates of other institutions up and down the country know where to eat, where to sleep, where to work, and where to piss.

All told, I spent eighteen months in Wandsworth and Coldingley jails. I kept my nose as clean in the English prisons as I ever had on Terminal Island and put my all into being accepted as suitable for early parole.

Serving the end of my sentence in a British jail meant that I could at last see my children again. I had not been in the same room and breathed the same air as them now for nearly eight years. It was wonderful to see them, albeit awkward at first (prison visiting rooms are no place to rebuild a family) but just being in the same city as them, knowing they were mere miles away rather than across an ocean, offered me some of the hope that had begun to fade from my life in my cell in San Pedro, California.

My parole was finally granted on 15 January 2001. When I first received the letter I stared blankly at the words on the page for a full minute before registering what they meant. When I was finally released, taking into account my time at Brixton, Belmarsh, Terminal Island, Wandsworth and Coldingley prisons I had spent eight years in jail. I left prison in a taxi with £18 and a travel voucher in my pocket. The rest of the possessions I left with, everything I had in the world, barely half filled the clear plastic carrier bag stamped with Her Majesty's Prisons logo I had been issued as I signed out.

After walking along Bayswater Road, past Notting Hill underground station and along Portobello Road I arrived at the address that May and the kids now called home, the address the Prison Service expected me to stay at from that point on. There was no one there.

By now it was night. I watched as groups of people headed to and from the bars and restaurants, which seemed to be everywhere. I marvelled at their carefree smiles and easy laughter as the nervousness and anticipation of seeing my family again threatened to overwhelm me. Eventually May returned alone to find me waiting on the doorstep. She was less than pleased to see the man who had caused her so much heartache but willing, through the goodness of her heart, to provide him with a home. May had served me with divorce papers while I was in prison, and I didn't blame her. I had signed the papers and assumed that was that, as had my soon to be ex-wife. But it wasn't. May had been so thrown by the whole affair that the papers needed to complete the divorce, to make it absolute, were never processed. Although we were still technically married May was not ready to welcome me with open arms just yet, but over time I felt the healing begin. It's an ongoing process.

For me, readjusting to the outside world was a huge task but one that I had no option but to face. My children had grown in my absence, Nicholas was seventeen now, Nigel was fifteen; both of them had become young men without me. At nineteen, Nicole was already a woman. I had a lot of work to do, I had bridges to build with all of them. I had put my wife through hell. She, along with my children, had paid a huge price for the choices I had made and repairing the damage they had caused would take time. But I had plenty of that.

After a few weeks I contacted the friends I'd made in Camden. It had been a long time and I was nervous and excited to see them all again but unsure if they would even remember me. It turned out that they did, and as soon as I got in touch a meeting was hastily arranged. We were to get together in Earls Court, at a restaurant they'd chosen knowing it had a decent wine list and served fine king prawns in garlic sauce, a favourite of mine from way back. I stepped sheepishly into the restaurant to find them all in attendance. Ed and Steph were there, Chris and Adrian had come along, as had Toby, Dan and Andreas. I hadn't heard back from Gareth yet and could only presume that having hidden the truth of my past from him while we were in business together, and then severing the partnership by being carted away in a police car, had been a bit too much to bear.

Things were a little awkward for me at first. Since last seeing these people I had spent eight years in prison in both England and America and was still finding my feet in the world I had been released into. Sure enough though, once the first couple of bottles of wine had been opened and my barriers dropped a little the conversation began to flow, the jokes were coming thick and fast, and so too were the questions. Had I really made all that cash? Was it true what the papers had said, that I'd been busted for smuggling seventy-odd tons of weed into America? Well, yes, that was all true, and much more besides.

Having paid the price and served the time for my criminal adventure I was now in the position to be able to talk about it freely, and that felt good. Of course they refused to believe that all that cash had passed through my hands and my bank accounts and I hadn't squirrelled away a red cent. Surely, they said, surely there's a bank account somewhere that you've forgotten about, surely you hid one of those cardboard boxes of cash and you're just waiting for the right moment to go and collect? Well, sadly no. But still they didn't believe me. One by one they caught me and pulled me to one side, daring me to tell them the truth about the missing millions. But the truth was there were no missing millions. I told them I made it out of the smuggling game with nothing to show for it except a book full of memories. Some of the memories are good, some not so good, and some downright awful, but I had earned all of them, every last one.

They told me how much dope had changed since I'd gone away. Smuggling the stuff was a dying art, much of what was available now was grown in attics and spare bedrooms in Liverpool, Manchester, Essex. The new weed was cultivated beneath hydroponic lights, strains and seeds were cross-fertilized and mutant varieties were born. Skunk weed, inducing mild psychosis and intense paranoia, had replaced the gentle euphoria and mellow Thai high. Ironically, as the weed became stronger the case for, if not legalization, then at least reclassification to grade C began to be taken more seriously. The newspapers, my friends told me, were full of calls for changes to the law and many considered it just a matter of time before they were heeded.

Camden market was much altered too. A few of the old guard remained but most had moved on to Spitalfields or Greenwich. The faceless high street chains were edging into Camden High Street and busily ripping out the heart and soul of the place, replacing it with

Starbucks and identikit pubs where you couldn't smoke. My friends had long since left, moved on to the next ports of call on their own journeys. Ed and Steph were married now, living aboard their houseboat with their daughter Betty. Toby had married a girl called Katie, Dan was getting serious with a girl called Anna and even Adrian had met a teacher and settled down. Andreas told me tales of the time he'd spent travelling through India with his friend Frank, and said he'd just met a girl he liked whose name made me smile. She was called Diana.

Looking around the table I saw that they were all completely different people now, and not one of them had changed a single iota. It was beautiful.

As the night drew to a close, Andreas took the place next to me at the table by now strewn with empty wine glasses and full ashtrays, listening to the conversations around us and taking in the sights while he rolled himself a cigarette from a duty-free pouch of Drum Mild and I broke the bad news to the group yet again that there really, no *honestly*, there really was nothing left. He went quiet for a moment as he prepared to ask me the question I'd asked myself a million times, the question I was still no nearer an answer to.

'In the end, Mike . . .' he said.

I knew what was coming, so I watched Andreas finish rolling his cigarette and artfully insert a filter before lighting up. It looked like a small joint. I took a moment to register that his hair was a tad longer these days, that there may even have been a hint or two of grey at the temples, like Lietzman had the last time I saw him. I took in his single-breasted motorcycle jacket, the one he'd worn at Camden when I'd first strolled through there a decade before. I noted how the stitching was beginning to fray at one or two of the seams at the shoulders, how the suede that lined the collar at the neck had worn down to a smooth glossy shine. I looked then at the patterns in his fifties gabardine shirt, long sleeved with flapped pockets, the fabric made up of swirling oriental dragons in browns, greens and golds, breathing fire with eyes that took me back to a temple mask in Bangkok. How long ago was that now? As Andreas lit his cigarette I flashed back to flying over Robert Lietzman's ranch in his helicopter at midnight, miles of empty America beneath us. I watched a curious smile break across Andreas's face, eyes first . . .

'After all that, was it . . . was it worth it?'

I held his stare for a beat then took in the scene. A table full of my friends, laughing, drinking, smoking, swapping stories like I'd never been away. For some reason I flashed back to San Francisco, to a Sunday morning over a decade before.

We'd worked through the night, another load had got through and we had, as we always did, gone at it non-stop, reweighing and repacking the dope before selling it on to Rod and the hippie connection. It was the four of us – me, Lietzman and the two Colflesh brothers – and by the time the sun came up we were tired and hungry and ready for breakfast. There was a restaurant that we used; it wasn't particularly close to the warehouse but it wasn't too far either so we climbed into a car and headed off. It was another perfect Californian day, hot, clear and blue and the trip passed quickly amid lively discussion of how much our newly arrived weed was worth.

At the restaurant we ordered what we always ordered: eggs Benedict times four, champagne with orange juice and strong coffee; leave the pot. The restaurant had a laid-back feel to it, half inside and half out, there was a lot of wood around, gnarly trees and big stone pots with flowers growing in them and butterflies drifting through on the warm morning breeze. The waitresses there knew us by now and smiled a lot and the chef sang Neil Young songs as he worked at slicing our salmon and beating our eggs. We had elected that morning to sit outside, overlooking the orange trees and listening to the birds. The food and drink arrived and, pausing from taking the piss out of one another, we raised our glasses in a toast. To what though, I couldn't for the life of me remember. To another successful load, perhaps? To the good life? To the freedom to do what we wanted, when we wanted?

As I tried to remember what we'd drunk to, the faces of my old partners changed and suddenly I was sitting at a different table, looking into the eyes of my children, of my wife. I breathed in the London air and looked over at the bar and with his question still hanging in the air between us, I looked back at Andreas.

And I didn't even know where to start.

FURTHER READING

Smokescreen by Robert Sabbag
Mr Nice by Howard Marks
High by Brian O'Dea
Grass by Phil Sparrowhawk, with Martin King and Martin Knight
Reefer Men by Tony Thompson

ACKNOWLEDGEMENTS

My most fervent acknowledgements and sympathies are for my co-defendants. By dint of length of sentence, Brian Daniels, the cool Godfather, thank you, and my partners, Robert and Samuel Colflesh. It was Robert and Samuel's tireless energy and consummate intelligence that provided the momentum which swept us all along. I was privileged to spend ten intimate years as 'shadow' to the formidable twins, and to whom I felt the deepest affection. Whether or not the outcome was to everyone's satisfaction – the journey was mind-blowing. Thank you both from the bottom of my heart . . .

I would also like to acknowledge the individual and exceptional skills of: Abraham; Anthony; Beng Seng; Bernahrd; Bobby; Gary; George; Ian L; Ian W; Jeffrey; Joe; Jupri; Keith; Mark; Mike O'; Nelson; Nico; Rick; Rusfi; Sam; Saptu; Terrence; Wuthi and their innocent partners. Thank you too, Russell Aoki, for your guidance and for the attention beyond the legal jousting. To Captain Jim (R.I.P.) and Moira for the years of parental surrogacy and producing, directing and featuring in 'Living the Delphino Dream'.

A particular thanks to an under-mentioned colleague who made my life easier for his unquestioning dedication; whom I could count upon anytime; a man I would be proud to call family. My love and thanks for ever Terry. Forgive me if I have under-reported your importance, it is only to save your blushes. You were there, in the action, on every page. *Thank You . . .*

To my co-author. How do you translate a twelve-year retrospective into a fresh real-time true adventure? Well you will need someone with multi-skills that include: unbelievable patience, an accountant's dedication to research, a detective's perseverance to weaning out the truth from tenuous strands of evidence, the discipline of a psychiatrist delving into the archives of memory, a writer to sort the words onto the page in a fashion that implores us to turn the next page in anticipation, rather than taking the dog for a walk and a man with a director's vision for a final product. Lee Bullman is a man who embodies all these qualities and more. Lee has been an absolute pleasure to work with. I looked forward to the sessions on the couch with avid enthusiasm and now that I am cured, I look forward to continuing my friendship with Lee in a more balanced relationship.

Special thanks go to the wonderful and charitable couple, Stephannie & Eduard who recognized Lee's potential and matched us up along with a lot more besides. It has been a long journey, but worth every step. Much love and thanks Lee.

My last thoughts are for the person who brought me into this world and who has believed in the sunny side of her little boy all of her 87 years . . . It would have been a pointless and barren life without my Mother's unconditional love, I love you Mum.

MICHAEL FORWELL, 2008

TO US AND THOSE LIKE US

To my friend Michael Forwell. For smuggling tons of marijuana into the United States of America and putting up with my constant questions about the exercise with consummate grace, trust and patience. To Sandra Diane and Thomas William Bullman. To Sister Liberty, Jon and all the Slaters, and to Cheryl. To Ernest Hemingway in a shark-skin suit, Mr K *('it's good, dude, but it needs more sex')* and his Loco Go-Go Gomez. To Mrs Nics. To Jake Arnott and The Velvet Underground. To Daniel, Victor and Anna, down there in God's country. To Jo Perfect and Betty Evans (x), Matty, Atom, Archie and Betty's mum. To Isabel Atherton at Creative Authors and to James Duffett-Smith, the rock 'n' roll lawyer. To Ingrid Connell for saying yes and guiding me through it all with an encouraging smile and free books. To Lorraine, Dusty, Tania, Bruno, Iram, Catherine, Stuart the artist, and to all at Pan Macmillan. To Mary Bekhait and Limelight. To Katie O'Connor and the winter medley, Eloise, Harvey Wallbanga, Dominic, Mel and all of the Crouches. To everyone at Cotton Productions, Coalition, and Compass DSA. To Selina, Mikey and Harper Bone. To Charlotte, Pavo and Oscar, the little drummer boy. To The Coach and Horses, The Russell Cotes, Hank Williams and The Clash. To Roger Bentley, Bobbie Gentry and Bea in the

Bongo Van. To Andy Eastwood, Salena Godden, and David Thomas. To Pav, Henri, Mo and Stella, and to DIGS over in New York. To Martin Lloyd Edwards, Roy Watson and to Sheila Bell. To Jude Davies, Neil McCaw and Nick Rowe. To everyone in jail for smuggling, selling or smoking marijuana. To Michael Kilcline, David Griffin, Little John and Mark Paxman. To Tom Waits, The Special AKA, Robert Sabbag, Damon Runyon and James Ellroy. To my goddaughter Honey. To Amber, Andy and Adele. To Texas Johnny McNabb, Terry Razor and to all the true believers. To Gene Vincent and the Blue Caps, to Piers Thompson, Jim Thompson, Howard Marks, and to Natalie and Luisa. To Toby, Katie, Ruby and all the Powells. To Justin Murphy, to Chris, Adrian and Sven. To Christine and Dave Howson, and to Jean Warren. To the Pearce, Riley and Miles families, and to Abigail and the kids.

To MWC and my wife Janine. For putting up with a husband on the night-shift, for the honeymoon dance and so much more besides, you're on every single page.

And lastly but by no means leastly, to Betty, Steph and the kindly king Ed Vermatt, for giving away the idea.

Peace be upon you all,

Fortes fortuna adiuvat, baby.

LEE BULLMAN, 2008

extracts reading groups
competitions books new
discounts extracts
competitions
books new
events books
extracts
new reading groups
interviews
events extracts
discounts
new books events
events new
discounts extracts discounts
www.panmacmillan.com
extracts events reading groups
competitions books extracts new

www.ingramcontent.com/pod-product-compliance
Ingram Content Group UK Ltd.
Pitfield, Milton Keynes, MK11 3LW, UK
UKHW040640280225
455688UK00002B/46